PRE-INTERMEDIATE
coursebook

Lindsay Clandfield

with additional material by Amanda Jeffries

About Global

Lindsay Clandfield is a teacher, teacher educator and lead author of Global. He was born in England, grew up in Canada, taught at a university in Mexico, lives in Spain and has trained teachers from around the world. He is also the creator of the popular blog **Six Things** (www.sixthings.net), a collection of lists about ELT.

Six quotes that inspired global

True education means fostering the ability to be interested in something.
Sumio Iijima, Japanese physicist

It is books that are the key to the wide world; if you can't do anything else, read all that you can.
Jane Hamilton, American author

The English language is nobody's special property. It is the property of the imagination…
Derek Walcott, Caribbean poet

The important thing is not to stop questioning.
Albert Einstein, German-American physicist

The mind is not a vessel to be filled, but a fire to be kindled.
Plutarch, Greek historian

If you are going to write another coursebook for the English language, please try to do something a bit different.
An English teacher who wishes to remain anonymous

Global Pre-intermediate by numbers:

10 units   160 pages   10 extracts from famous novels   53 vocabulary sections   35 explanations of English grammar   10 functional English lessons   27 accents from around the world in Global Voices   200 audio clips   30 video clips   150 interactive activities   100s of curious and interesting facts

Content highlights

1 Individual & Society
Surprising origins and facts about everyday objects
Six Degrees of Separation by John Guare
CCTV is watching you!

2 Eating & Drinking
Tastes Comforting
Secrets of the world's top kitchens **The people behind the drinks** Water and the human body

3 Art & Music
Discovered! Works of art found in unexpected places
The Picture of Dorian Gray by Oscar Wilde
The history of sound recording *High Fidelity* by Nick Hornby

4 Hopes & Fears
When I grow up… children's hopes for the future The aid worker: a profession of hope Famous dystopias in literature Reactions to… *An Inconvenient Truth*

5 Work & Leisure
Profile: An Indian call centre worker Bad bosses and work issues The serious leisure perspective Ten facts about amusement parks

6 Science & Technology
The science of happiness The worst jobs in science *Frankenstein* by Mary Shelley Going, going, gone … Online auctions

7 Time & Money
A brief history of time zones *A Tale of Two Cities* by Charles Dickens A lifetime of financial concerns A different kind of bank

8 Home & Away
Famous homes and their infamous occupants *Dracula* by Bram Stoker The cat came back *The Beach* by Alex Garland New kinds of tourism

9 Health & Fitness
The common cold Milestones of modern medicine Olympic tales

10 New & Old
Brave New Words by Kerry Maxwell New places in a new world Old but loved: the Trabant Two classic board games

Global English
by **David Crystal**

page 15	Same language but different
page 39	The power of music
page 63	All work and no play
page 87	The English language and the number four
page 111	Sports English

Contents

		Grammar	Reading texts	Listening texts	Vocabulary	Speaking and Pronunciation
UNIT 1	**Individual** page 6	Word order in questions (p7) / *What* and *How* questions (p9)	Surprising origins and facts: The identity (ID) card (p7)	Descriptions of people (p8)	Everyday objects (p6) / Describing people (p8) / EV *look* and *look like* (p8)	Describing people (p8) / False identities (p9) / P The alphabet (p7)
	Society page 10	Present simple, frequency adverbs (p11) / Present continuous (p13)	It's a small world … the six degrees of separation theory (p10) / Readers' response CCTV is watching you (p13)	Descriptions of personal relationships (p10) / Explanation of the six degrees of separation theory (p10)	People you know (p10) / EV *in touch* (p10) / EV *place* (p12)	Family and friends (p11) / Arguments for and against CCTV (p12) / P Linking words (p13)
		Function globally: Common social expressions (p14) / Global English: Same language but different (p15)		Writing: A personal description / Study skills: Being a good language learner	(p16) (p17)	
UNIT 2	**Eating** page 18	Countable / uncountable nouns, quantifiers (*some, any*) (p19) / Quantifiers (*a lot of, a little, a few, not enough, much, many*) (p20)	Tastes comforting (p18) / Ten secrets … from the world's top kitchens (p20)	Talk on Zao Shen (p21)	Food (p18) / In the kitchen (p21) / EV *taste* (p18)	Food questionnaire (p18) / How do you make it? (p19) / Food tips (p20) / Describing a kitchen (p21) / P /k/ and /tʃ/ (p21)
	Drinking Page 22	The infinitive (p23) / The infinitive of purpose (p24)	The people behind the drinks (p22)	Talk on water and the human body (p24)	Containers and drinks (p22) / The human body (p24)	What do you like to drink …? (p22) / Drinks questionnaire (p25) / P /tə/ and /tuː/ (p25)
		Function globally: Eating out (p26) / Global voices: Food that makes you think of home (p27)		Writing: A description of food and drink / Study skills: Evaluating your language learning	(p28) (p29)	
UNIT 3	**Art** Page 30	Past simple and past continuous (p32)	Discovered! True stories of how valuable works of art were found in unexpected places (p30) / The Picture of Dorian Gray by Oscar Wilde (p33)		Works of art (p30) / Furniture and furnishings (p32) / EV *discover* (p30)	Describing works of art (p30) / Retelling stories (p32) / P Past simple regular verbs (p33)
	Music page 34	Used to (p35)	High Fidelity by Nick Hornby (p37)	Lecture on the history of sound recording (p35) / Talk on music in film and TV (p36)	Audio and video (p34) / Feelings (p36) / EV Saying and writing decades (p35) / EV *just* (p37)	Describing pictures (p34) / P Used to (p35) / Music (p37)
		Function globally: Agreeing and disagreeing (p38) / Global English: The power of music (p39)		Writing: A scene from a short story / A review / Study skills: Conversation partners	(p33) (p40) (p41)	
UNIT 4	**Hopes** page 42	Future hopes and plans (p43) / Future plans and intentions (*be going to*, present continuous) (p45)	When I grow up … (p42) / Pandora's box (p45)	Interview with two aid workers (p44)	Adjectives and synonyms (p42) / Global issues (p44)	My hopes and plans (p43) / Foreign aid (p44) / Hope (p45) / P Word stress (p44)
	Fears page 46	Prediction and ability (*will, be able to*) (p47) / Future time clauses (p49)	Things will get worse … famous dystopias in literature (p46)	Conversation about *An Inconvenient Truth* (p48)	Phrasal verbs with *get* (p47) / Geographical features (p48) / EV *-ed / -ing* adjectives (p48)	Climate change questionnaire (p49)
		Function globally: Making offers and decisions (p50) / Global voices: Reasons why people learn English (p51)		Writing: An email to a friend / Study skills: Using your dictionary: finding the right entry	(p52) (p53)	
UNIT 5	**Work** page 54	Have (p55) / Modal verbs (p56)	Profile of an Indian call centre worker (p54)	Conversations between bosses and employees (p56)	Work (p54) / Work issues (p56) / EV *job* and *work* (p54)	Jobs (p54) / Job characteristics (p57) / P Contractions (p57)
	Leisure page 58	*-ing* verbs (p59) / Present perfect, *have been / have gone* (p60)	Ten facts about … amusement parks around the world (p60)	Presentation about 'The serious leisure perspective' (p58)	Leisure activities (p58) / EV *play* (p58)	Ten questions about leisure (p61) / P /ŋ/ (p59) / P Past participles (p61)
		Function globally: Turn-taking (p62) / Global English: All work and no play (p63)		Writing: Leisure time / A CV / Study skills: Recording new words and phrases	(p59) (p64) (p65)	

EV - Extend your vocabulary   P - Pronunciation

		Grammar	Reading texts	Listening texts	Vocabulary	Speaking and Pronunciation
UNIT 6	Science page 66	Comparatives with -er and more (p67) Comparatives (a bit / much / as … as) (p68)	The science of happiness (p66) Fitter Happier (p67) Frankenstein by Mary Shelley (p69)	Conversation about the worst jobs in science (p68)	Noun formation (p69) EV Metaphors for happy (p66)	Happiness (p66) Guessing jobs (p68) Dangerous knowledge (p69) P The schwa (p67)
	Technology page 70	Superlatives (p70) Phrasal verbs and objects (p73)	Going, going, gone … (p70) The Luddites (p73)	Website addresses (p71) Conversations about computer problems (p72)	Compound nouns (p70) Phrasal verbs (p72) EV Other ways of saying yes (p72)	Website addresses (p71) Modern technology (p73) P Phrasal verbs, sentence stress (p72)
		Function globally: Finding things in common (p74) Global voices: The most important technological advance (p75)		Writing: Describing advantages and disadvantages Study skills: Personalising language learning		(p76) (p77)
UNIT 7	Time page 78	Present perfect with for and since (p79)	A brief history of time zones (p78) A Tale of Two Cities by Charles Dickens (p81)	Talk on the concept of time (p80)	Prepositions of time (in, on, at) (p78) Time expressions (p80)	The best time to … (p78) Time-saving inventions (p81) It is the best of times because … (p81) P /aɪ/ and /eɪ/, sentence stress (p80)
	Money page 82	Present perfect with yet and already (p82)	A lifetime of financial concerns (p82) A different kind of bank (p84)		Money, verb phrases (p82) EV borrow and lend (p85)	Describing pictures (p84) A bank loan (p85) P /ʌ/ (p83)
		Function globally: Shopping in a market (p86) Global English: The English language and the number four (p87)		Writing: Giving your opinion Study skills: Managing your study time		(p88) (p89)
UNIT 8	Home page 90	Passive voice (p91)	Bram Stoker's Dracula (p91) The cat came back (p92)	Famous homes (p90)	Animals (p92) Prepositions of movement (p93) EV house and home (p90)	A tour of your home (p90) Animals (p92) P /h/ (p90)
	Away page 94	First conditional (p95) Second conditional (p97)	Travel guidebooks (p94) The Beach by Alex Garland (p95) New kinds of tourism (p96)	Conversations with travel guides (p94)	Adjectives and prepositions (p96) EV Words that mean trip (p94)	Beach resorts (p95) Describing photos (p96) If you could go anywhere … (p97) P Sentence stress (p97)
		Function globally: Speaking on the telephone (p98) Global voices: Homes where you live (p99)		Writing: A dialogue A description of a town Study skills: Learning words with prepositions		(p91) (p100) (p101)
UNIT 9	Health page 102	Modal verbs of advice (p103) Could / couldn't, had to / didn't have to (p105)	Milestones of modern medicine (p104)	Talk on the common cold (p102) Advice on cures for the common cold (p103)	Feeling ill (p102) Medical treatment (p104)	The common cold (p102) P ch and gh (p102) P Word stress (p104) Sports questionnaire (p107)
	Fitness page 106	Past perfect (p107) Reported statements (p109)	Olympic losers (p106)	Conversation at the doctor's (p108)	Sport (p106) Say, tell and ask (p109) EV win and beat (p106)	A visit to the doctor (p108) Fitness questionnaire (p109)
		Function globally: Describing illness (p110) Global English: Sports English (p111)		Writing: A sick note An online post Study skills: Using your dictionary: exploring collocations		(p103) (p112) (p113)
UNIT 10	New page 114	Defining relative clauses (p115) Definite article (the) (p117)	Brave New Words by Kerry Maxwell (p114) New places in a new world (p116)	Interview with Kerry Maxwell on Brave New Words (p114)	New words in context (p114) Places (p116) EV Words that mean new (p116)	Famous quotes (p117)
	Old page 118	Verb form review (p119) Both, neither (p120)	Old but loved: the Trabant (p118)	Two classic board games (p120)	Transport (p118) Games (p121) EV Words that mean make (p120)	Transport (p118) Driving questionnaire (p119) A board game (p121) P Consonant clusters (p118) P Sentence stress and intonation (p121)
		Function globally: Ending a conversation (p122) Global voices: Your favourite words in English (p123)		Writing: Definitions game A report on studies Study skills: Evaluating your pronunciation		(p115) (p124) (p125)

Communication activities:
Student A: (p126)   Student B: (p128)

Additional material: (p130)   Grammar focus: (p132)   Audioscript: (p152)

Contents   5

Unit 1: Individual & Society

Part 1

Vocabulary
Everyday objects

Reading
The Identity Card

Grammar
Word order in questions

Pronunciation
The alphabet

Vocabulary

1 Look at the pictures and read the information. Match each object to a word in the box. There are three words you do not need.

chewing gum   credit card   glasses
key ring   lipstick   mobile phone
pen   umbrella

2 Do you have any of these things with you today? Which ones? Tell a partner.

Reading

1 🔊 1.01 Read and listen to the text on page 7 about another everyday object: the identity card. What kind of information about an individual can you find on an identity card?

2 Read the text again and find examples of …

1 a historical reason for ID cards.
2 countries with no ID cards.
3 a material used in ID cards.
4 information on an ID card.
5 biometric information on an ID card.

3 Does your country have identity cards? What information do they contain?

Surprising origins and facts: Everyday objects

Origin: Egypt, more than 5000 years ago
Cleopatra used one made from dead insects.

a

Origin: United States, 1973
The first model weighed 0.79 kg and measured 25cm.

b

Origin: United States, 1950
The first one was the Diner's Club card. People used it to pay in New York restaurants.

d

Origin: Mexico, 1860
It comes from the chicle plant. The original idea was to use it to make car tyres.

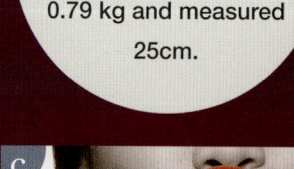
c

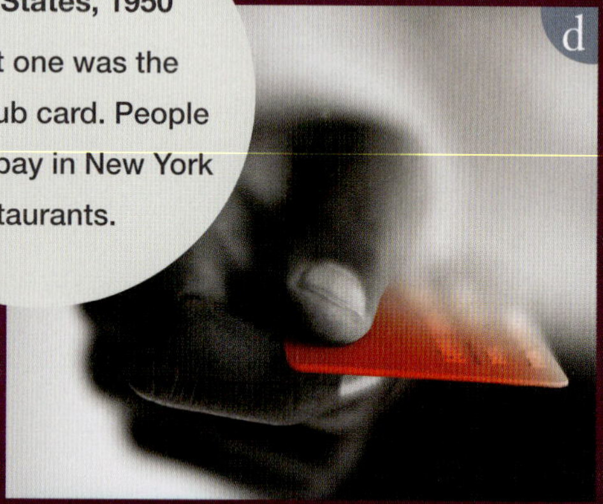

Origin: Italy, 13th century
The early models helped people to see but they caused headaches because they were so heavy.

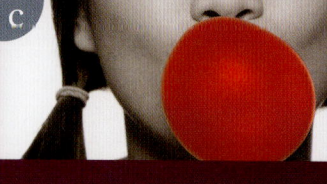
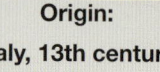
e

Unit 1 Individual

Surprising origins and facts: The identity (ID) card

Grammar

Are ID cards obligatory?
Do all countries **have** ID cards?
What is a biometric ID card?
What did people **use** ID cards for?

- in questions the verb goes before the subject
- in present simple or past simple questions, the auxiliary verb *do / did* goes before the subject and the infinitive goes after the subject
- question words (*What, Where, Who*, etc.) go at the start of a question

1 Complete the questions by putting the words in the correct place.

1	do you do?	what
2	you speak any foreign languages?	do
3	what your name?	is
4	what's phone number?	your
5	you have any children?	do
6	where you born?	were
7	where did you to school?	go
8	where do live?	you
9	you married?	are
10	what your date of birth?	is

2 Match the questions in exercise 1 to the topics in the box.

Name	Profession
Address	Marital status
Phone number	Children
Date of birth	Education
Place of birth	Languages

3 Choose five questions from exercise 1. Work in pairs and ask each other the questions.

G **Grammar focus** – explanation & more practice of word order on page 132

What were the first ID cards?
The first ID cards were, in fact, paper identity documents, which appeared in the 18th century.

What did people use the first ID cards for?
People used the first ID cards to travel to different countries. The ID card was the first passport.

Do all countries have ID cards?
No, they don't. There are more than a hundred countries in the world with ID cards. But several English-speaking countries don't have a national ID card system. These countries include the UK, the US, Canada, Australia, Ireland and New Zealand.

What do ID cards look like?
ID cards are usually made of plastic and can fit inside a person's wallet.

What information do governments put on ID cards?
Most ID cards contain the person's name, date of birth, signature and a photograph. Some cards contain other information such as the person's address, phone number, nationality, profession and marital status.

What is a biometric ID card?
More modern ID cards now contain biometric information, for example, fingerprints or digital images of people's eyes.

Pronunciation

1 🔊 1.02 Listen to three people spelling personal information. Write the words they spell.

2 Work in pairs. A: spell the words to B.

- your last name
- the name of the street you live on
- two words from this lesson

3 Swap roles and repeat.

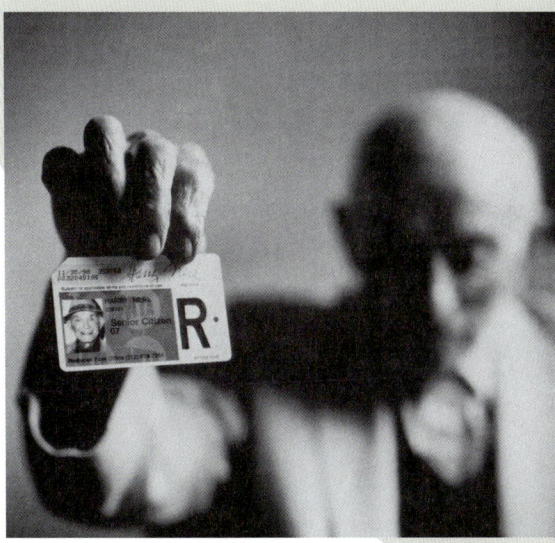

Individual Unit 1

UNIT 1 Individual & Society

Part 2

Speaking & Vocabulary
Describing people

Listening
Identity parade

Grammar
What & How questions

Speaking
False identities

Speaking and Vocabulary

1 Think of someone you know very well and describe this person to a partner. Use the phrases below to help you.

- This is …
- He's / She's …
- He's / She's got … eyes and … hair.
- He's / She's … years old.

2 Write the words in the box under the correct headings below.

> bald   beard   blond   curly   fair
> in her twenties   medium-height
> middle-aged   overweight   scar   short
> shoulder-length   slim   straight   young

3 Think about the person you described in exercise 1. Can you add any more details to the description?

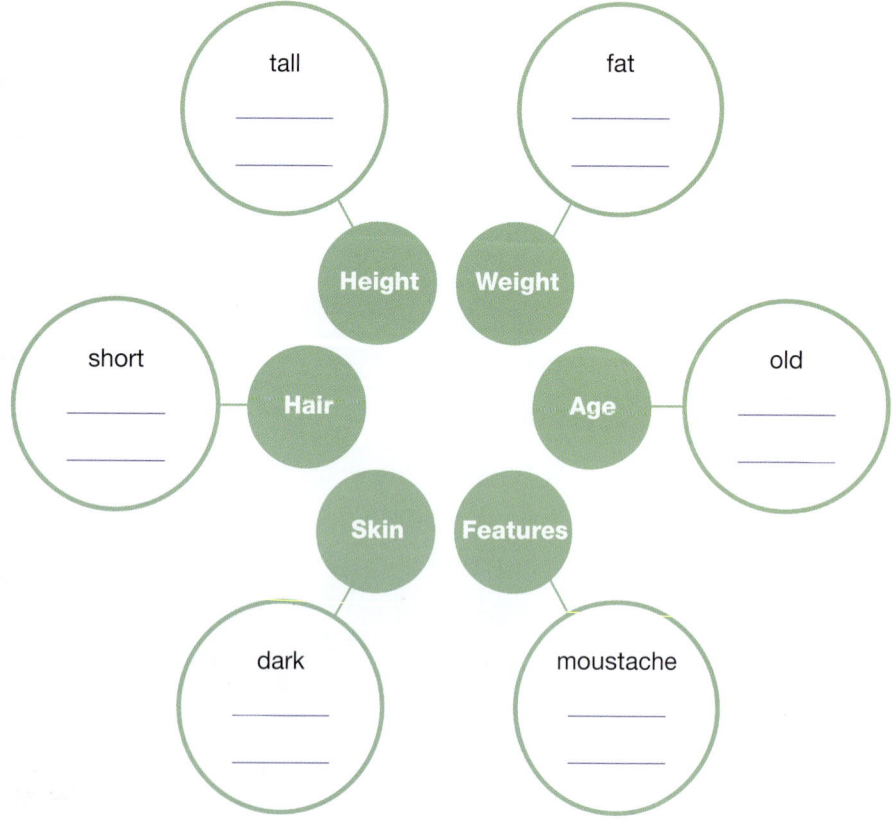

Listening

1 🔊 1.03–1.06 Listen to four conversations and choose the correct photo a–j on page 9 for each one.

2 Listen again and answer the questions. There is one question for each conversation.
1. Does the woman like the photo?
2. How old is the baby?
3. What is different about Bella?
4. What colour is the man's hair?

3 Work in pairs. A: choose one of the photos and describe it to your partner. B: try to guess the correct photo. Then swap roles and repeat.

Extend your vocabulary – *look* and *look like*

We use *look* + adjective to describe a person's appearance.
He looks thin.
She looks good.

We use *look* + *like* + noun phrase to compare someone's appearance to someone or something else.
She looks like her mother.
He looks like a film star.

Choose the correct option in each pair of sentences.

1. He looks like his father.   He looks his father.
2. Are you OK? You look like tired.   Are you OK? You look tired.
3. I look horrible in this photo.   I look like horrible in this photo.
4. That chair doesn't look like comfortable.   That chair doesn't look comfortable.

8 Unit 1 Individual

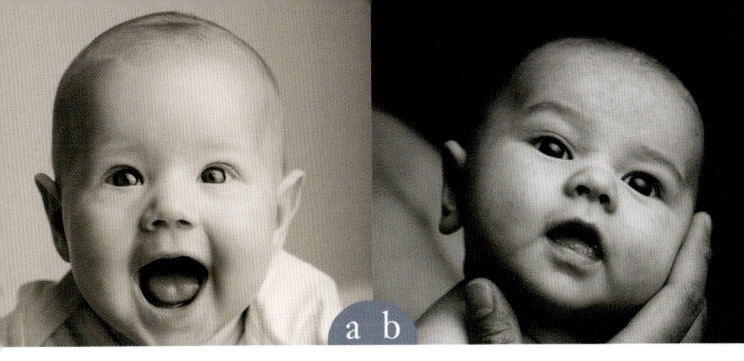

Grammar

How old is he?
What kind of car does he drive?
What colour are his eyes?

- use *how* + adjectives such as *old, tall, long* to ask for more detail
- use *what* + *kind of / sort of* + noun to ask for information about the noun
- also use *what* + *colour / time / size* to ask for specific detail

1 Complete the questions below with the correct question words.

how	how many	how much
what kinds	what sort	

Q&A: IDENTITY THEFT

1 _____ safe is your identity?
The answer is: not safe, if you look at the statistics for identity theft.

2 _____ of crime is identity theft?
Identity (ID) theft occurs when someone steals your identity. It's one of the biggest new crimes in the world today.

3 _____ people are victims of identity theft every year?
Experts think that millions of people are victims around the world. In the US alone, it's around nine million people every year.

4 _____ does identity theft cost?
ID theft is big business and costs billions of dollars to national economies.

5 _____ of identity theft are there?
There are different types: using your credit card; getting a phone in your name or getting a government document, eg a driving licence, are some examples.

2 Put the words in the correct order to make questions.

1 colour are your eyes what?
2 hair colour what your is?
3 hair how long your is?
4 month what birthday is your?
5 old you how are?
6 street live you do on what?
7 tall you are how?

G Grammar focus – explanation & more practice of *what* and *how* on page 132

Speaking

1 Write this information on a piece of paper and give it to the teacher.

- your full name
- your address
- your birthday

2 You are going to *steal* someone's identity. Take a piece of paper from the teacher and do not show it to anybody. This is your new identity.

3 Work in pairs and ask each other questions from exercise 2. Find out your partner's false identity.

Individual Unit 1

UNIT 1 Individual & Society

Part 3

Vocabulary & Listening
People you know

Listening & Reading
Six degrees of separation

Grammar
Present simple, frequency adverbs

Speaking
Family & friends

Vocabulary and Listening

1 Work in pairs and make a list of the people you know in the class. Tell each other what you know about them.

2 🔊 1.07 Listen to a woman talking about people she knows. Write the words in the box under the correct names.

| acquaintance | classmate | colleague |
| friend | neighbour | |

Sofia   **Hans**
_____   _____

Becky Fleming

Ken   **Pilar**
_____   _____

3 Listen again and answer the questions.
1 Where is Becky's neighbour?
2 Does Becky know Hans well?
3 Does she work with Ken?
4 How does she know Sofia?

4 Copy the diagram above and write the names of people you know. Write the relationship underneath each name. Then work in pairs and tell each other about the people.

This is Louise. She's my neighbour.
Jorge is a colleague from work.

Listening and Reading

1 🔊 1.08 Read and listen to the extract from the play *Six Degrees of Separation* on page 11. Do you know this theory?

2 🔊 1.09 Listen to an explanation of the theory. Draw lines between the names below to show which people are connected.

```
         you
John           Jane
   The Ambassador
              Mary
Robert   The Secretary
         General of the
         United Nations
         Mr Smith
```

3 Listen again. Explain the link between …
1 you and John.
2 Jane and Robert.
3 Mr Smith and the Ambassador.

4 Work in pairs and discuss these questions. Do you think this theory is true? Are you connected to a famous person in any way? Tell your partner.
My wife's sister has met the President.
I work with a man. His son's teacher went to school with a famous singer.

Extend your vocabulary – *in touch*

If you are *in touch* with someone you see, speak to or write to them.
He is often in touch with important people.
You can *lose touch* with a person if you don't see, speak or write to them any more. You are then *out of touch* with that person.
I lost touch with a lot of my school friends many years ago. We are out of touch now.
Keep in touch or *stay in touch* are informal expressions you can use to tell someone you want to be in contact.
See you soon. Let's keep in touch.

Complete the sentences with an expression using *touch*.
1 She's still _____ with her grandmother. She writes to her every week.
2 I'm _____ with my school friends. I never see them.
3 A: See you later.
   B: OK, _____.
4 He doesn't want to _____ with his family. He calls them every month.

10 Unit 1 Society

It's a small world ... the six degrees of separation theory

I read somewhere that everybody on this planet is separated by only six other people. Six degrees of separation between us and everyone else on this planet. The President of the United States, a gondolier in Venice, just fill in the names. … I am bound – you are bound – to everyone on this planet by a trail of six people.

From *Six Degrees of Separation* by John Guare.

Grammar

*Robert **works** for a big hotel in the city centre.*
*Mr Smith **knows** many people.*
*He **sometimes has** lunch with the ambassador.*
*He **is often** in touch with important people.*

- use the present simple to talk about habits and routines and for things that are always true
- add *s* to regular verbs when talking about *he / she / it*
- use frequency adverbs to say how often something happens
- frequency adverbs go between the subject and the verb except with the verb *to be*

1 Complete the text about online social networks using the correct form of the words given.

Keeping in touch

One way people often _____ (keep) in touch with friends and family is using the internet. People _____ (use) social networking sites. These are special websites. Every member _____ (have) their own page.

Let's look at Jim, for example. Jim _____ (be) always in touch with his network of friends. He _____ (not write) emails, he _____ (put) information on a social networking site every day. Jim often _____ (take) photos of his family and _____ (put) them on his webpage. His friends _____ (look) at Jim's page and _____ (see) the information and photos. They then _____ (send) him messages.

2 Complete the sentences by putting the word or phrase in the correct place.
1 Becky talks to her parents on the phone. (*three times a week*)
2 She is very friendly with the neighbours. (*always*)
3 She goes out with her colleagues. (*often*)
4 She uses the internet to keep in touch with people. (*every day*)

G **Grammar focus** – explanation & more practice of the present simple on page 132

Speaking

Work in pairs.
A: turn to page 126.
B: turn to page 128.

Society Unit 1 11

UNIT 1 Individual & Society

Part 4

Speaking & Reading
CCTV is watching you

Grammar
Present continuous

Pronunciation
Linking words

Speaking and Reading

1 Read the information below about CCTV cameras and answer the questions in pairs.
1 Do any of the facts surprise you?
2 Do you have CCTV in your town? Where?
3 Do you think that CCTV cameras are a good idea?

2 Quickly read *Readers' response* on page 13. What kind of texts are they?
a advertisements in a newspaper
b letters to a newspaper
c emails to a company
d messages from the government

3 Read the texts again and answer the questions.
1 Who works at night in a shop?
2 Who thinks the article is not fair?
3 Who talks about the police?
4 Who mentions other ways of watching people?

4 Work in pairs. Find two arguments in favour of and two arguments against CCTV cameras in the texts. Which arguments do you agree with?

Meaning: Closed Circuit Television
Origin: 1942, to watch German rocket launches
Early uses: government buildings and banks
Modern uses: shops, airports, buses, hospitals, schools, streets, underground train systems
Largest number of CCTV cameras in one place: Singapore Airport (more than 3,000)
Most common place for a CCTV camera: at a cash machine
City with most CCTV cameras: London, England
Times per day that the average English person is on camera: 300

Extend your vocabulary – expressions with *place*

Place is a very common word in English expressions.
If something *takes place*, it happens.
The festival takes place in October.
If something is *out of place* it does not belong or is uncomfortable.
I felt out of place there, I didn't know anybody.
Look at the highlighted expressions in the texts on page 13. Match them to their meanings or uses 1–5 below.
1 to explain the first point in an argument
2 instead of
3 everywhere
4 a particular position or part of town
5 that something is not appropriate for you

Readers' response
CCTV is watching you

First identity cards, and now cameras all over the place. They are watching our every move. Soon they will listen to our phone calls and read our emails and letters. Do we have any private life left?

Rajit Gadh

So we have CCTV cameras in our neighbourhood. I really don't understand it. This is a very quiet place and there are no problems here. Personally I believe that this is just another example of government invasion of our privacy.

Martha Klein

Your article, CCTV is watching you, gives a very negative view of CCTV cameras. In the first place, the truth is that we are living in a dangerous society and people need to feel safe. You also don't mention how crime is going down in neighbourhoods with CCTV. You only give one side of the argument!

Philip Richards

The problem with the cameras isn't the technology, it's how people are using the technology. If the police are using the cameras to find information about criminals, what is the problem with that? It's not our place to say how they should do their job.

Kenneth Thomas

My co-workers and I agree with CCTV cameras. We work in a 24-hour shop and I usually work late. We have two cameras in the shop and we are putting in two more now. We don't have a lot of money. The cameras give us protection in place of security guards.

Tatyana Ivanov

Grammar

*CCTV cameras **are watching** you.*
*We **are putting** in two more cameras now.*
*We **agree** with CCTV cameras.*

- use the present continuous to talk about things that are happening now or around now
- use the present continuous to talk about temporary situations
- we do not usually use stative verbs such as *agree, believe, know, like, need* with the present continuous

1 Underline the correct form of the verbs in the letter.

I am looking / look out of my window at work right now and I can see two CCTV cameras. These cameras are belonging / belong to the company, and they watch our every move. I am not understanding / don't understand why we are needing / need them. I am not liking / don't like them.
Lola Sule

2 Think of three people you know. For each person, write two or more sentences about …
- what they do.
- what they are probably doing now.

My brother Graham works as a secondary school teacher.
He's probably teaching a history class right now.

3 Work in pairs and compare your sentences. Ask one question about each person on your partner's paper.

Where is your brother teaching?

G Grammar focus – explanation & more practice of the present continuous on page 132

Pronunciation

1 🔊 1.10 Listen to five sentences. How many words do you hear in each? (contractions = two words)

2 Listen again and write the sentences. Then practise saying them. Pay attention to linking the words together.

3 Work in pairs and imagine a context for each sentence. Think about:
- Who is speaking?
- Where are they?
- What do they say next?

Society Unit 1

Function globally common social expressions

a   b   c d

Warm up

Work in pairs and choose two or three situations from the list below. Roleplay a short conversation for each situation.

Situations
1 You are meeting for the first time.
2 You are friends. It's late and you would like to go home.
3 A is working and B is the customer. B: you want some help.
4 You work together. It's A's first day. B: introduce yourself.
5 You are classmates. It's the end of the week and you are saying goodbye.
6 A: it's your birthday. B gives you a present.
7 You don't know each other. A: you bump into B who drops something.

Useful phrases
- How are you?
- Nice to meet you.
- Have a good weekend.
- Excuse me.
- Thank you very much!
- See you tomorrow.
- I'm sorry.

Listening

🔊 1.11–1.14 Listen to four conversations. Match each one to a picture and a situation.

Language focus: social expressions

Read the phrases and cross out the response that is **not** correct.
1 How are you?
   a Fine thanks.   b Very well, thank you.
   c I'm nice.
2 Hi, I'm George.
   a Fine to meet you.   b Nice to meet you.
   c Pleased to meet you.
3 Have a good weekend.
   a You too.   b Thanks.   c Yes, please.
4 Excuse me.
   a Yes, can I help you?   b You're welcome.
   c Yes?
5 Thanks for everything.
   a You're welcome.   b No problem.
   c Yes, please.
6 See you tomorrow.
   a You too.   b Bye.   c See you.
7 I'm sorry.
   a That's all right.   b It's OK.
   c You're welcome.

Speaking

Work with a new partner and choose **one** of the tasks below.

A Repeat the warm up activity using the new expressions you have learnt.

B Look at the audioscript on page 152 and choose one of the conversations. Practise it and try to memorise it. Then continue the conversation.

Global English

Same language but different
by David Crystal

We use language to express our thoughts, form relationships with others, and build communities. The focus is always on the individual. If you study language you study people, and people are as different as chalk from cheese. So their language will be different too.

Sometimes it's regional background that makes the difference. If you
5 hear someone say *That's a bonny wee child*, the speaker is probably from Scotland, because words like *wee* (little) and *bonny* (pretty) are hardly ever used anywhere else. And someone who says *My car's hood and windshield were damaged* probably has an American background; someone from the UK would say *bonnet and windscreen*.

10 Often it's social background that makes the difference. In the 1950s in Britain there was a lot of publicity about how upper-class (U) people used different words from those used by other classes (non-U). U speakers had *luncheon* (or *lunch*) in the middle of the day and *dinner* in the evening. Non-U speakers had *dinner* in the middle of the day. *Luncheon* is rare today, but there is a still a social divide between
15 *lunch* and *dinner*.

Above all, these days, it's the technology that makes the difference. The internet allows people to express their individuality in ways that were inconceivable a few years ago. Emails vary from highly formal (*Dear Professor Crystal*) to highly informal (*Yo, Dave!!*). Older people often keep the rules of punctuation and capitalisation they once learned;
20 younger people often try out new ways (*i dont think so – LOL*).

But times are changing. As more older people start to use the internet, they are also using the latest abbreviations more and more. BRB (Be right back).

> **Glossary**
>
> **background** (*noun*) – the type of family, social position or culture that someone comes from
>
> **BRB** (*verb*) – internet abbreviation for *Be right back*; you use this to say informally that you will return soon
>
> **LOL** (*verb*) – internet abbreviation for *laughing out loud*; you use this to say informally that you think something is funny

Warm up

1 Are these sentences true (*T*) or false (*F*) for you?
- I speak more than one language.
- I speak differently at work to how I speak at home.
- My language has many different dialects.
- There is more than one language in my country.
- Rich people speak differently to poor people.

2 Work in pairs and compare your answers. Do you agree?

Reading

1 Read the text *Same language but different*. What three factors does the author mention?
a differences in geography   c differences in diet
b differences in social class d differences in technology

2 Read the text again and decide if these sentences are true (*T*) or false (*F*).
1 People are very different, so language is different.
2 *Hood* and *windshield* are British English words.
3 U speakers had lunch in the evening.
4 Technology always makes language very formal.
5 Young people don't use capital letters in the same way as older people on the internet.
6 Young people are inventing new ways of using capital letters.

Language focus

Find words or expressions in the text with these meanings.
1 to be very different (lines 2–3)
2 uncommon (line 14)
3 most importantly (line 16)
4 impossible to think about or imagine (line 17)

Speaking

Do you think the differences in English that the author talks about are true for your language? Think of some examples. Use the questions below to help you.

- How do people start and finish emails in your language? Is it formal or informal?
- Are there different parts of your country that use different words to mean the same thing? Can you give an example and explain it in English?
- Are there abbreviations on the internet in your language like *LOL* or *BRB*?

Writing a personal description

Reading

1 Read Constanza's description of herself.

Is it …
a an email to a friend?
b an introduction for a social networking site?
c a letter of application for a job?

2 Is there anything in the description that's true for you?

Hi! My name is Constanza Ximena Jara Castro, but people call me Coti for short. I'm twenty years and single. I born in Valdivia, in the south of Chile, but now I live in Santiago, the capital city. I study journalism in the university and I like very much this course.

We are five people in my family – my parents, my two elder sisters and me. We also have got a dog called Kalu. My father's job is a photographer and my mother is teacher.

In my free time I like swimming, listening music and seeing friends. In the future I hope to go to USA for do a Master's and my ambition is to work as a journalist for a national newspaper.

Writing skills: looking for errors in your work

1 Read a corrected copy of Constanza's description and find twelve differences.

2 Which of these errors do you sometimes make?

3 Do you usually check your writing for errors before giving it to a teacher?

Hi! My name is Constanza but people call me Coti for short. I'm twenty years old and single. I was born in Valdivia, in the south of Chile, but now I live in Santiago, the capital city. I am studying journalism at university and I like this course very much.

There are five people in my family – my parents, my two elder sisters and me. We also have a dog called Kalu. My father is a photographer and my mother is a teacher.

In my free time I like swimming, listening to music and seeing friends. In the future I hope to go to the USA to do a Master's and my ambition is to work as a journalist for a national newspaper.

Language focus: joining sentences

1 Join the sentences using *and*, *but* or *so*.

I have a dog called Lucky. I have a cat called Mimi.
I have a dog called Lucky and I have a cat called Mimi.

1 I'm short and slim. I have long curly black hair.
2 My sister trained as a teacher. She's unemployed at the moment.
3 I'm thirty years old. I'm married with two children.
4 Clodagh isn't a common name. People often don't know how to spell it.
5 I have three sisters. I don't have any brothers.
6 I was born in a small village. I find living in a big city very strange.

2 Read the joined sentences. Cross out any words that you don't need.

I have a dog called Lucky and I ~~have~~ a cat called Mimi.

Preparing to write

Make notes about yourself for a social networking site. Use the topics in the box to help you and include your own ideas.

| Name | Age | Birthplace | Town | Occupation |
| Family | Free time | Ambitions | | |

Writing about names

- My full name is Alejandro Gustavo Donoso Jimenez.
- People call me Alex for short.
- My nickname is Chacho.
- I was named after my grandfather.
- I have a sister called Andrea and a brother called Pablo.
- I have a dog whose name is Pepe.

Writing

Write your description and check it for errors. Then work in pairs and swap your descriptions. Try to correct each other's work.

Global review

Grammar

1 Complete the questions with the correct words.
1 _____ married? No, I'm single.
2 _____ speak English? Yes, a little.
3 _____ your phone number?
  It's 07051-459-216.
4 _____ you do? I'm a teacher.
5 _____ is your car? It's red.

2 Complete the sentences with the correct form of the verb in brackets.
1 A: Excuse me, can you help me?
  B: I'm sorry, I _____ (try) to work right now.
2 I _____ (not / know) many people in this town.
3 My brother _____ (not/ like) his boss, so he _____ (look) for a new job.
4 My mother _____ (not / speak) any foreign languages.

Vocabulary

1 Find and correct six spelling mistakes.

acquaintance	bald	clasmate	colleage	freind
heigth	identity	keyring	middle-aged	neigbour
proffesion	umbrella			

2 Look at the pictures. Correct three mistakes in each description.
1 This is Carlos. He's bald and overweight, and he's got a beard.
2 This is Veronica. She's middle-aged, with short dark curly hair.

Speaking

Work in groups of three. A: throw a dice to choose a person in the box. B and C: ask questions about the person. Ask about name, age, job, family and what they look like. Then swap roles and repeat.

1 A good friend
2 A neighbour
3 A family member
4 Your first friend
5 A new colleague or classmate
6 A good teacher

Study skills

Being a good language learner

1 Read the learning questionnaire. How often are these statements true for you? Give yourself a score for each question. Not usually = 0 points   Sometimes = 1 point   Usually = 2 points

* I try to practise using English as often as I can outside the classroom. ___
* I am willing to take risks and am not afraid of making mistakes. ___
* I am organised in the way I manage my learning. ___
* I think about how I learn best. ___
* If I don't understand something, I try to guess. ___
* I notice my mistakes and try to learn from them. ___
* I set goals and monitor my progress. ___
* If I am not sure about something, I ask for help. ___
* I regularly review what I have learnt. ___
* I try to use English to communicate my ideas. ___

2 Add up your total score and read what it means below.

16–20	Congratulations! You are already an excellent language learner. Keep up the good work!
11–15	You already have some very good language learning strategies. Now think how you can improve even more.
6–10	You are starting to use the right strategies but need to be more consistent.
0–5	Maybe you are finding it difficult to make progress. Try some of the strategies above and you could see a big difference.

3 Work in pairs and discuss the questions.
• Which of the strategies in the quiz do you use most?
• Which do you need to use more?
• Give your partner suggestions about things to do.

4 Write two new things you will try to become a better language learner.

UNIT 2 Eating & Drinking

Part 1

Vocabulary & Speaking
Food

Reading
Tastes comforting

Grammar
Countable / uncountable nouns, quantifiers (*some*, *any*)

Speaking
How do you make it?

Vocabulary and Speaking

1 Write the words in the box under the correct heading below.

bitter	breakfast	cook	dinner
eat	fresh	lunch	salty	serve
snack	spicy	sweet	taste

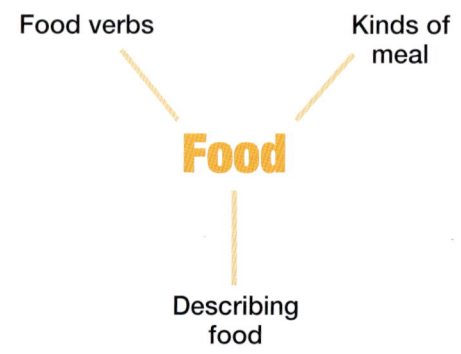

Food verbs Kinds of meal

Food

Describing food

2 Work in pairs and choose five questions from the list below. Then ask each other the questions.
- What meals do you eat with your family?
- Who prepares the food in your family?
- What do you like to eat on special occasions, eg your birthday?
- What did you have to eat last night?
- How often do you buy food? Where do you do the shopping?
- Do you eat out a lot? What kind of food do you like to eat at a restaurant?
- What did you have to eat this morning?
- Do you have a favourite food when you are sad? What is it?

A: *I'm going to ask you some questions about food and eating.*
B: *OK.*
A: *What meals do you eat with your family?*
B: *I usually have breakfast and dinner with my family. I have lunch at work.*

Reading

1 1.15 Read and listen to *Tastes comforting* on page 19. Do you have a name for this kind of food in your language?

2 Read the text again and make notes about each kind of comfort food under the headings *name*, *country* and *ingredients*.

3 Work in pairs and tell each other about the four kinds of comfort food in the text.

4 Do you have a comfort food? Tell your partner about it.

5 You are going to read more information about comfort food in different countries. Work in pairs. A: turn to page 126. B: turn to page 128.

Extend your vocabulary – *taste*

You can use the noun *taste* when you describe a flavour.
This chocolate has a very sweet taste.
It is also the name of one of the five senses (*sight, hearing, smell, touch* and *taste*).
You can use the verb *to taste* in the following ways:
taste + adjective
taste + *like / of* + noun
It tastes sweet / bitter / delicious / awful.
It tastes like chicken.
This water tastes of apples.
You can say *It tastes delicious* to give a compliment about food.
Complete the sentences with your own ideas.
- … has a sweet taste.
- I like food that tastes …
- I think … tastes awful.

tagine

Grammar

*It's **a dish** of pasta and meat. We are making **two dishes** like this.*
*There is **some meat** in the dish.*
*I like **coffee**. Can I have **a coffee** please?*
*We have **some meat** but we don't have **any vegetables**.*

- countable nouns can be singular or plural
- uncountable nouns do not have a plural form
- some words can be countable or uncountable
- use *some* and *any* with plural nouns or uncountable nouns
- we usually use *some* in affirmative sentences and *any* in negative sentences and questions

Tastes comforting

The expression comfort food is only around forty years old. It means a kind of familiar, simple food. People associate comfort food with good feelings, with childhood or with home.

Comfort food exists in all cultures. Some examples of popular comfort food from around the world include:

Roti – a kind of bread served with vegetables or lentils (popular in India).
Ramen – a dish of noodles with vegetables and meat in a soup (popular in Japan).
Tagine – a slowly cooked dish of meat and vegetables (popular in North Africa).
Poutine – a dish of fried potatoes with cheese and meat sauce (popular in French Canada).

1 Look at these words from the texts. Decide if each one is countable, uncountable or if it can be both.

bread	casserole	cheese	chocolate	cracker
lentil	meat	noodle	pasta	pizza	potato
sandwich	steak	sweet	toast	vegetable

ramen

2 Choose the correct word to complete the texts.

My comfort food

When I'm feeling sad, I always eat *any / some* chicken soup. Very hot chicken soup with pasta. There isn't *any / a* better dish for me.

Last summer I studied English in Scotland and stayed with *a / some* host family. Scottish food was OK, but they didn't have *a / any* good bread. Two weeks later a friend from Germany visited and brought me *some / any* delicious *Roggenbrot* bread. It was my comfort food.

Every time I go back to my village in Turkey, I ask my mother to prepare baklava for me. It's *a / any* special cake, with *a / -* honey and *any / -* nuts.

Speaking

1 Think of a dish that you like and make some notes about it. Use the headings below to help you.

Ingredients
Who usually prepares it
When you eat it
Why you like it

2 Work in pairs and tell each other about your dishes.

I'm going to tell you about arroz con costra. It's a Spanish dish and it's one of my favourites. It's a rice dish. My father usually makes it in the summer. You cook it with some meat …

G **Grammar focus** – explanation & more practice of nouns on page 134

Eating Unit 2

UNIT 2 Eating & Drinking

Part 2

Reading & Speaking
Ten secrets ... from the world's top kitchens

Grammar
Quantifiers (*a lot of, a little, a few, not enough, much, many*)

Vocabulary & Speaking
In the kitchen

Pronunciation
/k/ & /tʃ/

Listening
Zao Shen

Reading and Speaking

1 Work in pairs and ask each other these questions.
1 Can you cook?
2 Do you like cooking?
3 What dishes can you make?
4 Who is the best cook you know?

2 1.16 Read and listen to *Ten secrets ... from the world's top kitchens*. Which secret or secrets are about ...
a food preparation?
b food storage?
c eating?
d cleaning?
e the kitchen?

3 Did you know any of these tips? Tick (✔) the ones you knew.

4 Do you know any other good food tips? What are they?

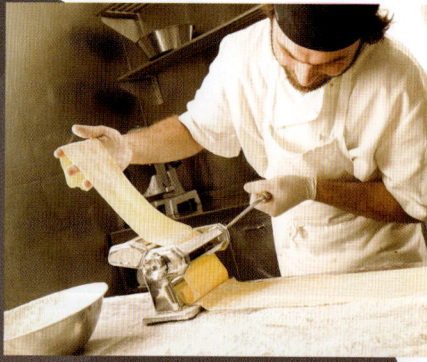

1 To give soup a beautiful golden colour, add some onion skin. Remember to take it out of the soup before you eat it.
2 Too much salt in a sauce? Add a little sugar or sparkling water.
3 Eggs will stay fresh if you store them with the pointed end down.
4 To clean a pan after cooking fish, put some cold tea in the pan for ten minutes first.
5 If you want a lot of juice from a lemon, cut it in half and put it in the oven for a few minutes first.
6 Lots of green bananas? Leave them in a bowl with a red tomato next to them.
7 When you cut an onion, put some bread under your nose. You may feel silly, but you won't cry.
8 Do you eat too much food at mealtimes? Turn off the lights. Dim lighting makes you want to eat less.
9 To see if pasta is cooked, throw a piece against the fridge. If it sticks on the fridge, it's cooked.
10 To make your kitchen smell good, put a little orange peel in the oven at 180°C for fifteen minutes.

Ten secrets ... from the world's top kitchens

Grammar

*Do you eat **too much food** at mealtimes? Put it in the oven for **a few minutes**. If you want **a lot of juice** from a lemon ... **Too much salt** in a soup?*

- use *a little* and *much* with uncountable nouns
- use *a few* and *many* with plural countable nouns
- use *a lot of* and *(not) enough* with plural nouns and uncountable nouns
- use *too much / many* to say there is more than you want

1 Read the sentences below about a busy head chef. Match the sentences 1–5 to the meanings a–e.
1 He is always a few minutes late for work.
2 He has a lot of friends at the restaurant.
3 He eats too many cakes and biscuits.
4 He doesn't get enough sleep.
5 He has enough work at the moment.
a He doesn't need any more.
b He should eat less.
c He isn't early.
d He's often tired.
e He has eight or nine.

2 Complete the questions with *much* or *many*.

In a typical day ...
- how _____ meals do you eat?
- how _____ coffee do you drink?
- how _____ time do you spend in the kitchen?
- how _____ portions of fruit do you eat?
- how _____ water do you drink?
- how _____ junk food or fast food do you eat?

3 Work in pairs and choose **four** questions from the list above. Then ask each other the questions. Use the expressions in the box to help you.

| a little | a lot | not many |
| not much | too many | too much |

G **Grammar focus** – explanation & more practice of quantifiers on page 134

20 Unit 2 Eating

Vocabulary and Speaking

1 Describe the differences between these three kitchens.

Useful language

- bowl
- glass
- oven
- spoon
- fire
- kettle
- saucepan
- toaster
- frying pan
- mug
- sink

Useful phrases

- This kitchen looks like it's in …
- There are … in this kitchen and … in that kitchen.
- I think this picture is more interesting. I prefer …

2 Which kitchen do you prefer? Why?

Pronunciation

1  1.17 Listen to the words below. Which have the /k/ sound, which have the /tʃ/ sound and which have both? Which word does not have a /k/ or a /tʃ/ sound?

| chill | chocolate | cloth | cook | cup |
| fork | knife | picture | quick | watch |

2 Listen again and repeat. What are the common spellings for /k/ and /tʃ/?

Listening

1 Look at the picture of Zao Shen. Which country do you think he is from? Who do you think he is?

2 1.18 Listen to a short talk about Zao Shen and answer the questions.
1 Who is Zao Shen?
2 Can you name one thing he does?
3 Where can you see pictures like this?

3 Are there any important beliefs about food or kitchens in your culture? What are they?

Eating Unit 2 21

UNIT 2 Eating & Drinking

Part 3

Speaking & Vocabulary
Containers and drinks

Reading
The people behind the drinks

Grammar
The infinitive

Speaking and Vocabulary

1 Work in pairs. How many correct phrases can you make with the words in the box?

a	glass cup mug bottle carton can	of	coffee cola juice milk tea beer water wine

Language note: some uncountable nouns can be countable if we believe there is a container, eg *two coffees* means *two cups of coffee*.

2 Work in pairs and ask each other these questions.

What do you like to drink …
- on a hot summer's day?
- in the morning, with breakfast?
- after dinner?
- in the winter, when it's cold outside?
- when you feel sad or miserable, as a comfort drink?

What other drinks do you like? When?

Reading

1 Look at the photos and names of different people on page 23. Do you know any of the names? What drinks are they associated with?

Useful phrases

- I don't know this name.
- I think this is …
- This is the name of a kind of coffee / water / beer.

2 1.19 Read and listen to the text *The people behind the drinks*. What do all the drinks have in common? Choose the best answer.

a They are all more than 100 years old.
b They are all cold drinks.
c They are not English drinks.

3 Read the text again and complete the sentences with the names of the drinks.

1 _____ sponsors a famous book.
2 _____ and _____ are from France.
3 _____ and _____ are hot drinks.
4 _____ was given as a present.
5 _____ and _____ were named after monks.

4 Do you know any of these drinks? Which ones?

22 Unit 2 **Drinking**

The people behind the drinks

Grammar

*He **wanted to make** a new drink.*
*It was **difficult to understand**.*

- use the infinitive after some verbs:
  agree, forget, need, try, want
- use the infinitive after adjectives

1 Read the extract from George Orwell's *A nice cup of tea*. Complete the rules by writing *to* or nothing (–) in each gap. Do you agree with his rules?

A nice cup of tea

It isn't easy to make a good cup of tea.
First of all, you should _____ use Indian or Ceylonese tea.
It's important _____ make tea in small quantities – in a teapot.
You need _____ make the teapot hot first.
Don't _____ put hot water in a cold pot.
Strong tea is the best kind of tea. One strong tea is better than twenty weak teas.
After you _____ put the tea in the pot, stir it. Or shake the pot.
Try _____ use a good breakfast cup for your tea. Tea is best in a good cup.
Don't forget _____ put the tea in the cup before you _____ put the milk in.
Tea is meant _____ be bitter. Don't put sugar in a nice cup of tea.

2 Write some rules for how to make a drink or some food that you know.

3 Work in pairs and tell each other your rules.

A nice …
It's important to …
You need to …
The best … to eat/drink is …
Try to use …
Don't forget to …

G **Grammar focus** – explanation & more practice of the infinitive on page 134

Perrier

Dr Louis Perrier was a doctor and politician in the south of France. At the end of the 19th century he got a job with a company that made special mineral water in a bottle. The water was originally popular in the UK and the US, but is now available around the world.

Cappuccino

The espresso coffee with hot milk has always had the Italian name cappuccino. It is more than three hundred and fifty years old and is now famous around the world. The name comes from a group of monks in Italy, the Capuchin monks.

Guinness

In 1759 an Irishman called Arthur Guinness started making beer in a small brewery in Dublin. He eventually created a dark beer called Guinness, which became Ireland's national beer. The Guinness company now owns many different products, the most famous being the *Guinness Book of World Records*, first published in 1955.

Earl Grey Tea

The Earl, Charles Grey, was British Prime Minister from 1830–1834. During his time in office, he received some special tea as a gift from China. The tea became very popular in Britain, and eventually people gave it the name Earl Grey tea.

Dom Pérignon

Dom Pérignon (1638–1715) was a blind Benedictine monk from Épernay, France. His senses of taste and smell helped him to improve the wines made at his monastery. It was Dom Pérignon who put the bubbles in champagne.

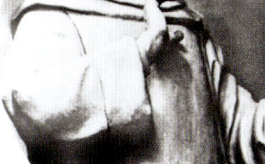

Glossary

blind (*adjective*) – unable to see
brewery (*noun*) – a place where people make beer
monk (*noun*) – a man who lives in a religious community away from other people

Drinking Unit 2 — 23

UNIT 2 Eating & Drinking

Part 4

Vocabulary
The human body

Listening
Water & the human body

Grammar
The infinitive of purpose

Pronunciation
/tə/ & /tuː/

Speaking
Drinks questionnaire

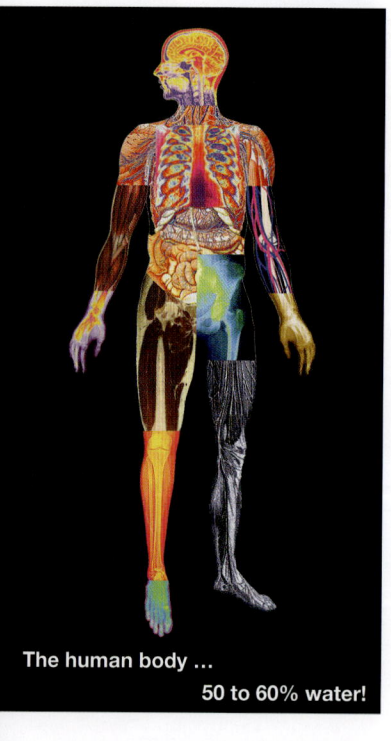

The human body …
50 to 60% water!

Vocabulary

1 How many parts of the body can you name in English? Work in pairs and complete the words below.

_ rm	b _ ck	e _ r
elb _ w	f _ ng _ r	f _ _ t
ha _ r	h _ nd	he _ d
k _ ee	l _ g	n _ se

2 Look at the words in the box. Decide if each part is inside (I) or outside (O) the body. Write I or O.

blood ___	bone ___	brain ___
heart ___	muscle ___	
nails ___	skin ___	

3 Work in pairs. How many parts from exercise 2 can you see in the picture?

Listening

1 You are going to hear a talk about water and the human body. First check you understand the words in the box.

| breathe | convert | factor |
| nutrients | temperature | waste |

2 1.20 Listen to the talk and write the parts of the body that you hear.

3 Listen again. What do the numbers mean?

| a few days | 2 | ⅔ | 22% |
| 75% | 85–95% | 92% | |

4 How much water do you drink? Do you think you drink enough water? Tell a partner.

Grammar

*Human beings need to drink water **to live**. What does water do **to help** the body?*

- we use the infinitive to say why we do something

1 Look at the pictures of different objects below. Describe what each object is for using the phrases in the box.

breathe underwater	drink with
make ice cubes	purify water
serve drinking water	water plants

You use this to water plants.

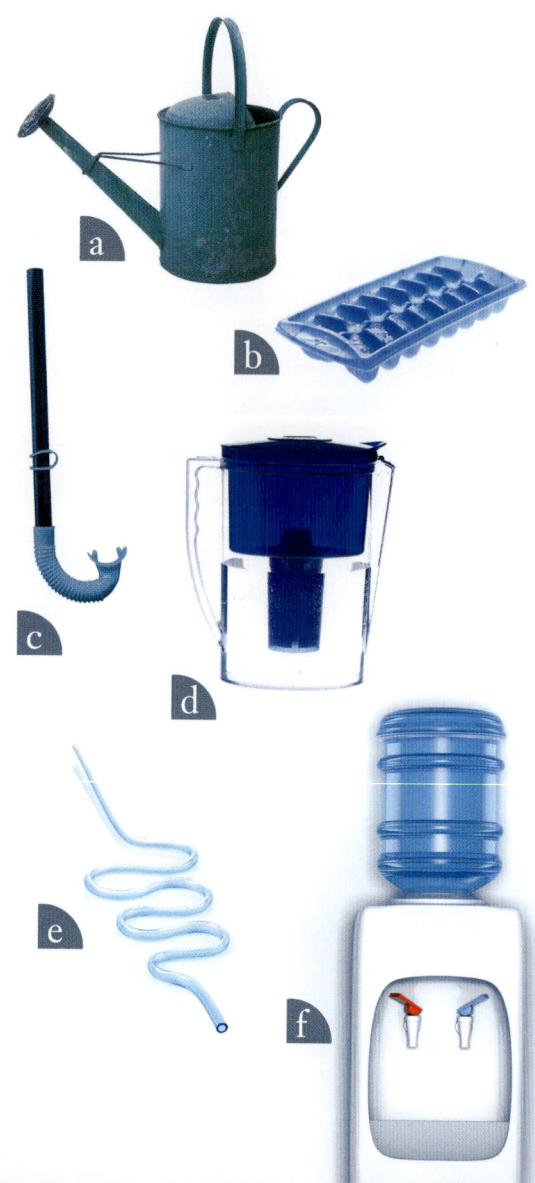

24 Unit 2 Drinking

2 Complete *More water facts* with *to* + a verb from the box.

flush   grow   have   produce   provide

More water facts

Around 2.5% of the planet's water is fresh water. The rest is salt water.

It usually takes between 50 and 100 litres _____ a shower.

It takes 5 to 10 litres _____ the toilet.

You need 1,900 litres of water _____ one kilogram of rice.

You need 100,000 litres of water _____ one kilogram of beef.

On average, it costs €23 _____ safe and clean water for one person.

About 1.1 billion people do not have access to clean drinking water. That's about 1 in 6 people.

3 Work in pairs. Complete the sentences in as many different ways as you can.

I went to the shop to …
People use water to …
He's learning English to …

G **Grammar focus** – explanation & more practice of the infinitive of purpose on page 134.

Pronunciation

1 🔊 1.21 Listen and circle how the underlined word is pronounced in each sentence.

It's <u>too</u> cold.   /tə/   /tuː/
You need <u>to</u> drink more water.   /tə/   /tuː/

2 🔊 1.22 Listen to the story below then practise saying the sentences. Pay attention to the pronunciation of /tə/ and /tuː/.

Last summer I went to Tunisia

It was too hot, and I needed something to drink.
I was hungry too.
I went to a shop to buy some water.
I didn't know how to ask for water.
I didn't have enough money to pay for it.
I spoke to the owner.
And he gave it to me for free.
He gave me some oranges too.

Speaking

1 Use the prompts to make questions.
- How much water / every day?
- Do / too little water?
- Do / water before you go to bed?
- Do / bottled water or tap water?
- How many bottles / week?

2 Work in pairs and choose one of the tasks below.

A Ask each other the questions from exercise 1.

B Make a similar questionnaire about a different drink, eg tea or coffee. Use the questions in exercise 1 to help you. Then interview another pair.

Drinking Unit 2   25

Function globally eating out

Warm up

1 Look at the pictures of four different places to eat. Work in pairs and describe the similarities and differences between them.

Useful language
- fast food
- self-service buffet
- flight attendant
- tray

Useful phrases
- I think this is in …
- It looks like a / an …
- In this picture they're … and in this picture they're …
- This one looks the most comfortable / expensive / interesting.

2 Have you been to any places like these? Which photo do you like the best?

Listening

1 🎧 1.23–1.25 Listen to three conversations. Match each one to a photo. There is one photo you don't need.

2 Listen again and answer the questions.

Conversation 1: Who is the reservation for?
Who is ready to order: the man or the woman?

Conversation 2: What is the problem with the food?
What size drink does the man have?

Conversation 3: Does the woman have anything else to drink?
Where does she have to pay?

Language focus: eating out

1 Put the words in the correct order to make useful phrases. Which phrases do customers say? Mark them with a **C**.

1 would to order you what like?
2 here think I there's a mistake.
3 the I have could bill?
4 your meal you did enjoy?
5 medium small, or large?
6 reservation we've a got.
7 over have to pay you there.
8 thanks lovely, it was.
9 for two, table please a.

2 🎧 1.26 Listen and check your answers. Then listen and repeat the phrases.

Speaking

Work in groups of three. A and B: you are customers. C: you work in a restaurant.

Turn to page 130 and choose a restaurant menu. Then roleplay a conversation. Use the new expressions you have learnt.

Global voices

Warm up

1 Complete the sentences with the words in the box. Use a dictionary to help you.

beetroot boil candy fry kebab lamb sweets

1 _____ is a kind of meat.
2 A _____ is a sort of meat dish.
3 _____ is a kind of vegetable.
4 _____ and _____ are sweet food made with sugar.
5 _____ and _____ are two ways of cooking food.

2 What other words could you use to complete these sentences?

Listening

1 You are going to listen to six people talking about food that makes them think of home. Try to match the names of food to the countries.

borsch candy kebab pizza schnitzel tortilla

1 Iran _____
2 Italy _____
3 Russia _____
4 Germany _____
5 US _____
6 Spain _____

2 1.27–1.32 Listen and check your answers.

3 Listen again and match the speakers 1–6 to the phrases a–f.

Speaker 1: Mo, Iran _____
Speaker 2: Gianfranco, Italy _____
Speaker 3: Elena, Russia _____
Speaker 4: Marlies, Germany _____
Speaker 5: Matt, US _____
Speaker 6: Sonia, Spain _____

a And it is very tasty really.
b I think it is a very simple dish.
c Of course not Pizza Hut but Napoli pizza.
d They remind me of growing up in the United States.
e Typical traditional food.
f You most often have it with French fries.

Language focus: listing ingredients

Choose the correct sentence.
1 a It consists of rice and lamb.
  b It consists with rice and lamb.
2 a It's made from eggs and potatoes.
  b It's made for eggs and potatoes.
3 a It's of vegetables, and meat and pasta.
  b It's made with vegetables, and meat and pasta.
4 a It is got rice and fish in it.
  b It has got rice and fish in it.

Speaking

1 Choose three of the topics below. Write one example of each on a piece of paper.
- a typical food or drink from your country
- a food or drink that you don't like
- a food or drink that you liked when you were a child
- a food or drink from another country that you like

2 Work in pairs and swap your lists. Can you guess the categories?

3 Tell each other more about the food or drinks on your lists.

Useful phrases
- It consists of …
- It's made from …
- It's delicious! / It tastes really good.

Mo, Iran Gianfranco, Italy Elena, Russia
Marlies, Germany Matt, US Sonia, Spain

Unit 2 Writing a description of food and drink

Reading

1 Read Gustavo's description of food in Brazil. Choose the best title for each paragraph.
a Drinks in Brazil
b Mealtimes
c Invitation to Brazil
d Food around Brazil

2 Complete the statements.
1 In Brazil, people tend to eat _____ meals a day.
2 The main meal of the day in Brazil is _____.
3 The national dish is _____.
4 The most typical drinks are _____.
5 Food and drink in Brazil are _____.

1 _____
In my country, people normally have three meals a day: breakfast, lunch and dinner. We also tend to have a lot of snacks between meals. For breakfast, we usually have coffee with milk and eat bread. We also like to eat fruits such as bananas, papaya, melon or watermelon, and to drink juice or yoghurt. Lunch is the main meal of the day. We generally eat a portion of beans and rice with beef, chicken or fish and salad. Dinner is similar to lunch but we tend to eat quite late, between seven and ten in the evening.

2 _____
The food in Brazil varies from region to region. Here in São Paulo, we like to eat feijoada with rice and meat on Wednesday or Saturdays. Feijoada is our national dish and it is cooked with beans and dried meat. In Minas Gerais, cheese bread is a speciality. In Bahia, the food is very spicy and hot. In the north of Brazil, people eat a lot of fish but in the south, it is common to have barbecues and to drink a kind of tea that is served very hot.

3 _____
I think that coffee is the most typical beverage in Brazil. People drink coffee almost all the time; for breakfast, at work, in restaurants and so on. We also like to drink beer, and on special occasions or for celebrations, we drink caipirinha. Caipirinha is a drink made with pinga or vodka mixed with sugar or honey and crushed lemons.

4 _____
If you come to Brazil, you will enjoy our delicious and varied food and drink. Welcome to Brazil!

Language focus: describing habits

1 Notice how we describe habits.
We *normally / generally / usually* have coffee with milk.
People *like to / tend to* eat quite late.
It is *common / customary* to have barbecues.

2 Complete the sentences.
1 We _____ to have our main meal in the evening.
2 It is _____ to use chopsticks when we eat.
3 On special occasions, people _____ to eat out.
4 People _____ have a sandwich for lunch.
5 It is _____ for families to eat together.
6 We _____ use fresh ingredients to prepare meals.

Writing skills: using commas

Use commas …
a to separate prepositional phrases.
In my country, people normally have three meals a day.
b to separate items in a list.
breakfast, lunch and dinner

1 Find more examples of a and b in the text.

2 Add commas to these sentences.
1 In China typical dishes are rice noodles and dumplings.
2 Noodles are made with flour eggs and water.
3 For breakfast people tend to have coffee bread and jam.

Preparing to write

1 Make notes about food and drink in your country. Use the paragraph titles to help you.

Mealtimes   Typical dishes   Drinks

2 Work in pairs and share your ideas.

Describing meals and dishes

- The main meal of the day is …
- Our national dish is …
- A speciality / typical dish is …
- Our main / staple food is …
- Our most typical drink is …
- On special occasions, we have …

Writing

Write a description of food and drink in your country for a class magazine. Use your notes and the useful phrases above to help you.

Global review

Grammar

Correct the mistakes in eight of these sentences and tick (✔) the two that are correct.
1 I need get more sleep.
2 English people drink a lot tea.
3 You drink too many coffee.
4 I use a coffee machine for make my coffee.
5 How much biscuits do you want?
6 Could I have a few sugar in my tea, please?
7 This chocolate tastes bitter.
8 I have too little eggs to make a cake.
9 Don't forget buy some noodles.
10 It's important to eat enough fruit and vegetables.

Vocabulary

Circle the correct option to describe each picture.
1 *bottle / carton / can* of juice
2 *mug / glass / cup* of coffee
3 *plate / frying pan / saucepan*
4 *spoon / fork / knife*
5 *oven / sink / microwave*
6 *finger / arm / elbow*
7 *knee / foot / back*
8 *nail / muscle / bone*
9 *casserole / vegetable / toast*
10 *cook / serve / taste*

Speaking and Writing

1 Work in groups of three and ask each other the questions.
 • What did you eat and drink yesterday?
 • Do you have a healthy diet?

> **Useful phrases**
> • I eat a lot of …
> • I eat / drink too much / many …
> • I don't eat enough …

2 Work in pairs. You are going to have a party for everyone in the class. Write a list of the food and drink you need to buy. Then compare your list with another pair.

Study skills

Evaluating your language learning

1 Work in pairs. Look back at the unit you have just studied. Tell each other which parts you found easy or difficult.

2 Think about what you have learnt in this unit. Mark the statements a, b, c or d.
a confidently and accurately
b quite confidently and accurately
c with help from my notes or my teacher
d with difficulty

> I can ...
> * describe my eating and drinking habits ____
> * ask about eating and drinking habits ____
> * talk about quantities ____
> * describe things in a kitchen ____
> * pronounce the sounds /k/ and /tʃ/ ____
> * find information in a short reading text ____
> * talk about containers and drinks ____
> * understand a simple listening passage ____
> * describe how to make a dish or drink ____
> * describe purpose using *to* + infinitive ____

3 Work in pairs and compare your answers.

4 Look at how Stefan has evaluated his language ability. Underline the phrases which describe ability.

> *I think I'm quite good at understanding reading texts in the book. Sometimes I find it difficult to understand the listening passages. I'm not very good at grammar but my pronunciation is quite good. I need to expand my vocabulary, especially everyday English. I need more practice in speaking.*

5 Work in pairs and describe your ability in the areas below. Make suggestions about how to improve.

Grammar   Reading
Vocabulary   Listening
Pronunciation   Speaking
Social situations   Writing

6 Write a letter to your teacher. Say what you have found easy and difficult in the classes so far. Describe your general language ability.

UNIT 3 Art & Music

Part 1

Vocabulary & Speaking
Works of art

Reading
Discovered!

Speaking
Art

Vocabulary and Speaking

1 Match the words to the pictures a–h.

cave art   old manuscript   painting
photograph   sculpture   self-portrait
sketch   statue

2 Work in pairs and describe the pictures. Use the words in exercise 1 and the useful phrases to help you.

Useful phrases

- This picture shows …
- I think this is a picture of …
- It looks as if + clause …
- This is from + time / place …
- I (really) like / don't like this picture …

Reading

1 🔊 1.33 Read and listen to *Discovered!* on page 31 and match each text to a picture. There are four pictures that you do not need.

2 Read the texts again and complete the sentences with one or more words.
1 The *Venus de Milo* is a statue of _____.
2 The *Venus de Milo* is now in _____.
3 Some Mexican workers discovered a sculpture while they were installing _____.
4 The sculpture is now in _____.
5 The couple from Milwaukee thought their Van Gogh painting was _____.
6 *Vase with Flowers* sold for _____.
7 The man found the Declaration of Independence while he was shopping at _____.
8 The manuscript was inside a _____.

Extend your vocabulary – *discover*

Words in the same family:
discover – verb
discovery – noun
discovered – adjective
undiscovered – adjective

Complete the sentences with the correct form of *discover*.
1 The archaeologists made an important _____ near the town castle.
2 We only want to _____ the truth.
3 News flash: Picasso sketches _____ in church basement.
4 The painting was _____ until the dealer noticed it on the wall.

Speaking

Work in pairs and choose **one** of the tasks below.

A Tell your partner about an object that is important in your family. Use these questions to help you prepare.
- What is the object?
- How old is it?
- Where did it come from?
- Why is it important to you?

B Ask each other these questions.
- Do you like art?
  What kind of art do you like?
- Do you have any art in your house?
  What is it? Who is it by?
- Have you ever been to an art gallery?
  Which one?

a

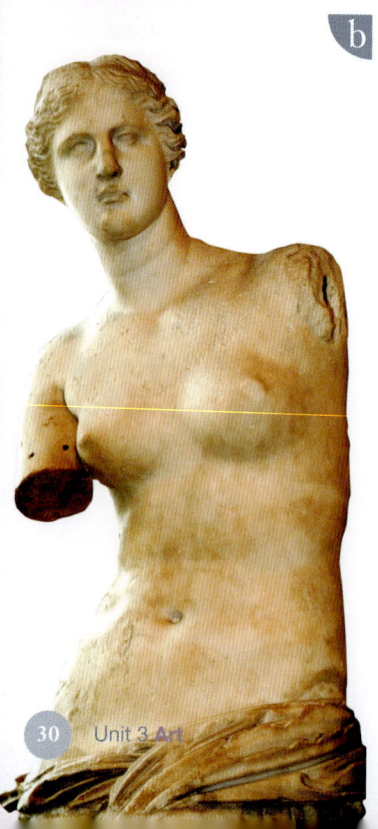
b

c

d

Discovered!
True stories of how valuable works of art were found in unexpected places

In a field
In 1820 a Greek peasant named Yorgos was working in his field on the island of Milos when he found several blocks of stone. Under the stones were four statues: three figures of the God Hermes and one of Aphrodite, the goddess of love. Three weeks later a group of French archaeologists arrived by ship. They bought the Aphrodite and took it to France. The king, Louis XVIII, called it *Venus de Milo* and gave it to the Louvre. It is now one of the most famous works of art in the world.

Under a street
On February 21, 1978, workers were putting down electrical cables on a busy street corner in Mexico City when they discovered a huge sculpture of the Aztec moon goddess Coyolxauhqui. It was more than four hundred years old and is now in the Museum of the Great Temple in Mexico.

On a wall
A man and his wife from Milwaukee, US, asked an art dealer to look at a painting they had in their home. While he was walking through the house, the dealer saw a different painting. The couple thought this was a reproduction of a Vincent Van Gogh, but it was in fact the original. On March 10, 1991, the painting *Vase with Flowers* sold for $1.4 million.

At a market
A man from Philadelphia was shopping at a flea market when he saw a wooden picture frame he liked. He paid $4 for it. When he got home he took the old picture out of the frame and found an old document behind it. It was a copy from 1776 of the American Declaration of Independence. The copy sold for $2.4 million in New York in 1991.

Glossary
archaeologist (*noun*) – a person who studies ancient societies
dealer (*noun*) – a person who sells a particular product
flea market (*noun*) – a market where old things are sold at low prices
peasant (*noun*) – a poor person who works on another person's farm
reproduction (*noun*) – a copy of something

Art & Music

UNIT 3

Part 2

Speaking
Retelling stories

Grammar
Past simple & past continuous

Vocabulary
Furniture & furnishings

Reading
The Picture of Dorian Gray

Pronunciation
Past simple regular verbs

Writing
A scene from a short story

Speaking

1 Work in pairs. Tell each other what you remember about the works of art from page 31. Use the phrases below to help you.

A Greek peasant was working in his field when …

In 1978 a group of Mexican workers were putting down electrical cables when …

One day an art dealer went to visit a man and his wife in Milwaukee. While he was walking through the house …

A man from Philadelphia was shopping at a flea market when …

2 Check your answers in the texts.

Grammar

1 Write the past simple form of the verbs in the box. All the verbs are in the text on page 31.

| arrive | ask | buy | discover | find |
| get | pay | see | sell | take |

2 Put the verbs into two groups, regular and irregular verbs.

*Three weeks later a group of French archaeologists **arrived** by ship.*
*Yorgos **was working** in his field.*
*While he **was walking** through the house, the dealer **saw** a different painting.*

- use the past simple to talk about completed actions in the past
- use the past continuous to talk about an action in progress in the past
- the past continuous is common with a simple past action when one action interrupts the other

3 Complete the texts with the past simple or past continuous form of the verbs in brackets.

In a hole in the ground

In 1978 workers _____ (dig) behind an old casino in Dawson City, Yukon when they _____ (discover) more than 500 films from 1903 to 1929. The films _____ (be) in perfect condition because of the cold temperatures.

In an attic

In 1990 Barbara Testa, a librarian, _____ (find) 665 pages of an old book while she _____ (look) through a trunk in her attic. The book _____ (be) the original manuscript of the great American novel *Huckleberry Finn* by Mark Twain.

As a bicycle rack

Every day employees of the God's House Tower Museum in Southampton, UK _____ (put) their bicycles against a black rock in the basement. In 2000 two Egyptologists _____ (visit) the museum. They _____ (examine) other items when they _____ (see) the black rock. They _____ (identify) it as a 2,700-year-old statue of the Egyptian King Taharqa.

 **Grammar focus** – explanation & more practice of past tenses on page 136

Vocabulary

1 Which of these things can you see in the picture on page 33?

armchair   carpet   coffee table
curtains   lamp   mirror   shelf
sofa   wall   window

2 Which things do you have in your house? Where are they?

The Picture of Dorian Gray

Dorian decided to go to bed and went slowly towards his bedroom. He walked along the hall and through the library. Basil's portrait of Dorian was on a wall in the library. Suddenly Dorian stopped and looked at the portrait. He was surprised. The painting looked different. The face in the painting had changed. Yes, it had changed! Quickly, Dorian opened the curtains. Sunlight came into the room. Dorian looked closely at the picture and saw that the face was different. It looked unkind and cruel. A huge mirror hung on another wall. Dorian looked in the mirror at his own face. He saw a beautiful young man. He had not changed. What was happening to the picture?

Suddenly Dorian remembered the day that Basil finished the picture. Dorian remembered his wish. He remembered his own words.

'I wish that I could always be young. I wish that picture could grow old instead of me. I would give anything and everything for this to happen. I would give my soul!'

Why did the face in the picture look cruel and unkind? Was his wish coming true? Was the picture changing?

The Picture of Dorian Gray (1890) is one of Oscar Wilde's most famous novels. The main themes are the purpose of art and the obsession with youth and beauty.

Glossary

cruel (*adjective*) – causing pain to people
huge (*adjective*) – extremely large
soul (*noun*) – the spiritual part of a person
wit (*noun*) – the ability to use words in a clever way that makes people laugh

Reading

1 🔊 1.34 Read and listen to an extract from the book *The Picture of Dorian Gray*. What was happening?

2 Work in pairs. Choose two of these questions and then discuss them.
- Have you read this book? Would you like to?
- Dorian makes a wish by saying: 'I wish that I could always be young. I wish that picture could grow old instead of me.' Would you make the same wish as Dorian? Why?
- Do you think people are too concerned with being young in today's society?
- 'Your personality is written on your face.' What does this quote mean? Do you agree with it?

Pronunciation

1 🔊 1.35 Listen to some sentences from the text. Tick (✔) the verbs that have an extra syllable in the past tense.

1. decide – decided ___
2. walk – walked ___
3. stop – stopped ___
4. look – looked ___
5. open – opened ___
6. remember – remembered ___

2 Practise saying the verbs and the past tense forms.

3 How do you pronounce the past tense of these verbs?

asked	discovered	hated	finished
listened	loved	needed	started
wanted	worked		

Writing

1 Read the opening sentences from four short stories.

Mark was sitting in the most comfortable armchair when he heard the strange noise again.

I was happy when I received the sculpture, but I didn't know its secret.

As she was looking at the photograph, she was certain she saw the eyes move.

It was the most beautiful painting, and the most dangerous.

2 Choose one of the sentences and continue the story. Write two or three more sentences.

3 Work in pairs. Swap your stories and add another sentence to your partner's story. Then return the story to your partner.

Oscar Wilde (1854–1900)

Oscar Wilde was an Irish writer of plays, poetry and novels. He was famous for his wit and commentary on the society of Victorian London.

Art Unit 3 33

UNIT 3 Art & Music

Part 3

Speaking
Describing pictures

Vocabulary
Audio & video

Listening & Writing
The history of sound recording

Grammar
Used to

Pronunciation
Used to

Speaking

1 Look at pictures a and b. Make some notes on the differences between them. Use the useful language and phrases to help you.

Useful language

- classical music
- conductor
- guitarist
- play
- concert hall
- drummer
- orchestra
- rock group

Useful phrases

- This looks like …
- The picture at the top / bottom shows …
- Maybe / perhaps it's in …

2 Work in pairs and describe the differences between the pictures.

3 Work in pairs and ask each other these questions.

- What kind of music do you like?
- Where do you usually listen to music? At home, at work, on the bus etc?
- Do you listen to music while you are working or studying? What kind of music?

Vocabulary

1 Rearrange the letters to make the correct words.

  ⏩

yapl   wirend   staf wadfror

⏹ ⏸ ⏏

pots   saupe   cejet

2 🔊 1.36 Listen and check your answers. Then repeat the words.

3 Match the words to the pictures on page 35.

audio cassette   ____
CD   ____
DVD player   ____
headphones   ____
MP3 player   ____
record   ____
record player   ____
video cassette   ____

Do you have any of these things at home?

4 🔊 1.37 Complete the instructions with the words in the box. Then listen and check your answers.

| button | down | off | on | plug | up | watch |

Right, to use this DVD player, first you _____ it in here. To turn it _____, just press this _____. Now press eject and put the disc in the tray. Close the tray and press play to _____ the film. To turn _____ the volume, use this button. If it's too loud, turn _____ the volume with this button. And, to turn it _____, press here.

5 Work in pairs. Make a similar set of instructions for a CD or MP3 player.

34   Unit 3 **Music**

 a
 b c
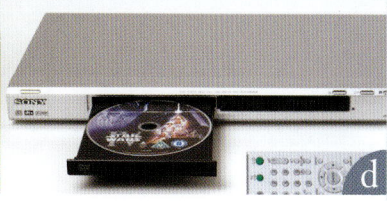 d
 e
 f
 g
 h

Listening and Writing

1 You are going to hear a lecture about the history of sound recording. Before you listen, list the words from vocabulary exercise 3 in order from oldest to newest.

2 🔊 1.38 Listen to the lecture and check your answers.

3 Listen again and complete the notes.

History of sound recording

The first: Thomas Edison in _____.
Edison predicts sound recordings for office dictation, speaking _____, education, talking _____ and music.
1900s: people play _____ on _____ players.
1920s: first films with sound – called _____.
_____: Philips introduces audio cassette.
1963: first _____ opens in Los Angeles.
1970s–1980s: VHS video, cassette Walkman and _____ – ends era of the record.
Early 1990s: DVD
1996: first digital music player sold in _____.
2001: Apple iPod, a popular _____, appears.
Current music devices can store _____ songs, video and _____.

Extend your vocabulary – saying and writing decades

In English we can use the phrase *the nineties* to describe the years from 1990 to 1999.
I was at university in the nineties.
In informal writing we can write *the 90s*.
The years 2000 to 2010 are sometimes called *the noughties*.
Complete the sentences with the correct decades.
1 I don't like music from _____ (1980–1989).
2 I was born in _____ (1960–1969).
3 I was at school in _____ (1970–1989).

Grammar

*People **used to** listen to music on vinyl discs.*
*Vinyl records **used to** be popular.*
*They **didn't use to** have CDs.*

- use *used to* to talk about regular actions in the past which don't happen now
- use *used to* to talk about situations in the past which aren't true now
- the negative of *used to* is *didn't use to*

1 Look at the picture below and rewrite the sentences with *used to*.

In those days families were bigger.
In those days families used to be bigger.
1 Most women were housewives.
2 People didn't have lots of things.
3 Most families didn't have a television.
4 Some families had a radio in the living room.

2 Make questions with *did* and *use to*. Add two more questions.
1 What music _____ you _____ listen to?
2 Where _____ you _____ go to school?
3 _____ you _____ have long hair?

3 Work in pairs and ask each other the questions.

G **Grammar focus** – explanation & more practice of *used to* on page 136

Pronunciation

1 🔊 1.39 Listen and repeat these sentences. Pay attention to the stressed words.

My <u>brother</u> <u>used</u> to <u>play</u> the <u>guitar</u>.
I <u>didn't</u> <u>use</u> to <u>listen</u> to <u>classical</u> <u>music</u>.
In connected speech, *used to* is pronounced /juːstə/.

2 Underline the stressed words in grammar exercise 1.

3 🔊 1.40 Listen and check your answers. Then repeat the sentences.

Music Unit 3 35

UNIT 3 Art & Music

Part 4

Vocabulary
Feelings

Listening
Music in film & TV

Speaking & Reading
High Fidelity

Vocabulary

1 Match the words in bold to the words in the box with similar meanings.

I was feeling **cheerful** today because …
… makes me feel very **calm**.
Last week I was **miserable** because …
I'm **frightened** of …
… makes me **sleepy**.
I'm always **anxious** when …

| angry | bored | excited | happy |
| relaxed | sad | scared | tense | tired |

2 Complete the sentences in exercise 1 so they are true for you.

3 🔊 1.41 Listen to four short pieces of music. How do they make you feel?

4 Imagine one of the short pieces of music is part of a scene from a film. Listen again and answer the questions.
- Where is the scene?
- Who is in the scene?
- How do they feel?
- What is happening?

5 Work in pairs and tell each other about the scene you imagined.

Listening

1 🔊 1.42 Listen to the composer Andy Price talking about how he uses music in films and TV programmes. Tick (✔) the feelings he mentions.

| angry | calm | excited | happy |
| sad | safe | scared | tense |

2 Listen again and choose the correct answers.

Music *used to be / has always been* an important part of film and television.

If you want an audience to feel *scared / angry* then use violins, played very quickly and on a high note.

Gentle music on a guitar, piano or violin is good for *love scenes / death scenes*.

Choral music (people singing) can make an audience feel *tense / sad*.

When the character of Robin Hood appears in the programme you can hear *trumpets / guitars*.

The orchestra *used to play / usually plays* in front of a large screen showing the film.

3 Work in pairs and compare your answers.

Andy Price is a composer for theatre, film, television and advertisements. His work includes the music to the BBC programmes *Robin Hood*, *Score* and *The Six Wives of Henry VIII*. He has won many awards for his work.

Extend your vocabulary – using *just*

You can use *just* in spoken English in different ways.
For emphasis:
Just turn it off!
To mean *only*:
It just makes me bored.
To mean *exactly*:
He is just like his father.

Put *just* into the following sentences. What does *just* mean in each one?
1 Be quiet, please.
2 It was a mistake.
3 Thank you for the CD, it's what I wanted.

Speaking and Reading

1 Work in pairs. Write down the names of all the pop groups you can think of in one minute.

2 Work with another pair and compare your lists. Then answer these questions.
- Is pop music popular in your country?
- Who listens to pop music?
- Do you like pop music?

3 1.43 Read and listen to the extract from Nick Hornby's *High Fidelity*. How does pop music make the writer feel?

4 Work in pairs and discuss these questions.
- Do you think the author is being serious or funny?
- The writer thinks British people are very scared of violence in videos.
Do people in your country worry about this? Do you think it is a problem?

High Fidelity

What came first, the music or the misery? Did I listen to music because I was miserable? Or was I miserable because I listened to music? Do all those records turn you into a melancholy person?

People worry about kids playing with guns, and teenagers watching violent videos; we are scared that some sort of culture of violence will take them over. Nobody worries about kids listening to thousands – literally thousands – of songs about broken hearts and rejection and pain and misery and loss. The unhappiest people I know are the ones who like pop music the most …

Nick Hornby (1957–)
Nick Hornby is one of Britain's most popular contemporary authors. He frequently writes about sport and music. Many of the characters in his books have aimless or obsessive personalities.

High Fidelity (1995) is set in London and is about Rob, a man who works in a record shop. His girlfriend has left him. In the rest of the book, Rob examines his past relationships with women and with music. There was a film of the book in 2000 and a Broadway musical in 2007.

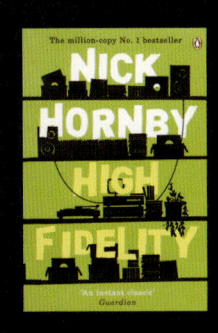

Glossary:
melancholy (*noun*) – a feeling of being very sad and having no hope
miserable (*adjective*) – extremely unhappy

Function globally agreeing and disagreeing

Warm up

1 Work in pairs and look at the pictures from four different films. Match the pictures to the types of film in the box.

| action | comedy | drama | horror | musical |
| romantic comedy | science fiction | thriller |

2 Describe the similarities and differences between the pictures.

3 What kinds of films do you like?

Useful language
- costumes
- in black and white
- martial arts

Useful phrases
- I think this one is a / an …
- I've seen / I've never seen …
- This could be from India / Germany …

Listening

1 1.44–1.46 Listen to three conversations about films and match each one to a situation. There is one situation you don't need.

a An interview situation, perhaps on television or on radio.
b A couple deciding what to rent at a DVD shop.
c Two friends coming out of the cinema.
d A teacher giving his opinions about films to a class.

2 Listen again and answer the questions.
Conversation 1: Did they both like the film?
Conversation 2: What kinds of films do they talk about?
Conversation 3: What kind of film does the woman want to see?

Language focus: agreeing and disagreeing

1 Read the sentences and mark *A* for agreeing, *D* for disagreeing or *I* for in between.

I agree. ____
Absolutely. / Definitely. ____
I don't agree (at all). ____
Well, maybe but … ____
You're absolutely right. ____
That's what I think too. ____
Oh please! ____
That's right. ____
I sort of agree / disagree but … ____
Exactly. ____

2 1.47 Listen and check your answers. Then listen and repeat the phrases. Try to copy the intonation.

Speaking

Work in pairs and choose **one** of the tasks below.

A Complete these sentences with your own ideas.
- Two great films are _____ and _____.
- Two great actors are _____ and _____.
- The best musician from my country is _____.
- The worst kind of music today is _____.

Compare your ideas with your partner. Do you agree or disagree?

B Decide how much you agree or disagree with these statements.
- Music used to be much better.
- Hollywood always produces the same kinds of films.
- There is a lot of exciting new art around today.
- Art galleries and museums are important for society.

Compare your opinions with your partner. Do you agree or disagree?

Global English

The power of music
by David Crystal

Music has the power to engage all the emotions – from excitement to relaxation, from tears to laughter. But why does it have such power over us? The clue lies in babies.

The word *lullaby* has been in English since the Middle Ages. It's one of several, such as *rockaby* and *hushaby*, which show how generations of mothers have helped their children fall asleep through music.

5 Babies can hear in the womb about two months before they're born. Newborns prefer their mother's voice to that of a stranger. And they show preferences in music too. One research study played the same tune to a group of mothers every day throughout pregnancy; another group of mothers didn't hear the tune. When all the babies were born, their heart-rate was monitored while the tune was played to them. Only the 'musical' babies reacted to the tune.

10 There's something special about the music of the voice. From the moment a baby is born, the mother talks to it in an unusual way. Her voice ascends and descends from very high to very low – almost like singing in speech. And infants soon copy. You can hear them trying to sing from around nine months of age.

Melody, of both speech and music, is especially
15 significant. In another study, infants were shown two pictures of their mother. In one she was singing and in the other she was speaking. They looked for longer at the singing one.

Singing also simplifies our vocal behaviour: words are
20 often shorter, sounds are clearer and repeat more often, and they often rhyme. Nursery rhymes work so well because they combine these effects – clear rhythm, repeated sounds and rhyme. In the music of speech lies the foundation of poetry.

Glossary

clue (*noun*) – a piece of information that helps you to understand something

longer (*adverb*) – more time

monitor (*verb*) – to regularly check something

stranger (*noun*) – someone who you do not know

Warm up

1 Complete the nursery rhyme with the words in the box. Do you know this rhyme?

| all | blows | fall |

Rock-a-bye baby on the tree top,
when the wind ___
the cradle will rock,
when the bough breaks
the cradle will ___,
down will come baby,
cradle and ___.

2 Can you remember any nursery rhymes in your language? What are they?

Reading

1 Read the text. Which sentence is the best summary?
a Music and poetry are linked.
b We are affected by music from a very young age.
c Babies are more sensitive to music than adults.
d Lullabies are an English invention.

2 Read the text again. What do these words refer to?
1 it (line 2)
2 It (line 3)
3 that (line 6)
4 it (line 11)
5 them (line 12)
6 one (line 18)
7 they (line 21)
8 they (line 22)

3 Which of the facts in the text do you think are the most interesting? Compare your ideas with a partner.

Language focus

Look at the words in the box and put them into two groups: *music* or *babies*. Then translate them into your language.

| born | infant | melody | musical | nursery |
| pregnancy | rhyme | singing | tune | womb |

Speaking

Work in pairs and ask each other these questions.
When you were a child …
- did your mother or father sing to you? What songs?
- did you have a favourite record or group? What was it?
- did you play an instrument? Which one?
- did you have music class at school? Did you enjoy it?
- did you use to sing? What songs?

Writing a review

Reading

1 Read Stefano's review of a concert he went to and answer the questions.
1. Who gave the concert?
2. What sort of singer is he?
3. Where was the concert held?
4. What happened during the concert?
5. Did Stefano enjoy the concert?

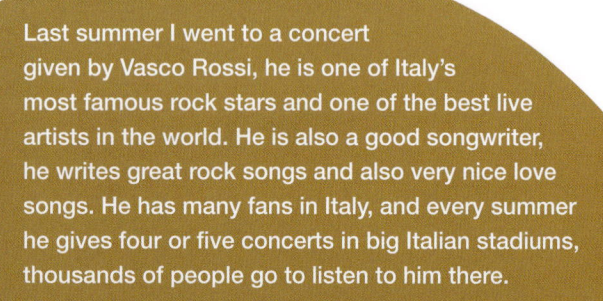

Last summer I went to a concert given by Vasco Rossi, he is one of Italy's most famous rock stars and one of the best live artists in the world. He is also a good songwriter, he writes great rock songs and also very nice love songs. He has many fans in Italy, and every summer he gives four or five concerts in big Italian stadiums, thousands of people go to listen to him there.

The concert took place in Rome's Olympic stadium, there were very many people there, all the tickets were sold out. I arrived at the stadium at three o'clock in the afternoon, I had to queue for six hours, I was very excited to see Vasco Rossi. The concert started at 9 o'clock in the evening, it went on for a very long time, maybe three or four hours. When Vasco Rossi started the concert everybody shouted, in the middle of the concert the crowd sang with him, it was very nice.

When the concert finished there were many security guards, everybody went home very quickly but without problems. I was very tired, I also went straight home, I was happy because of the excellent concert.

2 Would you enjoy the concert? Why?

Writing skills: sentences

1 You cannot join sentences with a comma. You need to start a new sentence using a full stop and capital letter. Stefano wrote:

Last summer I went to a concert given by Vasco <u>Rossi, he</u> is one of Italy's most famous rock stars.

He should write:

Last summer I went to a concert given by Vasco <u>Rossi. He</u> is one of Italy's most famous rock stars.

2 Find 12 more places where Stefano has joined sentences with a comma.

3 Join some of the sentences using *and*, *but* or *so*.

Language focus: adjectives

Make your writing more interesting by avoiding words like *nice*, *good* or *great*. Use your dictionary to find different words.

Improve Stefano's writing by using these words in the text.

| moving | powerful | talented | tender and expressive |

Preparing to write

1 Think of a concert you have been to or would like to go to. Make notes about it. Use the useful phrases below to help you.

Paragraph 1: Who was the concert given by? Give some information about the performer.
Paragraph 2: Where did the concert take place? Who was in the audience? What happened during the concert? How did you feel?
Paragraph 3: What happened at the end? How did you feel?

2 Work in pairs and share your ideas.

Describing a concert

- The concert was given by …
- It was a live / open air / sell-out concert.
- It took place in a stadium / a concert hall / a field.
- The hall was full / packed / half empty.
- The audience cheered / clapped / shouted.
- The music was brilliant / powerful / moving.
- I felt excited / moved / happy.

Writing

Write a review of a concert. Use your notes to help you.

Global review

Grammar

1 Complete the sentences with the past simple or past continuous form of the verbs in brackets.

1. How much _____ (*you / pay*) for that painting?
2. I _____ (*not / pay*) anything. It was a present.
3. When we _____ (*arrive*) at the cinema, our friends _____ (*wait*) for us.
4. My grandfather _____ (*find*) a valuable manuscript while he _____ (*work*) in his attic.
5. He _____ (*sell*) it to the museum for more than half a million dollars.

2 Complete the sentences with the correct form of *used to* and the words in brackets.

1. What kind of music _____ (*you / listen*) to when you were a child?
2. I _____ (*listen*) to pop music. I _____ (*not / like*) classical music then, but I do now.

Vocabulary

1 Read the definitions and complete the words.

1. a large group of musicians who use instruments to play classical music — o _____
2. you can listen to live music here — c _____ / h _____
3. an image of a person or animal, made of stone, metal or wood — s _____
4. you usually put books on these — s _____
5. a comfortable object to sit on — a _____

2 Complete the sentences with the correct word.

1. I used to be *angry / tense / frightened* of horses.
2. Sanna always has a happy face – she's a *sad / cheerful / scared* person.
3. I hate exams – they make me *anxious / relaxed / sleepy*.
4. As a child I used to feel very *miserable / bored / excited* about going on holiday – it was the best week of the year.

Speaking and Writing

1 Work in pairs. You are ill in bed and feeling miserable. Tell your partner how to find your favourite music and play it on your music player. Then swap roles and repeat.

2 Work in small groups. Write four sentences about your childhood using *used to* or *didn't use to*. One must be false. Take it in turns to read out your sentences and try to guess which one is false.

Study skills

Conversation partners

1 Work in pairs and discuss these questions.
- How often do you speak English outside class every week?
- In what situations do you speak English? For example, with friends or family, at work, in social situations etc.
- What do you talk about?
- How can speaking outside class help to improve your speaking ability?

One way to practise speaking is to meet with a conversation partner between classes. Your partner can be someone from your English class. You can use some of your time together to practise what you have learnt in class.

2 Work in pairs. Make arrangements to meet as conversation partners this week.

* Decide on a time and place to meet.
  In school, before or after the class?
  In one person's house at the weekend?
  In a bar or café in the evening?
  On the phone?

* Decide how long you will meet for.
  For fifteen minutes?
  For half an hour?
  Some other length of time?

* Decide which of these topics you would like to talk about. Add your own ideas.
  Finding out about each other.
  Your taste in art, music or books.
  Things you used to do in a previous school.
  Feelings that you had this week.
  Some things that you did this week.
  Instructions for using something.
  _____

3 Make some notes after the meeting.
- What was the most helpful or interesting part of the meeting?
- What was difficult?
- What will you do differently next time?

UNIT 4 Hopes & Fears

Part 1

Vocabulary
Adjectives & synonyms

Reading
When I grow up ...

Grammar
Future hopes & plans

Speaking
My hopes & plans

Vocabulary

1 Look at the phrases below. Put them in order from most important (1) to least important (4). Compare your answers with a partner.

being **good-looking**   being **intelligent**
being **rich**   having **good** health

2 Match the words in bold in exercise 1 to the words in the box with similar meanings. There are two words in the box that you don't need.

awful   beautiful   clever   excellent
handsome   smart   terrible   wealthy
well-off   wonderful

3 Look at the two extra words. What are they synonyms of?

4 Look at your list from exercise 1. Do you think your order was different in the past? How about in the future? Complete the sentences and then compare with a partner.

When I was younger I probably thought … was more important.

… will be more important when I'm older.

Reading

1 Read the text *When I grow up*. What are the children talking about?
a Their hopes for their own lives and their families
b Their hopes for the world
c Both a and b

2 Read the text again. Which quotes are the most interesting for you? Choose two quotes and tell a partner.

3 Work in pairs. Choose two of these questions and then discuss them.
- Do you think these children are optimistic or pessimistic about the future?
- Do children in your country have similar hopes?
- Did you have similar hopes when you were a child?

WHEN I GROW UP ...

I'd like to be **super intelligent**.

I want to live with **my mum** as long as I can.

I hope to have a **rich** husband.

I hope that people in my area **say sorry** when they do something **bad**.

I'd like to have **lots of money**.

I hope we have more places where you can **sit and talk** without the sound of **cars**.

To put the **world's money** together and give Africa **water**.

I hope to have a **lot of money**.

I'm planning to **travel** and learn **different languages**.

I want to **help my father** pay for things.

I'd like thousands of people to **watch me on TV**.

My family is going to find a **box of treasure**.

I hope that my **mum** meets someone and **has a baby**.

42 Unit 4 **Hopes**

Grammar

*I **hope** to have a lot of money.*
*I **would like** to be super intelligent.*
*I am **looking forward to** being older.*
*I'm **going to** be a fun but good teacher.*

- use *hope*, *plan*, *want* and *would like* to talk about future hopes that aren't definite
- use the infinitive after *hope*, *plan*, *want* and *would like*
- use *look forward to* to talk about definite future plans
- use *be going to* to talk about things you have already decided to do

1 How many correct sentences can you make with the words in the table? Use the text to help you.

| I | 'm - | hope
going
looking
   forward
planning
want
would like | to | get
getting | a good
job. |

2 Complete the text using the correct form of the words given.

The hopes of children

In a survey of English schoolchildren, researcher Cathie Holden found that, for their personal future, the majority of boys and girls hope *to go / going* to university or college. They also all hope *getting / to get* a good job. More boys are planning *to pass / pass* their driving test than girls, and more girls are looking forward to *have / having* children.

For their local area, children in the report said they hope for less violence and fewer poor people. They also said that they would like *have / to have* more parks and places to play. The majority of boys and girls are looking forward to *living / live* in a world without wars and an important number of them said they would like things *to get / getting* better in the developing world.

G **Grammar focus** – explanation & more practice of future tenses on page 138

Speaking

1 Choose **three** of the ideas in the box that you would like to talk about.

- A place you hope to visit one day
- Something you hope you **don't** do in the future
- Something you're not looking forward to
- A person you'd like to meet one day
- A person you're going to see today

2 Work in pairs. A: tell B about your ideas. B: ask for more information.

3 Swap roles and repeat.

*I'm planning to have **one child** and spend **lots of time** with him or her.*

*I'd like my dad to **understand me** one day.*

*I want to be **good-looking**.*

No wars because my brother's dad will die, he's in the army.

*I'm going to be a **fun** but **good teacher**.*

*I'd like to have **less pollution** in my city.*

*I'm looking forward to being **older** and not having to **listen to my parents** any more.*

*I want to have a **nice house**.*

*I'm going to get a **good wife**.*

*I'd like people to grow up but **never die**.*

*I'd like to **make a difference**.*

*For the **world** to be more **human**.*

*I want to be **wise**.*

UNIT 4 Hopes & Fears

Part 2

Speaking & Listening
A profession of hope

Vocabulary & Pronunciation
Global issues, word stress

Grammar
Future plans & intentions (*be going to*, present continuous)

Reading & Speaking
Pandora's box

Josh Gross and Helle Hansen are based in Denmark. In terms of foreign aid, Denmark is one of the most generous countries in the world. There are many NGOs (Non-Governmental Organisations) in Denmark that work on projects in Latin America and Africa.

Speaking and Listening

1 Study the graph about foreign aid below. Then work in pairs and discuss the questions.

- Does anything about the graph surprise you?
- Do you know any aid organisations? What are they?
- Have you ever given money to an aid organisation?
- Do you think rich countries should give more money in foreign aid?
- Do you know anyone who works for an aid organisation?

2 1.48 Listen to two aid workers talking about their next job. Put the interviewer's questions and comments in the correct order.

How did you become aid workers? ___
What is the most important thing in your job? ___
So, tell us about yourselves. 1
Thanks for your time. ___
What are you going to do there? ___

3 Listen again. What do these words mean in the listening?

| Danish | Guatemala |
| two years ago | village |

4 Would you like to work for an aid organisation? Why?

Vocabulary and Pronunciation

1 Match the words in the box to the definitions below.

| disease | homelessness | hunger |
| natural disasters | pollution | poverty | war |

1 people do not have enough money
2 people do not have a place to live
3 people do not have enough food
4 people are sick
5 countries are fighting each other
6 weather or environmental problems such as floods (too much water) or earthquakes (when the earth moves)
7 the air, water or land is dirty

2 Complete the pronunciation chart with the words from exercise 1.

O	Oo	oO	Ooo	oOo
war	natural	___	___	___
___	___			

3 1.49 Listen and check your answers. Then repeat the words.

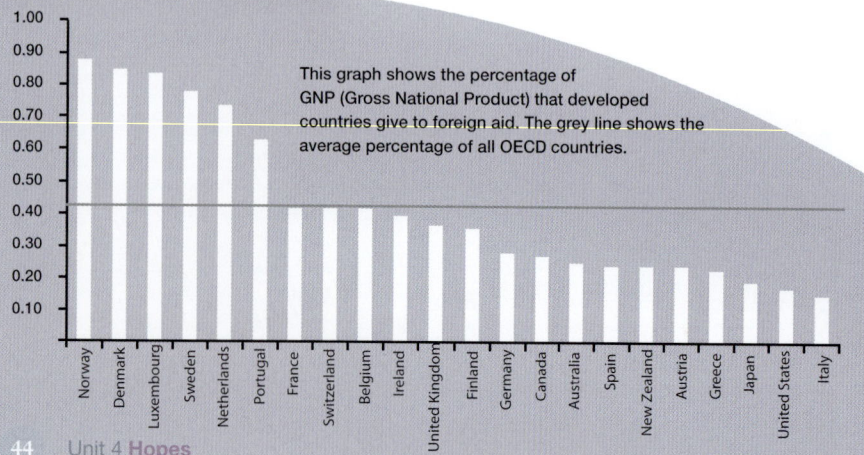

This graph shows the percentage of GNP (Gross National Product) that developed countries give to foreign aid. The grey line shows the average percentage of all OECD countries.

Countries (left to right): Norway, Denmark, Luxembourg, Sweden, Netherlands, Portugal, France, Switzerland, Belgium, Ireland, United Kingdom, Finland, Germany, Canada, Australia, Spain, New Zealand, Austria, Greece, Japan, United States, Italy

44 Unit 4 **Hopes**

Grammar

*We **are going to work** with the children there. The organisation **is starting** a new project in Guatemala next year.*

- use *be going to* to talk about things you have already decided to do
- use the present continuous to talk about future plans, often when they are already arranged

1 Read the text and decide if the underlined parts are correct or incorrect. Then correct the mistakes.

A new project

Susana works for a Spanish NGO in Madrid. The organisation <u>is start</u> a project next month in Ethiopia. Susana <u>is going for work</u> with a local women's organisation in the country. Together they <u>are going to develop</u> an educational project for pregnant women. Susana <u>is going to travel</u> to Ethiopia with a group of doctors. 'I'm a bit nervous, but I've been to Africa before and I know Ethiopia,' she says. '<u>It's going to being</u> a great project.'

2 Complete the questions with the present continuous or *be going to*.

1. A: What _____ (do) after class?
   B: Meeting a friend.
2. A: _____ you _____ (go) away next summer?
   B: No, I'm staying here.
3. A: _____ you _____ (read) an English book this year?
   B: Yes, I am. I have a detective novel I want to read.
4. A: _____ you _____ (work) tomorrow?
   B: Yes, I am. I start at 8am!
5. A: _____ you _____ (study) English next year?
   B: Yes, I think so.

3 Work in pairs and ask each other the questions from exercise 2.

G Grammar focus – explanation & more practice of future tenses on page 138

Pandora's box

In Greek mythology, the character Pandora had a large box. It contained all the troubles of the world. When she opened the box, she let all the troubles come into the world except one – hope. The Greeks thought that hope was also very dangerous. But without hope, people were filled with despair. Finally Pandora opened the box again and let out hope as well.

Reading and Speaking

Work in pairs. Read *Pandora's box* and then discuss the questions.

- Why do you think the Ancient Greeks thought hope was dangerous?
- Did people use to have more hope twenty years ago? A hundred years ago?
- Are you a person with a lot of hope? Why or why not?

Hopes Unit 4

UNIT 4 Hopes & Fears

Part 3

Reading
Things will get worse

Grammar
Prediction & ability (*will, be able to*)

Vocabulary
Phrasal verbs with *get*

Reading

1 Which novels do students in your country usually have to read at school? Did you read them?

2 Look at the titles below of three famous books that students in many English-speaking countries often study. Do you know any of these books?

3 1.50 Read and listen to the summaries and tick (✔) the features they have in common.
a The story happens in the future.
b The government controls everything.
c The story happens in England.
d People are happy.

4 Read the summaries again and decide if the sentences refer to *1984*, *Brave New World* (BNW) or *A Handmaid's Tale* (HT).
1 Women won't be able to have children. ___
2 There'll be only three countries in the world. ___
3 There will be a nuclear disaster. ___
4 We won't have wars. ___
5 Babies will be born in factories. ___
6 The government will control people's thoughts. ___
7 Love will be a crime. ___
8 People won't get sick from disease. ___

5 Look at the sentences in exercise 4. Do you think these things will happen in the future? Tell a partner.

Useful phrases
- It's possible.
- I don't think …
- Maybe …
- I'm sure … won't …
- I'm sure … will …
- I hope not.

Things will get worse …
Famous dystopias in literature

Nineteen Eighty-Four

The novel is set in the future, but it is the year 1984. Winston Smith lives in London, part of the country Oceania. There are three countries in the world: Oceania, Eurasia and Eastasia. Big Brother is the leader of Oceania. The government controls everything, even people's thoughts. Winston works for the government, but he is getting tired of his boring life. He meets Julia, another worker, and they fall in love – a crime in Oceania. The government discovers their secret, and Winston and Julia must go to the Ministry of Love, a centre for enemies of Big Brother.

The author: George Orwell (1903–1950), English

Brave New World

London, 600 years in the future. The Controllers are the rulers of the world. People don't know war, poverty, disease or pain. They enjoy leisure time, sports and pleasure, but they are not free. The Controllers create babies in factories. Adults are divided into five social classes, from the intelligent *alphas* to the worker *epsilons*. When a man from a wild area of the world gets to London, he criticises the society. In the end, he has to choose between joining them or dying.

The author: Aldous Huxley (1894–1963), English

Glossary
dystopia (*noun*) – imaginary place or situation where everything is very bad
infertile (*adjective*) – not physically able to have children
pollution (*noun*) – chemicals and other substances that have a harmful effect on air, water or land
revolution (*noun*) – a situation in which people completely change their government or political system
totalitarian (*adjective*) – controlling a country and its people in a very strict way
underground resistance (*noun*) – a secret organisation that fights against the group that controls their country

A Handmaid's Tale

In the future a revolution replaces the government of the United States with the totalitarian Republic of Gilead. Because of pollution and nuclear accidents, many women are infertile. New laws create the job of handmaid, a woman who can have babies for rich families.
This is the story of Offred, a handmaid. Offred works for Fred, a commander, and his family. She wonders if she can get away, and learns about an underground resistance from another handmaid. But there isn't much time. If Offred doesn't get pregnant soon, she knows they will send her to the dangerous colonies.

The author: Margaret Atwood (1939–), Canadian

46   Unit 4 Fears

Grammar

*There **will** be only three countries in the world.*
*Women **won't be able to** have children.*

- use *will* and *won't* to talk about future predictions
- use *will / won't be able to* to talk about ability or possibility in the future

1 Read the text about *Fahrenheit 451*. Complete the summary below by rewriting the underlined sentences with *will / won't* or *will / won't be able to*.

Fahrenheit 451

It is 24th century America. The government controls society through the media. It is criminal to be an intellectual. People can't read or own books, as books are against the law. The population gets all their information from the television. They don't know their history. Guy Montag is a fireman. Firemen don't stop fires, they start them. They burn books at a temperature of 451 degrees. One day Montag meets the young Clarisse, who makes him question the society he lives in. Soon Montag gets interested in the books he is supposed to destroy.

The author: Ray Bradbury (1920–), American

In Ray Bradbury's vision of the future …
the government will control society through the media.

2 Read the definition of *utopia*. Write five predictions for a future utopia.

utopia (*noun*) – an imaginary place or situation in which everything is perfect

G **Grammar focus** – explanation & more practice of prediction & ability on page 138

Vocabulary

1 Look at these phrases with *get* from the summaries. Write them next to the correct meanings of *get* in the table below.

1 Winston works for the government, but he is *getting tired* of his boring life.
2 When a man from a wild area of the world *gets to London* …
3 If Offred doesn't *get pregnant* soon …
4 The population *gets all their information* from the television.
5 Soon Montag *gets interested* in the books …

Meaning of *get*	Examples	
become	*getting tired*	
receive		
arrive		

2 Match the phrasal verbs with *get* to the correct definitions.

1 get around   a return (from a journey)
2 get away   b travel
3 get back   c get out of bed
4 get together d leave / escape
5 get up   e spend time with someone

3 Work in pairs and ask each other the questions.

Imagine it's a perfect, utopian world …

- What time do you get up every day?
- What time do you get back home from work?
- Where do you get away when you need a holiday?
- How often do you get together with friends and family?
- How do you get around? What kind of transport do you use?

Fears Unit 4   47

UNIT 4 Hopes & Fears

Part 4

Vocabulary
Geographical features

Listening
An inconvenient truth

Grammar
Future time clauses

Speaking
Climate change questionnaire

Vocabulary

1 Look at the pictures and complete the words with the correct vowels.

2 1.51 Listen and check your answers. Then repeat the words.

CLIMATE CHANGE the signs are here

EUROPE
Stronger st_rms and increased chance of fl_ _ ds

AFRICA
L_k_s and r_v_rs disappearing

NEW ZEALAND
_c_ _ns getting warmer

MEXICO, US
Numerous f_r_st fires

AFRICA
Area of d_s_rt increasing

GREENLAND
Glacial _ce melting

Listening

1 Look at the film poster on page 49. How does the poster describe the film? What do you think it is about?

2 1.52 Listen to people talking about the film and check your answer.

3 Listen again. Are the statements true (T) or false (F)?

Speaker 1: He saw the film a few years ago.
Speaker 2: She didn't know about global warming and climate change before she saw the film.
Speaker 3: He liked the film.
Speaker 4: He thinks it's a typical Hollywood film.
Speaker 5: She doesn't believe that climate change is happening.
Speaker 6: He thinks it's important for young people to see it.

4 Have you seen this film? Would you like to?

Extend your vocabulary – –ed / –ing adjectives

Terrified describes how we feel.
I was terrified by the film.
Terrifying describes things or situations that make us feel terrified.
It was a terrifying experience.
We can use this rule for many adjectives: *bored / boring, frightened / frightening, interested / interesting, surprised / surprising.*

Choose the correct words to complete the dialogues.

1 A: Did you see the film?
   B: Yes, I did. It was long, and really *bored / boring*.
2 A: So, was he angry?
   B: No. He was very *relaxed / relaxing* about the whole thing. I was *surprised / surprising*.
3 A: I'm a bit nervous about the heat this summer.
   B: I know what you mean. It's a *worrying / worried* situation.

Unit 4 **Fears**

Grammar

After you see this film, you will think differently.
If we reduce carbon emissions, we will reduce global warming.

- after future time clauses such as *after, before, when* and *if* we use a present tense

1 Complete the sentences with the present simple or future simple of the verbs in brackets.

1 If we _____ (not do) something now, we _____ (have) serious problems in the future.
2 If you _____ (look) at the ten hottest years, you _____ (see) they happened in the last fourteen years.
3 When this climate change _____ (happen) I _____ (be) dead.
4 You _____ (think) differently after you _____ (see) it.

2 Work in pairs and complete the sentences with your own ideas.

After class finishes …

I … before the end of this year.

If the weather is good tomorrow …

When I have enough money …

G **Grammar focus** – explanation & more practice of future time clauses on page 138

Speaking

1 Read the questions below and think about your answers.

How to reduce your carbon footprint
1 Do you use energy-saving light bulbs? How many?
2 Do you recycle anything? What?
3 Do you ever walk / take the bus instead of driving? How often?
4 Do you use a lot of hot water at home? What for?
5 Do you buy things with lots of packaging? What?
6 Have you ever planted a tree? When?

2 Work in pairs and ask each other the questions. If your partner answers *yes*, ask the follow-up question.

3 Look at the information in the table and tell your partner how much carbon they will save if they make these changes.

Action	Carbon saving
Change to energy-efficient light bulbs	68 kg per year
Recycle half of your household waste	1,095 kg
Walk instead of driving	0.5 kg per km
Wash your clothes in cold water	225 kg per year
Reduce your household waste by 10%	544 kg
Plant a tree	907 kg

Function globally making offers and decisions

Warm up

Work in pairs and choose three situations from the list below. Roleplay a short conversation for each situation.

Situations
1. A: you are talking to a friend (B). Your train to the airport leaves in 5 minutes. You're late!
   B: your car is parked outside.
2. A: you arrive at your destination and get off the train.
   B: you are carrying a very heavy bag.
3. A: you are in the train station café with a friend (B).
   B: you don't have enough money to pay for the coffees.
4. A: you are at the train station but have missed your train. You want to buy a ticket for the next train.
   B: you work in the ticket office.

Listening

1 1.53–1.55 Listen to three conversations. Match each one to a situation in the Warm up. There is one situation you don't need.

2 Listen again and answer the questions.
Conversation 1: How much is the bill?
Conversation 2: How is the man going to get to the airport?
Conversation 3: What train is the woman going to take?

Language focus: offers and decisions

1 Read the information in the table. What verb do we often use to make offers and decisions?

Offers	I'll carry those books for you.
	Shall I pay for this?
	Let me take that for you.
Decisions	I'll take the next train.
	I won't take the train. I'll take a taxi.

Language note: *shall* is usually used only in questions and with *I* or *we*.

2 Complete the offers or decisions with *will* or *shall* and a verb from the box. There is one verb you don't need.

| carry | have | help | pay | take |

1. A: Are you ready to order?
   B: Yes. I _____ a salad.
2. A: I don't understand this.
   B: That's all right. I _____ you.
3. A: The next train is in twenty minutes.
   B: _____ we _____ it or wait?
4. A: Here, let me take those bags.
   B: Thanks, but it's OK. I _____ them.

3 1.56 Listen and check your answers. Then listen and repeat the phrases.

Speaking

Work with a new partner and choose **one** of the tasks below.

A Repeat the warm up activity using the new expressions you have learnt.

B Look at the audioscript on page 154 and choose one of the conversations. Practise the conversation and try to memorise it.

Global voices

Warm up

1 Read ten reasons why people learn English. Choose the top 3 and the bottom 3 for you.

I'm learning English because …
1 I'd like to get a job with a multinational company.
2 I want to understand songs, TV programmes or films in English.
3 I hope to get a job with a company in the USA.
4 I'd like to be an English teacher.
5 It will be helpful for my career.
6 I'm planning to get a job in the tourism industry.
7 I want to meet other English-speaking people and make friends.
8 It's important for my studies.
9 It's a world language and it's important to know.
10 I like English and American culture.

2 Work in pairs and compare your answers. Can you think of any other reasons why people learn English?

Listening

🔊 **1.57–1.62** Listen to six people talking about why they are learning English. Which reasons from exercise 1 do they give? Write the numbers.

1 Abdul, Libya ___
2 Olga, Russia ___
3 Mert, Turkey ___
4 Naif, Saudi Arabia ___
5 Arthur, France ___
6 Dain, South Korea ___

Language focus: synonyms

Read the sentences from the listening. Which word in the box has a **different** meaning to the word in bold?

1 Well I believe English is very important **nowadays**.
Naif, Saudi Arabia

| actually | currently | now | these days |

2 I'm learning English because it will be helpful for my **career**. Abdul, Libya

| job | profession | university studies | work |

3 We need to study English. It is **essential**.
Dain, South Korea

| important | necessary | obvious | vital |

Speaking

1 Read the questions about learning English. They are typical questions from international English speaking exams. Choose three questions you can answer.
- How long have you been learning English?
- Why are you learning English?
- How important is English in your country?
- How will English be useful to you in the future?

2 Think about your answers and practise what you want to say.

3 Work in pairs and ask each other the questions.

Unit 4 Writing an email to a friend

Reading

1 Read two emails between friends. What do they arrange to do?

Hi Pamela,

I am writing to invite you to go to the cinema with me this weekend. I would like to see *La Vie en Rose*.

It is a drama starring Marion Cotillard and it has had very good reviews. It is the true story of the famous French singer, Edith Piaf. I have heard that the music is beautiful and the acting is brilliant.

We could meet in front of Cinemark at Higienópolis Mall at four o'clock on Saturday. Would that be convenient for you?

Yours sincerely

Laura

Hello Laura,

I would love to go to the cinema with you. That would be wonderful. I would really like to see this film. My sister has seen it and she says it is great. I will see you at four o'clock.

Pamela

2 Would you like to see this film? Why?

Writing skills: informal style

1 Are these statements true (*T*) or false (*F*)?

In emails to friends …
a do not use contractions such as *I'm*, *it'll*.
b use informal salutations such as *hi*, and endings such as *cheers*.
c we can miss out salutations and endings.
d we must write in paragraphs.

2 Laura and Pamela have not used contractions in their emails. Make 13 changes to the emails.

3 Mark these expressions formal (*F*), quite informal (*Q*) or informal (*I*).

Hello Laura	Dear Laura	Hi Laura
Best wishes	Cheers	Yours sincerely
Bye for now	Regards	Yours

Language focus: making invitations and arrangements

1 Mark these expressions formal (*F*) or informal (*I*).

1 I am writing to invite you to go to the cinema.
2 How do you fancy going to the cinema with me?
3 I'm afraid I'm busy tomorrow.
4 Unfortunately I am busy tomorrow.
5 Would it be convenient to meet on Friday evening?
6 What about meeting outside Pizza World?
7 I'd love to see the film.
8 I would very much like to see the film.
9 That would be wonderful.
10 That sounds great.
11 I look forward to seeing you on Friday.
12 See you on Friday.

2 Read the emails again and change any expressions that are too formal.

Preparing to write

Work in pairs and tell each other about a film you have seen recently. Use the useful phrases below to help you.

Describing a film

- It's a western / comedy / drama / thriller / musical.
- It's an action film / a horror film / a documentary.
- It's about …
- It's had brilliant / good / quite good / poor reviews.
- It stars Marion Cotillard and it's directed by Olivier Dahan.
- The acting / photography is wonderful / poor.

Writing

Work with a new partner. Write an email to your partner inviting them to see a film. Describe the film and suggest a time and a place to meet. Then swap your emails and write replies.

Global review

Grammar

Complete the sentences with the correct words.
1. What *do you do / are you doing* next weekend?
2. I hope *getting / to get* together with some friends.
3. I would like *to learn / learning* another language.
4. I *'ll buy / 'm going to buy* a new car at the weekend.
5. When I *buy / will buy* my new car, I *will able / will be able* to get around more.
6. Are you looking forward to *go / going* to university?
7. Next month I *will start / am starting* a new job.
8. If the world's temperature *gets / will get* warmer in the next few years, glacial ice *melts / will melt*.

Vocabulary

Put the words into the correct boxes. There are two words you do not need.

| clever | desert | flood | forest fire | homeless | lake |
| ocean | poor | storm | war | wealthy | well-off |

Natural disasters	People with a lot of money
People helped by aid organisations	Geographical features

Speaking and Writing

1 Work in groups of three. Ask each other about your plans for the times below.
- after class
- this evening
- the weekend
- next summer

Try to find one plan that is the same for everybody.

2 Work in pairs. Write a list of five things people could do to reduce their carbon footprint. Then compare your list with another pair.

Study skills

Using your dictionary: finding the right entry

1 Work in pairs and look at the phrases below. Which word would you look up in the dictionary to find the meaning of each phrase?
1. global warming
2. get away
3. fall in love
4. against the law

2 Look up the words to see if you were right.

* The most important word in an expression is called the *keyword*. Keywords are often nouns, but can also be verbs, adjectives or adverbs.
* Some words in a dictionary have more than one entry. This might be because the same word can belong to two classes:
  an *orange* dress   eat an *orange*
  (adjective)   (noun)

3 Find two different word classes for each of these words.
1. heat _____
2. pretty _____
3. fair _____

Sometimes words have the same spelling but different meanings or different pronunciations.

4 Find two meanings and pronunciations for these words.
1. tear _____
   _____
2. close _____
   _____

Some words have many meanings. These are listed at the beginning of an entry.

green (*adjective*)
1. like grass in colour   4. not ready to be eaten
2. with lots of plants   5. not experienced
3. caring for nature   6. of the Green Party

5 Choose the best meaning of *green* in the sentences below.
1. She is campaigning for **green** issues such as reducing packaging and the use of cars.
2. We need more **green** areas in our town.
3. He is too **green** to manage the company.

Work & Leisure

UNIT 5

Part 1

Speaking
Jobs

Vocabulary
Work

Reading & Speaking
Profile of an Indian call centre worker

Grammar
Have

Speaking

1 Read the quote about work in the United States.

"When you go to work, if your name is on the building, you're rich. If your name is on your desk, you're middle class. If your name is on your shirt, you're poor."
Rich Hall, American comedian and writer

2 Work in pairs and discuss these questions.
- What does this quote say about jobs in America?
- Is this true in your country?
- Look at the jobs in the box. Which ones would / wouldn't you like? Decide on the top three and the bottom three.

builder	doctor	disc jockey (DJ)
journalist	lawyer	
manager in a fast food restaurant		
musician	nurse	police officer
politician	security guard	shop assistant
teacher	waiter	

Vocabulary

1 Read the texts below and replace the underlined words and phrases with words in the box. Use your dictionary to help you.

| bonus | employ | hiring | an interview |
| salary | training | wages | |

Job possibilities at a multinational company
We <u>give work to</u> 6,000 people and need more
We offer a good starting <u>money</u>, plus end-of-year <u>extra money</u>
English and computer skills needed

Local supermarket is now <u>giving jobs</u>
No experience necessary, we will provide <u>teaching of the skills</u>
Excellent <u>money per hour</u> and good working environment
Contact Andrew Grau for <u>a talk about the job</u>

2 Work in pairs and discuss these questions.
- Have you ever been to a job interview? How was it?
- Is there a minimum wage in your country? What is it?
- Do you know anyone who works night shifts? What do they do?
- What is a good starting salary in your opinion?

Reading and Speaking

1 Read the introduction to *Profile of an Indian call centre worker* on page 55 and answer the questions.
1 Do you know what a call centre worker does?
2 Have you ever spoken to one?

2 Read the rest of the text. What does she say about …
1 her feelings about the job?
2 the hours she works?
3 the people she talks to?

Extend your vocabulary – *job* and *work*

You can use both *job* and *work* to talk about what someone does to get paid.
Do you like your job / work?
What kind of job / work do you do?
Work is uncountable with this meaning, so you cannot say *a work* or *works*.

Complete the sentences with *job*, *jobs* or *work*. Sometimes more than one answer is possible.
1 Rajeshwari has a good _____.
2 She likes her _____.
3 I have two _____.
4 Many young people don't have any _____.
5 Do you have a _____?

3 Work in pairs and choose **one** of the tasks below.
A Tick (✔) two pieces of information in the text you think are interesting or unusual. Then compare with your partner.
B How would you describe Rajeshwari? Write three words. Then compare with your partner.

54 Unit 5 Work

Profile of an Indian call centre worker

The English newspaper, *The Observer*, interviewed Rajeshwari Singh, a 20-year-old call centre worker. Rajeshwari lives and works in New Delhi, India. This is what she said about her work.

Companies like using call centres because they are cheaper and can give 24-hour service.

Call centre workers answer the phone or make telephone calls for large companies.

There are 350,000 call centre workers in India.

Many banks,ticket companies and telephone companies are using call centres in other countries.

I was so happy when I got this job. It was my first ever interview but they hired me. That night my dad bought chocolates and sweets and we had a small party. He was very proud.

With bonuses, my starting salary is 16,000 rupees (£190) a month.

I sell landlines to Americans. People can get angry. They say 'You people are taking the jobs from our hands.' I say that it's not my fault if Americans are expensive to employ.

My alias is Katie Jones. That's a little lie, I suppose, but a good lie. If I had to use my own name, I'd lose five minutes at the beginning of every call spelling it out, and I don't have a lot of time.

When you have voice training, you have to speak in an American accent all the time or you lose it. When I call home, my parents say 'I don't believe it, it's not you any more!'

Night shifts destroy your life. I don't get home from work until five in the morning, and I don't sleep until six.

You have to dress well even though people can't see you. It's a question of self-confidence. People can pick that up from your voice. And there are 4,000 people in the office to look at you.

There are a lot of Indians living in America and Britain. Sometimes you talk to people who say 'No English. Hindi? Hindi?' and you realise you're talking to an Indian, and often you get so confused you forget how to speak Hindi.

I miss my parents. I can't tell them when I feel upset because they'd come right away to Delhi and take me home.

Grammar

1 Look at sentences 1–8 and match them to the uses of *have* a–e below.

1. I have got a job as a call centre operator. **b**
2. I have worked at the company for ten years. ___
3. We had a small party. ___
4. I have voice training. ___
5. I have to use my own name. ___
6. I don't have a lot of time. ___
7. I have to speak with a US accent. ___
8. I have to dress well. ___

We can use *have*:

a. to talk about possessing or owning something.
b. as an auxiliary with *got* to talk about possessing or owning things.
c. as an auxiliary with *to* to say what is necessary or obligatory.
d. as an auxiliary in the present perfect.
e. to talk about actions or experiences.

> **Language note:** we can only use the contracted forms of *have* when it is the auxiliary verb, not when it is a main or modal verb.

2 Read the sentences with *have* and insert contractions where they are possible.

1. I have a brother and a sister.
2. I have never been to a job interview.
3. We have English class on Thursday morning.
4. I have got a good English dictionary.
5. I have had more than one job in my life.
6. I have breakfast with my family every morning.

G Grammar focus – explanation & more practice of *have* on page 140

Glossary

alias (noun) – a different name that somebody uses instead of their real name
landline (noun) – a telephone line that is not a mobile phone
pick up (phrasal verb) – to notice something that is not very obvious
upset (adjective) – sad, worried or angry about something

UNIT 5 Work & Leisure

Part 2

Listening & Vocabulary
Work issues

Grammar
Modal verbs

Pronunciation
Contractions

Speaking
Job characteristics

Listening and Vocabulary

1 Look at the cartoon about a bad boss. What is the joke? Do you think it is funny?

2 🔊 **1.63–1.66** Listen to four bosses talking to their employees. Number the topics in the order you hear them.

a meal ___   the computer ___
dress code ___   the weekend ___

3 Listen again and choose the correct alternative to complete each sentence.

Conversation 1: Someone has called (*in / out / for*) sick.
Conversation 1: You can take next Saturday (*away / off / on*).
Conversation 3: You are (*on / for / at*) company time, and you must respect that time.
Conversation 4: Of course you can go (*on / in / at*) your lunch break now.

4 Which do you think are bad bosses? Why?

Grammar

1 Look at sentences 1–6 and complete the rules a–d below.

1 You **have to** work this Saturday.
2 You **can** take next Saturday off.
3 You **mustn't** wear jeans to work.
4 You **don't have to** wear a jacket and tie.
5 You **can't** send personal messages with this computer.
6 You **must** arrive on time.

a We use *have to* and *must* to talk about rules and things that are necessary.
b We use _____ and _____ to say when something is not allowed.
c We use _____ to say that something is not necessary.
d We use _____ to say that something is possible or allowed.

Language note: modal verbs are followed by an infinitive without *to*.

> WELL, YOU HAVE TO START SOMEWHERE.

2 Complete the texts with the words in the boxes. Use each word only once.

| can   don't have to   must |

Dress-down Friday

In many financial companies in Britain, employees _____ wear a suit or other formal clothes. Some workplaces have a *dress-down* day, usually on a Friday. On this day, people _____ dress so formally. They _____ wear whatever they like.

| can   can't   mustn't |

Work computers

According to a 2006 survey by the American Management Institute, 78% of American companies have rules about email, instant messenger and blog use. Workers _____ use their computers for work, but they _____ send personal email messages or instant messages. Also, they _____ download programs onto work computers.

| can   don't have to   have to |

Flexitime

A study of the 68 biggest Australian companies found that 93% offered flexitime hours to their employees. Under flexitime, workers _____ work a fixed number of hours in a week, but they _____ start and finish at the same time every day. If they come to work earlier, they _____ leave earlier.

3 Complete the sentences about your job. If you do not work, use one of the jobs on page 54.

Every day I have to … at work.
I don't have to … at work.
At work, I can usually …
I can't … at work.

G Grammar focus – explanation & more practice of modal verbs on page 140

Pronunciation

1 1.67 Listen to the pairs of sentences. Can you hear the differences?

1 You can't wear that.
  You can wear that.
2 She can't come to class today.
  She can come to class today.
3 You must use your books.
  You mustn't use your books.

Language note: in British English, *can't* is pronounced /kɑːnt/.

2 1.68 Listen and circle the word you hear. Then practise saying the sentences.

1 Workers *mustn't / must* use the computers on the first floor.
2 You *can't / can* take your lunch break at two o'clock.
3 I really *must / mustn't* answer emails more quickly.

Speaking

1 Read the job characteristics in the box and tick (✔) the ones which are important to you.

What's important for you in a job?

You earn a lot of money.
You don't have to wear a uniform.
Your work is interesting.
You can work flexible hours (you can start and finish when you like).
You can take regular breaks.
You have to work with the public.
You can be your own boss.
You can work close to home.
You don't have to work on Saturdays or Sundays.
You have job security (you don't have to worry you will lose your job).

2 Work in pairs and share your ideas. Decide on the five most important characteristics of a job.

A: *For me, the most important things in a job are …*
B: *OK. For me, the most important things are …*
A: *What do you think the top five are?*
B: *I think …*

3 Work with another pair and compare your lists. Do you agree? Make a new list of the five most important characteristics.

Useful language

What do you think is the most important?
I think that … is more important than …
What about you?
I disagree. I think … is more important.
I agree. Let's put it on the list.

UNIT 5

Work & Leisure

Part 3

Vocabulary
Leisure activities

Listening
The serious leisure perspective

Grammar
-ing verbs

Pronunciation
/ŋ/

Writing
Leisure time

Vocabulary

1 Match the verbs in the box to the nouns.

| chat | collect | cook | do |
| go for | play | read | watch |

_____ books   the newspaper
_____ exercise   the gardening
_____ a walk   a drink with friends
_____ stamps   coins   things
_____ television a film   the news
_____ video games chess   sport
_____ with friends on the phone
_____ a meal   dinner   vegetables

2 Work in pairs and tell each other which of the activities you do.

I watch television every night.
I hardly ever read the newspaper.

3 Look at the chart showing how Americans spend their leisure time. Then work in pairs and discuss the questions.

- Is there anything that surprises you?
- Is it similar to how you spend your leisure time?

Listening

1 🔊 **1.69** You are going to hear a presentation about *The serious leisure perspective*. Listen and put the slides on page 59 in the correct order.

2 Listen again and answer the questions.
1 What are some examples of casual leisure?
2 Why do people enjoy casual leisure?
3 Why does leisure have a bad reputation?
4 What are some examples of serious leisure?
5 Why does the speaker think serious leisure is important?

3 Work in pairs and ask each other these questions.
- Which do you prefer, casual or serious leisure activities?
- Do you know anyone who has a serious leisure pursuit? What is it?

Extend your vocabulary – *play*

Words in the same family:
play – verb
player – noun
playful – adjective

Complete the sentences with the correct form of *play*.

1 He is an excellent football _____.
2 I _____ computer games until very late last night.
3 She is a very _____ child.

Leisure time on an average day

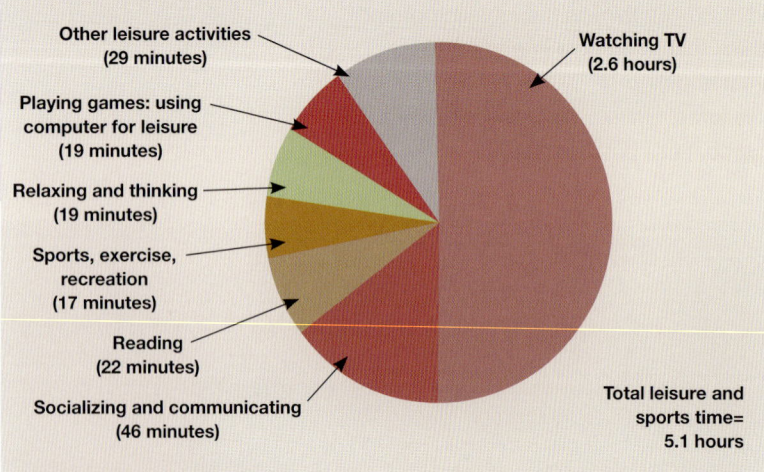

Other leisure activities (29 minutes)
Playing games: using computer for leisure (19 minutes)
Relaxing and thinking (19 minutes)
Sports, exercise, recreation (17 minutes)
Reading (22 minutes)
Socializing and communicating (46 minutes)
Watching TV (2.6 hours)
Total leisure and sports time = 5.1 hours

NOTE: Data include all persons age 15 and over. Data include all days of the week and are annual averages for 2006.
Source: Bureau of Labor Statistics

58 Unit 5 **Leisure**

Robert Macarthur

The Serious Leisure Perspective

Origins of the perspective – 1974
Robert Stebbins –
University of Calgary

Casual leisure and serious leisure

Grammar

1 Look at sentences 1–3 and answer the questions a–c below.
1 Watch**ing** television is casual leisure.
2 He's good at swimm**ing**.
3 People enjoy do**ing** leisure activities.

a What is the subject in sentence 1? Replace the subject with another activity from the listening.
b What kind of word comes before the -*ing* form in sentence 2?
c What other verbs can go before the -*ing* form in sentence 3?

2 Write the -*ing* form of the verbs in the box. Then put them into three groups according to their spelling.

cut	cycle	do	make	play
run	smoke	stop	swim	
take	watch	work		

3 Complete these sentences with your own ideas using the -*ing* form. Then work in pairs and share your ideas.

… is very relaxing.
I'm not very interested in …
I'm good at …
I don't enjoy … alone.
Some people find … a lot of fun, but I think it's boring.

G **Grammar focus** – explanation & more practice of -*ing* forms on page 140

Pronunciation

1 🔊 **1.70** Listen and repeat the sentences. Pay attention to the underlined sounds. What is the most common spelling of /ŋ/?

1 Rela<u>x</u>ing and watch<u>ing</u> TV are my favourite thi<u>ng</u>s.
2 I thi<u>n</u>k E<u>n</u>glish is a difficult l<u>an</u>guage.
3 No tha<u>nk</u>s, I'm stoppi<u>ng</u> smoki<u>ng</u>.

2 Work in pairs. Read your sentences from grammar exercise 3 to each other. Pay attention to the /ŋ/ sound.

Writing

1 Choose one of the activities in the box below and write a short paragraph about it.

- an activity you enjoy doing
- an activity you used to do but stopped doing
- a sport you like watching
- something you aren't very good at doing
- an activity you hate doing

2 Work in pairs. Swap papers and write two questions about your partner's activity. Then return the papers.

3 Read your partner's questions and rewrite the paragraph. Include the original information and the answers to your partner's questions.

Leisure Unit 5 59

UNIT 5

Work & Leisure

Part 4

Reading
Ten facts about ... amusement parks

Grammar
Present perfect, have been & have gone

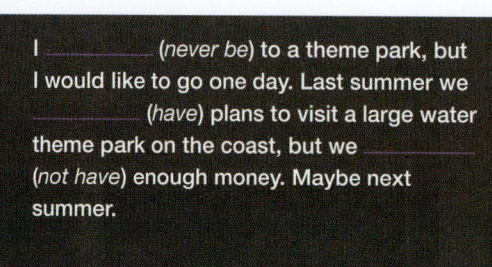

Pronunciation
Past participles

Speaking
Ten questions about ... leisure

Reading

1 Look at the two pictures. Do you like either of these things?

2 Quickly read *Ten facts about amusement parks around the world* and find the answers to the questions.
1 Where did the roller coaster come from?
2 Where was one of the first amusement parks?
3 What do modern amusement parks have?
4 How much money do amusement parks make?
5 What is the most popular amusement park outside the United States?
6 What is an *imagineer*?

3 Have you ever been to an amusement park? Is there one in your country?

Grammar

They **have built** eleven parks around the world.
I **have been** to an amusement park.
Have you **ever been** to an amusement park?

• use the present perfect to talk about an unspecific time in the past
• use the present perfect to talk about experiences
• use *ever* in questions about experiences
• *ever* means the same as *in your life*

Language note: She has **been** to Tivoli Gardens. This means she has come back.
She has **gone** to Tivoli Gardens. This means she is still there.

1 Complete the two texts with the past simple or present perfect form of the verbs in brackets.

Dale Johansson is a photographer of amusement parks. He _____ (visit) more than 50 different parks in 20 countries and _____ (take) photos of each one. He first _____ (become) interested in amusement parks when his father _____ (take) him to one when he was a child.

I _____ (never be) to a theme park, but I would like to go one day. Last summer we _____ (have) plans to visit a large water theme park on the coast, but we _____ (not have) enough money. Maybe next summer.

roller coaster

2 Complete the dialogues with *been* or *gone*.
1 A: Where has he _____?
   B: I don't know. He was here just a minute ago.
   A: Oh no.
2 A: We've _____ on this ride three times.
   B: I know, but it's great. Isn't it great?
   A: Hmmm.
3 A: Where's Marco?
   B: He's _____ on his break. He'll be back in fifteen minutes.
   A: He can't do that!
4 A: Have you _____ here before?
   B: Sorry, I don't understand. What?
   A: Is this your first time here?

3 Work in pairs. Imagine you hear one of the dialogues at an amusement park. Who is speaking? How do they feel? Add two more lines and then act out the dialogue.

Grammar focus – explanation & more practice of the present perfect on page 140

60 Unit 5 Leisure

Ten facts about ...
amusement parks
around the world

Amusement parks are leisure places for adults, teenagers and children.

People often think amusement parks are an American invention, but they originally come from Europe. Tivoli Gardens in Copenhagen, Denmark, is one of the oldest European amusement parks.

The first roller coaster was invented in Russia in the 1600s. People went down snowy hills on blocks of ice.

The world's fastest roller coaster is the *Formula 1 Racecoaster* at Germany's Nürburgring. It travels at 217 km per hour.

Modern amusement parks usually have rides, roller coasters and eating areas. There is often a common theme to make visitors feel as if they are in a different world.

Amusement parks are big business. In the United States alone, amusement parks make an annual profit of $11 billion. More than 30% of Americans have been to an amusement park.

Walt Disney created the first Disney theme park, an amusement park with several sections, in 1955 in California, US. The Disney Corporation has built eleven Disney theme parks around the world.

The most popular amusement park in the world is Walt Disney World in Florida.

The most popular park outside the US is Disneyland in Tokyo. Four of the top ten amusement parks are in Asia.

The people who invent Disney amusement park rides have a special name. They are called *imagineers*.

merry-go-round

Pronunciation

1 Put the past participles in the box into four groups depending on their sound.

been	bought	brought	come
done	driven	eaten	forgotten
ridden	seen	swum	taught	won

/ən/   /ʌm/ or /ʌn/   /ɔːt/   /iːn/

2 🔊 1.71 Listen and check your answers. Then repeat the words.

Speaking

1 🔊 1.72 Listen to the stress and intonation in this question.

Have you ever <u>been</u> to an <u>amusement park</u>?

2 Work in pairs. Look at the leisure questionnaire and say the ten questions. Use *Have you ever* + past participle. Pay attention to the stress and intonation.

3 Work in pairs and ask each other the questions. If your partner answers *yes*, ask two follow-up questions. Use the ideas in the box below to help you.

A: *Have you ever been to an amusement park?*
B: *Yes, I have.*
A: *Did you like it?*
B: *Yes, I loved it.*
A: *Who did you go with?*
B: *I went with my family.*

| Did you like it? | What? | When? |
| Where? | Who with? | Why? | Why not? |

Ten questions about ... leisure

1 ... be to an amusement park?
2 ... ride on a roller coaster?
3 ... buy tickets for a sports event?
4 ... be to a rock concert?
5 ... stay at a health spa?
6 ... see a circus?
7 ... do a dangerous sport?
8 ... drive a very fast car?
9 ... be to a water park?
10 ... visit a zoo?

Leisure Unit 5

Function globally turn-taking

a Business meeting
b Job interview
c Parent-teacher meeting
d Residents' association meeting

Warm up

Look at the pictures of four different meetings. Work in pairs and ask each other the questions.

- Who is speaking in each photo? What are they talking about?
- Have you ever been in one of these situations? When?
- Choose one of the pictures and think of two rules for that situation.
  At a business meeting people have to arrive on time.
  Somebody has to take notes.

Listening

1 1.73–1.75 Listen to three conversations and match each one to a picture. There is one picture you don't need.

2 Listen again and choose the correct answers.

Conversation 1: The woman wants to know about …
a the books.
b the children.
c his son.

Conversation 2: The man needs to arrive at …
a seven in the evening.
b seven in the morning.
c the European offices.

Conversation 3: The man doesn't like …
a the wages.
b the dress code.
c the woman.

Language focus: turn-taking

1 Read the audioscript on page 155. Find examples of a speaker turn-taking. This could be …
a asking a new question in the conversation.
b asking permission to speak.
c adding something to the conversation.

2 Make three turn-taking questions or sentences using the words in the box. You can use each word more than once.

| add | ask | a question | can | could |
| here | I | just | may | say | something |

Speaking

Choose **one** of the tasks below.

A Work in pairs and choose one of the conversations from the listening. Write the next three or four lines. Then read the conversation together. Use the new expressions you have learnt.

B Work in groups of three. A: choose a question and answer it. B: ask a question or give more information. C: continue. Use the new expressions you have learnt.

- What is most important in a job?
- What would be the ideal relaxing weekend?
- Is it necessary to speak English for work?
- Is it easy for young people to get jobs?
- Should there be more leisure facilities for young people?

Useful language

- Excuse me.
- Sorry, but …
- Pardon me.

Global English

All **work** and no **play**
by David Crystal

There's an old saying in English: *All work and no play makes Jack a dull boy*. Or Jill. Psychologists tell us we need a balance between work and play to have a healthy lifestyle. And it is the same for language.

One of the most noticeable features of work language is the technical vocabulary, or
5 jargon, that people use. Outsiders won't understand it. A doctor might look at the face of someone who's had a fall and say to a colleague 'That's a nasty perorbital haematoma'. If you were the patient, and heard this remark, you might be worried. But basically all it means is you've got a black eye.

Every profession has its jargon - law, banking, sport, physics, language teaching ...
10 Thousands of specialised terms might be used. They add precision. And they also make people feel they belong together. You know you're a member of a group when you can comfortably *talk shop*.

Jargon also saves time. That's why doctors say such things as *BP* and *SOB* (blood pressure, shortness of breath). It's quick and convenient.

15 But they shouldn't use such terms to the patient. Work language and leisure language are two very different things. That's the argument of the Plain English Campaign, which wants specialists to speak clearly when talking to the public.

20 It's easy for people to use jargon carelessly and annoy people. It's worse when it's used deliberately, to mislead the public. That's why we get so angry when we hear people using it to hide the truth. A politician once admitted that something he had said was 'an instance of plausible
25 deniability'. In other words, he'd told a lie!

Glossary
carelessly (*adverb*) – without thinking about what you are doing, so that you cause problems or damage
dull (*adjective*) – boring
mislead (*verb*) – to make someone believe something that is incorrect or not true
outsider (*noun*) – someone who does not belong to a group or organisation
talk shop (*verb*) – to talk about your work, especially in a way that is boring for other people

Warm up

1 Think of two or three examples of jargon in your language and write them on a piece of paper.

2 Work in pairs and share your ideas. Explain what your jargon means in English.

Reading

1 Read *All work and no play*. What is the main topic of the text?

a plain English
b technical vocabulary
c doctors and language
d radio and television

2 Read the text again and decide if the statements are true (*T*) or false (*F*).

1 Psychologists say that work is more important than play.
2 Jargon is language that everybody understands.
3 Jargon can be useful.
4 Jargon is precise language and it can make communication quicker.
5 The Plain English Campaign wants people to use more jargon.
6 We get angry when people use jargon to tell lies.

Language focus

Find words or expressions in the text with these meanings.
1 the correct relationship between two things (line 2)
2 to make something more clear or specific (2 words) (line 10)
3 easy (line 14)
4 people in general (2 words) (line 19)
5 used for saying something in another way (3 words) (line 25)

Speaking

Do you think there is too much jargon in your language? Can you think of some examples? Do you think campaigns like Plain English are a good idea?

UNIT 5 Writing a CV

Reading

Read the CV and put the headings in the correct places.

Date of birth	Email address
Education and qualifications	Interests
Referees	Skills	Work experience

CURRICULUM VITAE: Ahmed al-Qadi

(1) _____ : al-qadi22@hotmail.com

(2) _____ : 18-08-1987

(3) _____
2003–2005
Al Hussein College, Amman, Jordan
General Secondary Education Certificate
Average score: 88.5%

2005–2009
Applied Science University, Amman, Jordan
B.Sc. in Management Information Systems
GPA Score: 90.5% (Evaluation: Very Good)

(4) _____
2009–Present
Jordan Telecom: database assistant

(5) _____
English: intermediate
Jordanian driving licence
Modern programming and database management

(6) _____
Travelling, understanding other cultures, football

(7) _____
Mr Firas Al-Jabali, Head of Information Services, Jordan Telecom
Dr Omar Yassin, Head of Management Information Systems, Applied Science University, Amman, Jordan

Writing skills: setting out a CV

Correct the spelling and punctuation mistakes in this CV.

CURICULUM VITAE: Nathalie Baekelandt

Email adress   n.baekelandt @wanadoo.fr
Date of Birth   17 / 12 / 88

Education and Califications
University of Lille BA Hons Economics

Work Expereince
Personal Assistant to Project Manager, EDF Energy.
Duties – booking appointments, taking minutes, record-keeping

Skils   English: fluent   Interests   Aerobics, dance, swimming,
        Computer literate   photography, theatre

Referrees On request

Language focus: writing dates

Different countries write dates in different ways.
In Britain, the order is day, month, year.

16–01–2008   or   16/01/08
16 Jan 2008   or   16th January 2008

In the US, the order is month, day, year.

01–16–2008   or   01/16/08
Jan 16 2008   or   January 16th 2008

Complete the table.

UK	US
22nd November 1995	
	Feb 14th 2000
	05-28-1982
02-10-95	

Preparing to write

Work in pairs and make notes on what you would write under each of the CV headings.

Describing skills

- IT literate (Word, Excel, Powerpoint)
- French: fluent / intermediate / elementary
- Current driving licence
- Basic first aid

Writing

Write your CV. Use your notes and the useful phrases to help you.

Global review

Grammar

1 Complete the sentences with the correct form of the verb in brackets.

1. _____ (you /ever / be) to the US?
2. Yes, I _____ (go) there last year.
3. I hate _____ (write) letters, but _____ (chat) to friends on the phone is great fun.
4. I _____ (never / ride) a camel, but I _____ (see) one in a zoo.

2 Complete the job description for a shop assistant using *can*, *have to*, *don't have to* or *mustn't*.

1. You _____ be polite to customers.
2. You _____ have a driving licence.
3. You _____ arrive late.
4. You _____ earn a bonus if you sell a lot of goods.

Vocabulary

Match the words on the left to the ones on the right.

play	a walk
do	television
go for	a meal
chat	exercise
collect	on the computer
read	a magazine
watch	stamps
cook	on the phone

Speaking

1 Work in small groups. Think of three leisure activities you enjoy and mime them. The others try to guess the activities.

A: *I think you like playing tennis.*
B: *Yes, that's right. / No, that's not right.*

2 Work in small groups. Talk about a job you do or would like to do.
- Talk about the things you have to do.
- Talk about the good and bad parts of the job.

Study skills

Recording new words and phrases

1 Work in pairs and discuss these questions.
- Where do you write down new English words and expressions that you learn?
- When do you write down new words and expressions?
  a. In class?
  b. When you are reading?
  c. When you are doing homework?
  d. At some other time?
- What information do you write down about the words? Show your partner.
- How do you use your vocabulary notes when you have written them?

2 Look at how three Polish students have recorded new words from this unit. What are the differences between them?

---
upset = przygnębiony   take off = wziąć (sobie) wolne
chess = szachy   amusement park = park rozrywki

---
upset /ʌpˈset/ adj. sad, worried or angry about something. I miss my parents. I can't tell them when I feel upset.
take time off work = wziąć (sobie) wolne z pracy
You can take next Saturday off.

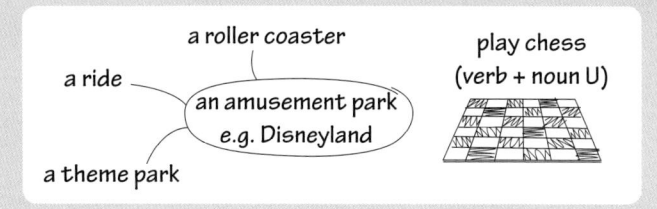

---
a roller coaster — an amusement park e.g. Disneyland — a ride — a theme park
play chess (verb + noun U)

---

3 Work in pairs and discuss the questions.
- Which method do you prefer?
- How can the different ways help?
- If you record words in a different way, why is that?

4 This week try recording vocabulary in a different way. How will you do it?

UNIT 6 Science & Technology

Part 1

Writing & Speaking
Happiness

Reading
The science of happiness

Grammar
Comparatives

Pronunciation & Reading
The schwa /ə/

Writing and Speaking

1 Write down five things that make you happy.

2 Work in pairs. Compare your lists and discuss these questions.
- Which items do you have in common?
- Is there anything you would like to change in your list?
- What do you think makes people happy?
- On a scale of 1 to 10 how happy are you?

Reading

1 Read the article *The science of happiness* and put the headings in the correct place.

Climate and happiness
Measuring happiness
Money and happiness
What makes people happy?

2 Read the text again. Look at the answers and complete the questions.
1 Q: How _____ _____ _____ happiness?
   A: By asking people how happy they are.
2 Q: Which _____ _____ _____ satisfied with their lives?
   A: Those who live in warmer parts of the country.
3 Q: Does money _____ _____ _____?
   A: If you have a home, food and clothes then no, it doesn't.
4 Q: What three things _____ _____ _____?
   A: Family and friends, belief in something and enjoyable objectives.

3 Match the highlighted words in the text to the definitions.
1 officially acceptable
2 something that makes you happy
3 meaning
4 your general view of things
5 to discover a number or result using mathematics

4 Do you agree with what the text says about happiness? Do you think it is possible to measure happiness?

Extend your vocabulary – metaphors for *happy*

We often use words that mean *high up* or *moving upwards* when we want to describe feeling happy or hopeful.

We often use words that mean *low down* or *falling* when we want to describe feeling sad.

Look at these expressions. Is each person feeling happy or sad?
1 That news really lifted my spirits.
2 My heart sank when I saw him.
3 I feel pretty low today.
4 I'm on top of the world.
5 I'm walking on air.
6 She's a bit down today.

The science of happiness

Everyone wants to be happy. Some argue that the main reason people do the things they do is to become happier. Others argue that happiness is a basic human right. But what is happiness? What really makes people happy?

1 _____
Social scientists usually calculate happiness simply by asking how happy people are. They ask people the question 'How happy are you from 1 to 10?' Ed Diener, an expert on happiness from the University of Illinois, says that this is a valid way of getting information about people's happiness.

2 _____
In one study, researchers asked people in different parts of a country 'How satisfied are you with your life?' People in parts of the country with nicer weather said they were more satisfied with their lives. They said they lived better than people from a city with bad weather.

3 _____
Researchers have examined the relationship between money and happiness for many years. They conclude that very poor people are less happy than rich people. But lots of money doesn't make you happier. If you have a home, food and clothes, extra money doesn't automatically make you more content.

4 _____
According to researchers, there are three things which make people happy:
1 Having close relationships with people – family and friends. The closer and deeper the relationships are, the better for your happiness.
2 Believing in something. This could be religion, a spiritual outlook or a special philosophy in life.
3 Having objectives that you find enjoyable and interesting. This means that your life has a purpose.

Grammar

*Lots of money doesn't make you **happier**. People with close family relationships were **more satisfied than** people with no family. People said they **lived better** in warm countries.*

- use comparative adjectives to compare two people or objects
- use adjective + *er* for short adjectives and *more* + adjective for longer adjectives
- use comparative adverbs to compare two actions

Complete the texts with the comparative form of the adjectives in brackets.

Health and happiness

Scientists say that happy people are _____ (*healthy*) than unhappy people. They also live _____ (*long*) and _____ (*good*) lives and are _____ (*fit*). One study found that _____ (*happy*) people live up to nine years longer.

Research in the United States suggests that married couples with children are _____ (*satisfied*) when their children are _____ (*young*). When researchers asked married couples about happiness with teenage children they said their lives were a lot _____ (*stressful*).

A survey of British men and women between 1993 and 2003 found that many people said their lives were _____ (*enjoyable*) as they became older. It showed that men were _____ (*content*) than women in their teenage years, but women were _____ (*happy*) than men _____ (*late*) in life.

G Grammar focus – explanation & more practice of comparatives on page 142

Pronunciation and Reading

1 2.01 Listen to the words and phrases. How are the underlined sounds pronounced?

fitt*er*   happi*er*   more pr*o*ductive
comfort*a*ble   regul*a*r exercise
pati*e*nt   bett*er* driv*er*

2 Listen again and repeat the words.

3 The words in exercise 1 come from a song by the English rock group *Radiohead*. Work in pairs. A: read the first line of the song. B: read the second line. Pay attention to the underlined schwa sounds.

4 The songwriter said that this song is about people in Britain in the 90s. Do you think he liked the 90s? Would you say the same about your country in the 90s?

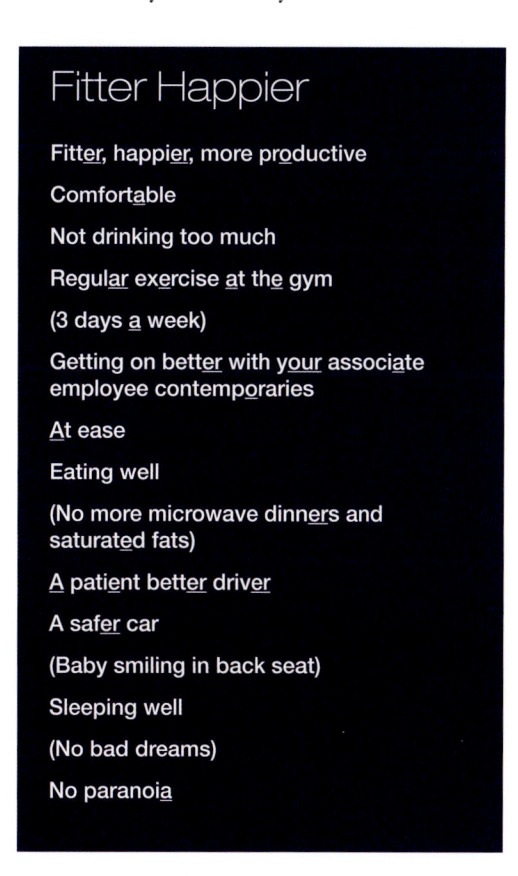

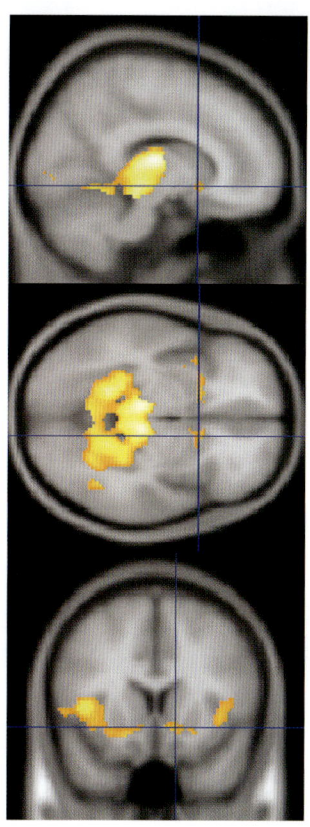

Fitter Happier

Fitt*er*, happi*er*, more pr*o*ductive

Comfort*a*ble

Not drinking too much

Regul*a*r exercise *a*t the gym

(3 days *a* week)

Getting on bett*er* with y*ou*r associ*a*te employee contemp*o*raries

*A*t ease

Eating well

(No more microwave dinn*er*s and saturat*e*d fats)

A pati*e*nt bett*er* driv*er*

A saf*er* car

(Baby smiling in back seat)

Sleeping well

(No bad dreams)

No paranoi*a*

UNIT 6 Science & Technology

Part 2

Speaking & Listening
Someone has to do it

Grammar
Comparatives (*a bit, much, as ... as*)

Vocabulary
Noun formation

Reading & Speaking
Frankenstein

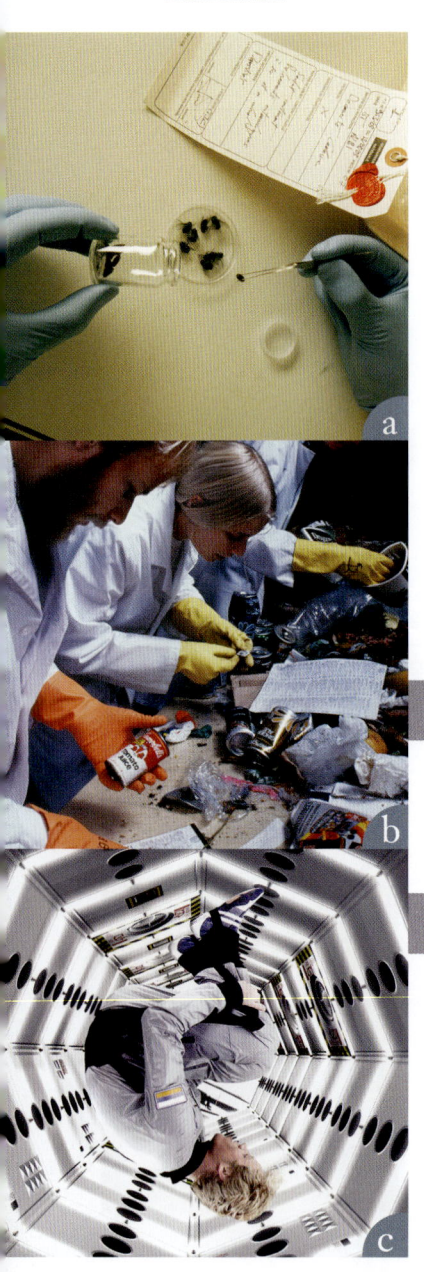

Speaking and Listening

1 Work in pairs. Look at pictures a–c and discuss what you think the jobs are.

2 Read the text below and match the jobs to the pictures. Then discuss what you think these people do in their jobs.

Someone has to do it ... in the name of science

The American magazine *Popular Science* looked at all the possible jobs you could have in science, and they picked out the worst ones. Here are three of them:

Garbologist – studies rubbish

Forensic entomologist – studies insects in the bodies of dead people

Gravity research subject – participates in experiments to study the effects of zero gravity on the human body

Language note: *garbage* is American English and *rubbish* is British English.

Useful language

- dirty
- flies
- rubbish
- experiments for space travel
- gloves
- turns around and around

Useful phrases

- Maybe he / she ...
- It looks like he / she works in ...
- He / she probably ...
- This looks ...

3 2.02–2.03 Listen to two people talking about their jobs. Which two jobs do they talk about?

4 Listen again and choose the correct answers.
1 Speaker 1 stayed in bed for …
 a the summer. b 50 days.
 c 15 days.
2 They paid speaker 1 …
 a $6,000. b $600. c $60,000.
3 Speaker 2 thinks her work …
 a is disgusting. b is interesting.
 c is boring.
4 Speaker 2 is finishing a project on …
 a office rubbish. b restaurant rubbish.
 c office and restaurant rubbish.

5 Do you think these jobs are bad? Which is the worst, in your opinion?

Grammar

*Office rubbish is **less disgusting** than restaurant rubbish.*
*It's **not as bad as** you think.*
*It's **a bit more difficult** than that.*
*She works **much faster** than him.*

- use *less* + adjective to mean not as much
- use (*not*) *as* + adjective + *as* to make comparisons
- use *as* + adjective + *as* to say that two things are the same
- use *a bit* or *much* to modify comparative adjectives and adverbs

1 Read the sentences from the listening and choose the alternative that is closest in meaning.
1 Office garbage is much less disgusting than restaurant garbage.
 a Restaurant garbage is much more disgusting than office garbage.
 b Office garbage is much more disgusting than restaurant garbage.
2 My job isn't as bad as people think.
 a My job is worse than people think.
 b My job is better than people think.

68 Unit 6 Science

2 Complete the sentences with your own ideas.

I speak English a bit better now than …
The weather today is a bit less … than …
English is a bit easier than …
I think … is much more … than …
I don't believe … is as … as people say.

3 Work in two groups. Group A: turn to page 127. Group B: turn to page 129.

G Grammar focus – explanation & more practice of comparatives on page 142

Vocabulary

1 Match each word to a suffix to make a new noun.

Word	Suffix	New noun
happy	-ist	happiness
science	-er	
relation	-ence	
exist	-ness	
research	-ship	

2 Make new nouns from the words in the box. Which noun endings are used for jobs?

| economy | friend | paint | nervous |
| silent | teach | tour | weak |

3 Complete the text with the correct form of the words.

The **NASA** researcher

My wife Karen is a _____ (*research*). She won a _____ (*scholar*) from NASA to research a special project. She is studying the possible _____ (*exist*) of life on other planets. She loves the work, except for the _____ (*lonely*). She works alone in a little office. She listens in complete _____ (*silent*) for unusual radio signals from space.

Reading and Speaking

1 2.04 Read and listen to the extract from the book *Frankenstein*. What was the problem with the science experiment?

2 Work in pairs and discuss this question.
- One of the themes of *Frankenstein*, and of many science fiction stories, is *dangerous knowledge*. Do you think scientific knowledge can be dangerous? Think of some examples.

Mary Shelley (1797–1851) was an English romantic novelist. She is best known for the novel *Frankenstein*, which she wrote when she was 19 years old. Some critics have called her the first English science fiction author.

Frankenstein tells the story of the scientist Dr Frankenstein and how he wishes to create life from a dead body, but how he creates a monster instead.

The body moved and I went nearer. I held out my arms and smiled. The man sat up and turned his head. His eyes were open.

I thought to myself 'Oh, God. What have I done? What has gone wrong?'

The man's skin was wrinkled and yellow. His eyes were yellow and dry. His thin, black lips opened in a terrible smile. I had made a Monster!

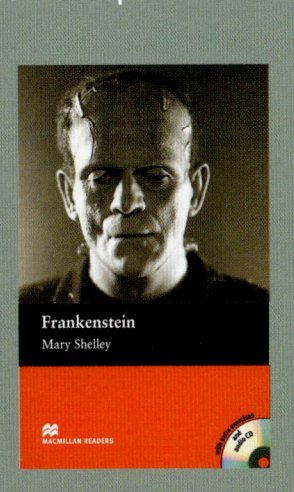

UNIT 6 Science & Technology

Part 3

Vocabulary
Compound nouns

Reading
Going, going, gone

Grammar
Superlatives

Listening & Speaking
Website addresses

Vocabulary

1 Look at the photo. How many of the things can you name in English?

2 Match the words in A to the words in B to make compound nouns. Which things can you see in the picture?

A	B
computer	phones
head	top
key	site
lap	screen
memory	board
mobile	message
mouse	stick
text	phone
web	pad

3 2.05 Listen and repeat the words. Underline the stress in each compound noun. Which one is different?

Reading

1 Work in pairs and ask each other the questions.
- Do you use the internet often? What for?
- Which websites do you often visit?

2 You are going to read about online auctions. Tick (✔) the words you think you will see.

businessman	buy	dangerous
expensive	global	internet
jet	kidney	river	sell

3 2.06 Read and listen to *Going, going, gone* on page 71 and check your answers.

4 Read the text again and answer the questions.
1 What do people do in online auctions?
2 How many people use eBay?
3 Name five unusual things that people have sold or tried to sell on eBay.

5 Have you ever bought or sold anything on the internet? Would you buy anything in an online auction?

Grammar

*Online auctions are among **the biggest** businesses on the internet.*
*Of all the online auction sites, eBay is probably **the most famous**.*
*It is one of **the most popular** websites I've heard of.*

- use superlative adjectives to compare two or more people or objects
- use adjective + *est* for short adjectives and *the most* + adjective for longer adjectives
- we often use superlatives with the present perfect tense

1 Complete the sentences with the correct word.

1 Online auctions are popular because you can find *the strangest / stranger* things there.
2 Many things online are *the cheapest / cheaper* than the same things in a shop.
3 I prefer buying from shops because I think it's *the safest / safer* than buying on the internet.
4 I think online shopping is *the best / better* way to get things.
5 The founder of eBay is one of *the richest / richer* men in America.

2 Complete the sentences with the superlative form of the adjectives.

1 What's _____ (long) time you've ever spent on the internet?
2 Who's _____ (funny) person you've ever spent time with?
3 What's _____ (cold) place you've ever been to?
4 What's _____ (strange) thing you've ever eaten?
5 What's _____ (good) film you've ever seen?

3 Work in pairs. Choose **three** of the questions from exercise 2 and ask each other.

G **Grammar focus** – explanation & more practice of superlatives on page 142

Unit 6 **Technology**

Going, going, gone ...

Online auctions and the eBay phenomenon

Online auctions are among the biggest businesses on the internet. These are sites that use the technology of the internet to allow people to buy things from each other. People can buy and sell almost anything online now. Of all these online auction sites, eBay is probably the most famous. Let's look at the numbers.

241,000,000 +

Ten years after eBay started in 1995 there were more than 241 million registered users, making it one of the most popular websites on the planet.

4th

With more than 200 million registered users, eBay's population is almost as big as that of Indonesia, which has the world's fourth biggest population.

£1.81

Many people have tried to sell fake items or silly things online. One man tried to sell the internet for a million dollars. Nobody wanted it. Another person tried to sell the meaning of life. It sold for £1.81.

$4.9 million

One of the most expensive items sold on eBay was a Gulfstream II private business jet for $4.9 million. One of the largest items ever sold was a World War II submarine. It was sold by a small town in New England that decided it did not need it any more.

50,000

In 2004 a 50,000-year-old mammoth appeared on eBay. The Dutch owner of the animal sold it for £61,000. It was one of the most unusual things sold on eBay.

1999

People have tried to sell all sorts of human body parts on the internet. In 1999 a human kidney went on sale on eBay. The website cancelled the auction and stops any auctions that aren't ethical.

Listening and Speaking

1 2.07 Listen and write the email and website addresses you hear. Which of these websites do you know?

Useful phrases

.	dot
/	slash
@	at
learn_English	learn underscore English
learn-English	learn dash English

2 Write five website or email addresses that you know – they can be real or invented.

3 Work in pairs and read the addresses to each other. Write the addresses as you listen.

Glossary

ethical (*adjective*) – considered to be right
fake (*adjective*) – made to look like something else
mammoth (*noun*) – an animal similar to an elephant with long hair that lived a very long time ago
submarine (*noun*) – a ship that can travel under the water

Technology Unit 6

UNIT 6 Science & Technology

Part 4

Speaking & Listening
Computer problems

Vocabulary & Pronunciation
Phrasal verbs, sentence stress

Grammar
Phrasal verbs & objects

Reading & Speaking
The Luddites

Speaking and Listening

1 Read the quotes about computers below. Work in pairs and tell each other if you agree with them and why.

> Computers are useless.
> They can only give you answers.
> *Pablo Picasso, Spanish artist*
>
> I do not fear computers. I fear the lack of them.
> *Isaac Asimov, American science fiction writer*
>
> Think? Why think? We have computers to do that for us.
> *Jean Rostand, French scientist and philosopher*
>
> Computers are like dogs. They smell fear.
> *Simon Alexander, American comedian*

2 2.08–2.12 Listen to five conversations about computer problems and number the problems in the order you hear them. There is one extra problem.

computer screen	email
internet connection	password
printer and printing	saving work

3 Listen again and choose the correct answers.
1 What did the man change in conversation 1?
   a a cable   b the mouse
   c the computer screen
2 How does the man feel at the end of conversation 2?
   a happy   b worried   c frustrated
3 What's wrong with the man's email in conversation 3?
   a there's a virus
   b there's too much email
   c he needs a password
4 Who saves their work in conversation 4?
   a the woman   b the man
   c the woman and the man
5 What happened to the woman's password in conversation 5?
   a she forgot it   b she changed it
   c she doesn't have one

Extend your vocabulary – other ways of saying *yes*

Here are some common ways of saying *yes*.
Yep and *yeah* are informal ways of saying *yes*.
Definitely is a stronger way of saying *yes*.
That's right is used instead of *yes* to respond to a question or statement.
I'm afraid so is used when you think the person hopes you will say *no*.

1 Look at the audioscript on page 155. Find an example of each way of saying *yes*.
2 Write five questions to ask your partner. You want them to answer *yes*.
3 Work in pairs and ask each other the questions. Answer *yes* in different ways.

Vocabulary and Pronunciation

1 Complete the sentences from the listening with the words in the box.

| down (x2)   in   on   out (x2)   up |

1 Now **log** _____ to the system.
2 **Shut** _____ the computer and leave it.
3 The laptop's **gone** _____ again.
4 **Type** _____ your username and password.
5 When I try to **print** _____ a document the computer **prints** _____ a different document.
6 You should really **back** _____ all your work.

2 2.13 Listen and check your answers.

3 Listen and repeat the sentences. Try to copy the stress.

72 Unit 6 **Technology**

Grammar

Turn on the computer.
Now *log on*.
Shut down the computer.
Shut the computer *down*.
Turn it *on*.

- some phrasal verbs such as *turn on* can take an object
- other phrasal verbs such as *log on* do not take an object
- when the phrasal verb takes an object, it can usually go before or after the particle
- if the object is a pronoun, it can only go between the verb and particle

1 Tick (✔) the sentences that are correct.
1. a Pick up the phone.
   b Pick it up.
   c Pick up it.
2. a Can you print out them please?
   b Can you print them out please?
   c Can you print out the documents please?
3. a Turn them off.
   b Turn off them.
   c Turn off all the computers.

2 Circle the object of the phrasal verb in the sentences below. Sometimes there is no object.

Please <u>sit down</u> and open your books. (no object)
Did you <u>plug in</u> the (computer)?

1. <u>Turn</u> the volume <u>up</u> please.
2. Philip isn't here today. He <u>called in</u> sick.
3. I forgot to <u>log on</u> to the school system.
4. <u>Look up</u> the words in the dictionary.
5. <u>Write</u> the words <u>down</u> in your notebook.
6. My flight <u>takes off</u> at seven o'clock tonight.

3 Look at the sentences again. If there is an object, replace it with a pronoun.

Did you plug it in?

G Grammar focus – explanation & more practice of phrasal verbs on page 142

The Luddites

One of the most famous anti-technology movements was the Luddite movement in 19th century England. The Luddites were organised groups of workers who were losing work to the new textile machines. They went out at night and destroyed the machines with hammers. Today the term *luddite* is used in English to talk negatively about people who are anti-technology.

Glossary
movement (*noun*) – a group of people who work together for a particular reason
textile (*noun*) – any type of woven cloth

Reading and Speaking

1 2.14 Read and listen to the text about the Luddites.
What kind of people were they?

2 Read the statements and mark your opinion next to each one. 1 = strongly disagree, 4 = strongly agree

Modern technology …

• makes us work harder, not less hard.	1 2 3 4
• is giving away our privacy.	1 2 3 4
• has taken away more jobs than it has created.	1 2 3 4
• has made us safer.	1 2 3 4
• is giving us too much information, so it's difficult to know what is true.	1 2 3 4
• has to be free for everyone.	1 2 3 4

3 Work in pairs. Discuss your opinions and try to give reasons for them. Are you a modern *Luddite*?

I agree that modern technology makes us work harder. In my job, I have to answer lots of emails and messages, and I have to do it more quickly than before.

Technology Unit 6   73

Function globally finding things in common

Warm up

1 Look at the pictures of four situations. Work in pairs and describe the similarities and differences between them.

Useful language

- chatting
- laptop
- on a train
- diary
- in an airport
- suit

Useful phrases

- I think they are on a train.
- They look like friends / colleagues / strangers.

2 What do you think the people in each picture are talking about? Choose one of the pictures and write a short conversation. Then present your conversation to another pair.

Listening

1 🔊 2.15 Listen to a conversation between two people in a taxi. Where are they going? What happens at the end?

2 Listen again and tick (✔) the things they have in common.

1 They are both going to the Technology Conference. ___
2 They have both been to San Francisco before. ___
3 They are both from Germany. ___
4 They both went to school in England. ___
5 They both work for ABT Technology. ___
6 They have both been to conferences before. ___
7 They are both staying at the conference hotel. ___

Language focus: finding things in common

Look at the highlighted expressions in the audioscript on page 155. Then complete the rules with *so*, *too* or *neither*.

We use **so / neither** when we have something in common.

Use _____ + auxiliary + I for affirmative statements.
Use _____ + auxiliary + I for negative statements.

We also use *me* + **too / neither**.

Use *me* + _____ for affirmative statements.
Use *me* + _____ for negative statements.

> **Language note:** when we don't have something in common, we can respond with the short form.
> A: *I am from Scotland.* B: *I'm not.*
> A: *I live in the city centre.* B: *I don't.*
> A: *I've never been to an art gallery.* B: *I have.*

Speaking

1 Look at the topics in the box. Write five true sentences about yourself. Use the phrases to help you.

Topic	Phrases
You & your family	I live with … I'm married / single …
Food & drink	I like / don't like … I don't eat / drink …
Art & music	I have / haven't read / seen … I listen to … I don't like …
Hopes & fears	I'm planning to … I'm afraid of …
Work & leisure	I work in … In my free time I …

2 Work in pairs. A: tell your partner about yourself. B: respond. Find three things you have in common. Use the new expressions you have learnt.

3 Swap roles and repeat the activity.

74 Unit 6 **Function globally**

Global voices

Warm up

1 Put the letters in the correct order to make words for technological advances.

| treniten | velsietoni | limboe nohep |
| pmretuco | lenap | |

2 Why are these advances important or useful? Complete the sentence for each of the advances above.

I think the … is important / useful because …

Listening

1 2.16–2.22 Listen to seven people talking about technological advances. Which advance from exercise 1 is each person talking about?

1 Honor, England _____
2 Arthur, France _____
3 Sara, Italy _____
4 Antonis, Greece _____
5 Maxim, Russia _____
6 Starla, England _____
7 William, Ghana _____

2 Listen again. Which speakers give reasons for their choice? What reasons do they give?

Language focus: *and*, *so*, *because*

1 Read what Guy says about another technological advance. Complete the sentences with *and*, *so* or *because*. Use the explanations in brackets to help you.

I think the most important technological advance – well for me personally recently has been a hard disk recorder for recording TV programmes [says his opinion]

1 _____ it means I can record everything very easily [gives a reason]

2 _____ I can see exactly what I have recorded by looking at everything on screen [adds another reason]

3 _____ I don't have to find lots of video tapes and different things like that [adds more information]

4 _____ it is much easier now to record TV programmes than it was in the past [explains a consequence]

5 _____ because of digital television we have lots more programmes to choose from [adds another reason]

6 _____ there's much more variety and choice [explains a consequence]

7 _____ that means you need to record even more programmes than in the past. [explains a consequence]

2 2.23 Listen and check your answers.

Language note: in spoken English, it is very common to add lots of clauses together with words like *and*, *or*, *so*, or *because*.

Speaking

1 What is the most important or useful technological advance? Why do you think so? Make a few notes.

2 Work in pairs and present your ideas. Try to speak for at least one minute.

Useful phrases

- For me personally, the most important technological advance is the …
- I think the most useful advance is the … because …
- … and …
- … so that means …

Global voices Unit 6   75

Writing describing advantages and disadvantages

Reading

1 Read Mohammed's essay on *The advantages and disadvantages of the internet*. Does he think there are more advantages or disadvantages?

2 Do you agree with his ideas? Can you think of other advantages or disadvantages?

The internet has revolutionised people's lives all over the world. People use the internet every day for their studies, to contact friends and family, and for pleasure. It has turned the world into a global village.

Using the internet has many advantages.

* You can send instant messages and contact people all over the world by email and in chat rooms.
* You can access huge amounts of useful information for your studies or for research.
* You can download games, music, videos, films and other software, often for free.

However, there are also certain disadvantages in using the internet.

* It can be dangerous to put personal information, such as credit card details, online.
* The internet is a good environment for hackers, who spread viruses and spy ware.
* There are some websites that are unsuitable for children.

In conclusion, despite the disadvantages, the internet brings huge benefits to our lives. It is hard nowadays to imagine a world without the internet.

Language focus: listing points

1 Look at a corrected version of the second paragraph of Mohammed's essay. What is different?

> Using the internet has many advantages. First of all, you can send instant messages and contact people all over the world by email and in chat rooms. In addition, you can access huge amounts of useful information for your studies or for research. Another important advantage is that you can download games, music, videos, films and other software, often for free.

2 Change the third paragraph in the same way. Use some of the useful phrases below to help you. Remember to use commas.

Listing points

- Firstly … / First of all …
- Secondly …
- In addition …
- As well as that …
- Another advantage is that …
- Finally … / Lastly …

Writing skills: getting ideas

Work in small groups and discuss this question.

When you want to get ideas for an essay do you …
* read a book or article on the subject?
* do a keyword search on the internet?
* speak to other people?
* brainstorm all you know and think about the topic?
* write freely to express your ideas?
* use mind maps?
* do something else?

All of these methods can help. Try using a different one next time you write an essay.

Preparing to write

1 Work in pairs and choose one of the topics below.

| clocks | mobile phones | satnavs | television |

2 Make a list of all the advantages and disadvantages.

3 Think about what to put in the introductory paragraph. For example, how and where the invention is used, its history, its effects on modern life etc.

4 Think about what you will write in the last paragraph. What is your conclusion? Are there more advantages or disadvantages? Why?

Writing

Write the essay. Use your notes and the useful phrases below to help you. Write four paragraphs:

a introduction, b advantages, c disadvantages, d conclusion.

Introducing advantages and disadvantages

- There are several advantages / disadvantages of …
- However, there are also some / certain disadvantages.
- One of the main advantages / disadvantages is …

Global review

Grammar

Circle the corrct options. Sometimes both are correct.

1. Where do I *plug in the computer / plug the computer in*?
2. If you don't want to lose your documents, it's a good idea to *back them up / back up them*.
3. Your computer is much *better / more better* than mine.
4. Tom works *harder / less hard* than his sister.
5. Shopping online is *more convenient / convenienter* than going to the supermarket.
6. The Nile is *the most long / the longest* river in the world.
7. Your job isn't *as well-paid as / as well-paid than* mine.
8. Time passes *faster / more fast* than you think.
9. Germany is a bit *less colder / less cold* than Norway.

Vocabulary

Read the definitions and put the letters in the correct order to make the correct words.

1. you use this to type documents on a computer
   yebadrok _____
2. you store and carry computer information on this
   rymome kicts _____
3. a small computer that you can carry around
   potpal _____
4. you use these to listen to music without making a noise
   nohapsheed _____
5. your computer sometimes does this if there is a problem
   thus wond _____
6. a relationship with a friend
   sprifidhen _____
7. the state of being happy
   shipspane _____
8. a person who does a study to find new information
   screeherra _____

Speaking

1 Work in pairs and find three differences between the items below. Which do you prefer and why?

- emails and text messages
- laptop computers and desktop computers
- mobile phones and landlines

2 Work in pairs. A: your partner has never seen one of the items below. Describe it and explain how it works. Then swap roles and repeat.

- a computer
- a printer

Study skills

Personalising language learning

1 Look at how Atsuko has recorded new words and grammar from the unit.

> *nervous (adj.) feeling excited and worried, or slightly afraid. Get nervous about / of something.*
>
> ** I get nervous when I have to speak in class.*
> ** My sister used to be nervous of ducks.*
>
> *outlook (n. sing.) Your general attitude to things. Share the same outlook on something.*
>
> ** Fumie and I share the same outlook on friendship.*
>
> *back up (verb T) to make a copy of information on your computer.*
>
> ** I must remember to back up my work on a memory stick.*
>
> _____
>
> **My hair is much longer than Fumie's hair.*
> **I prefer summer to winter because I love sunbathing.*

> If you can relate new language to yourself, your experiences or your ideas, it often makes it easier to remember.

2 Think of three words or phrases you have learnt this week. Write a true sentence about yourself or your life using each word or phrase.

1. _____
2. _____
3. _____

3 Write one true sentence about yourself or your life using a comparative structure and one using a superlative structure.

1. _____
2. _____

4 Work in pairs and read out your sentences. Ask questions to find out more information from your partner.

> Remember to write sentences personalising new language when you record it in your vocabulary notebook or grammar notes.

UNIT 7 Time & Money

Part 1

Vocabulary & Speaking
**Prepositions of time
(in, on, at)**

Reading
A brief history of time zones

Grammar
Present perfect with for & since

Vocabulary and Speaking

1 What do the letters mean? Solve the time puzzle.

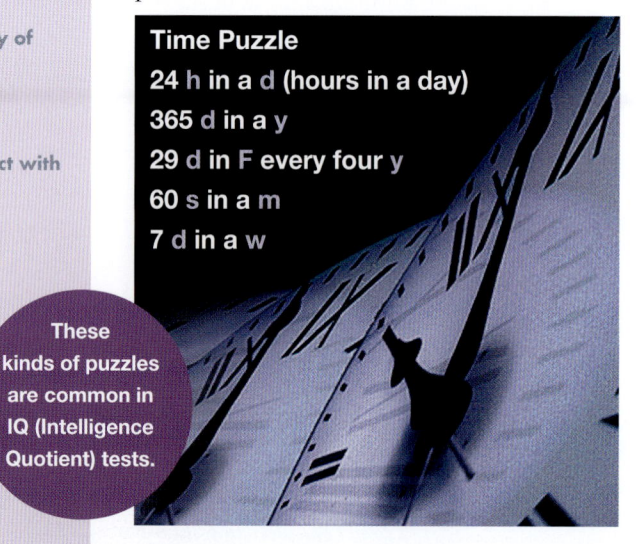

Time Puzzle
24 h in a d (hours in a day)
365 d in a y
29 d in F every four y
60 s in a m
7 d in a w

These kinds of puzzles are common in IQ (Intelligence Quotient) tests.

2 Here are three other *time numbers*. Can you make more puzzle items with them?

60   12   52

3 Complete the rules with the expressions in the box.

| dates (4th October, 12th March) | specific times (6 o'clock, eight-thirty) |
| seasons (summer, spring) | years (1999, 2005) |

Use **in** with months (*February, December*), times of the day (*the afternoon, the evening*), _____ and _____.
Use **on** with days (*Monday, Friday*) and _____.
Use **at** with _____ and certain time expressions (*the weekend, night*).

4 Choose five questions and write your answers on a piece of paper. Use a preposition + a time expression.

What's the best time to …
- go on holiday?
- wake up on a day when you aren't working?
- do homework or study?
- visit your home town?
- watch television for films or series?
- get married in your country?
- do exercise?

5 Compare your answers with a partner. Ask why.

A: *The best time to get married is in June.*
B: *Why?*
A: *Because the weather is always good in June.*

Reading

1 Work in pairs and discuss the questions.
- How many time zones are there in your country?
- Can you name a country where it is the middle of the night right now?
- Can you name a country that is one day behind you right now?

2 2.24 Read and listen to *A brief history of time zones* on page 79. Are these statements true (*T*) or false (*F*)?

1 Time zones have existed for 500 years.
2 Greenwich Mean Time and Coordinated Universal Time are the same thing.
3 China has always had the same number of time zones.
4 Jet lag makes you tired.
5 There is only one internet time.

3 Work in pairs and choose **one** of the tasks below.

A Choose three pieces of information from the text that you think are the most interesting. Compare with your partner.

B Discuss the questions.
- Have you visited a place with a different time zone? Where? When?
- Have you ever had jet lag?
- Do you know any good ways to avoid jet lag?

Grammar

*We **have had** standard time **for** less than 200 years.*
*Greenwich internet time **has existed since** 2000.*

- use *for* and *since* with present perfect to talk about unfinished time
- use *for* with a period of time
- use *since* with a point in time
- do not use *in* + a time expression with the present perfect tense

1 Complete the text with *for*, *since* or *in*.

A brief history of ... watches

The idea of a portable object that tells the time has been around _____ five hundred years.

_____ the past, people held watches in their hands. They were later called pocket watches, because you could put them in your pocket.

The wristwatch has existed _____ 1880, and electronic watches first appeared _____ the 1950s. Digital watches have existed _____ 1970.

Watches have been sold as jewellery _____ more than a hundred and fifty years. A watch is often considered a traditional gift idea for a man.

A brief history of time zones

Origin The idea of time zones has not existed for very long. People used to measure time using the shadow of the sun. For years, each country used its own time, and local times used to be very different from one place to another. After the 19th century people began to travel more. There was a lot of confusion about times. Countries needed a single, standard time. In 1884 members from 27 countries met in Washington, US to create a system of time zones. The world has had a time zone system for less than 200 years.

GMT, CUT, DST The time zone system starts with the Prime Meridian, an invisible line through Greenwich, England. This time is called GMT (Greenwich Mean Time) or CUT (Coordinated Universal Time). Many countries also observe daylight saving time, or summer time. This is the time of year when people change their clocks.

Different zones Some large countries have more than one time zone. The United States has ten time zones and Russia has eleven. China used to have five time zones but changed to one single zone in 1949. This means that when you cross the border from China to Afghanistan, you have to change your watch by four hours! Some countries have differences of less than one hour. For example, when you go across the border from India to Nepal you change your watch by only 15 minutes.

Jet lag If you travel across many time zones by plane, you may get jet lag. Jet lag is the feeling of being very tired because you have travelled across parts of the world where the time is different.

Internet time The spread of the internet has also increased communication between people from different countries. The Swiss company Swatch introduced internet time so that people on the internet would all use the same time. Greenwich has had its own internet time, called GET (Greenwich Electronic Time), since the year 2000.

2 Complete the sentences with the present perfect and *for* or *since*.

1. I _____ (*live*) in this town _____ ten years.
2. I _____ (*study*) English _____ I was twelve years old.
3. I _____ (*be*) in class _____ eight o'clock.
4. I _____ (*know*) the teacher _____ two years.
5. I _____ (*have*) my watch _____ my twentieth birthday.
6. I _____ (*know*) my oldest friend _____ we were at primary school together.

3 Complete the sentences with your own ideas and compare with a partner.

G **Grammar focus** – explanation & more practice of *for* & *since* on page 144

Time Unit 7

UNIT 7 Time & Money

Part 2

Vocabulary
Time expressions

Listening
The concept of time

Pronunciation
/aɪ/ & /eɪ/

Speaking
Time saving inventions

Reading & Speaking
A Tale of Two Cities

Vocabulary

1 Match the phrases in bold to the pictures. Which ones do you think are funny?

1 I think he **spends** too much **time** in front of the television.
2 It looks like Tom's worked **overtime** again.
3 Well, it **saves time** in the mornings!
4 Have you ever thought this job is a **waste of time**?
5 Advantage #1: lots of **free time**.

2 Look at the words and phrases in bold. What are they in your language?

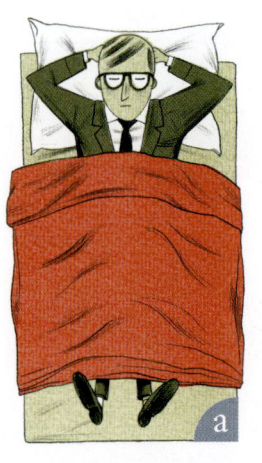

Listening

1 🔊 2.25 Listen to a talk about the concept of time in English. Finish the sentence to summarise the main point of the talk.

Time is …

2 🔊 2.26 Match 1–4 to a–d to make sentences. Then listen and check your answers.

1 The concept of time in the English language …
2 You can spend time and money …
3 You can give someone your time, …
4 We can convert time into money …

a and money into time.
b is connected to money.
c just like you can give them money.
d or save it.

3 Are there similar expressions for time in your language?

Pronunciation

1 🔊 2.27 Listen and repeat the sounds and words.

/aɪ/, time   /eɪ/, save

2 🔊 2.28 Listen and tick (✔) the word that has a different sound. Listen again and repeat the words.

1 fly   gym   why   eye
2 time   smile   life   machine
3 mobile   might   friend   height
4 save   waste   mail   money
5 great   break   meat   paper

3 Look at the words in exercise 2. What are some common spellings for /aɪ/ and /eɪ/?

4 🔊 2.29 Listen and repeat the proverbs. Do you have any similar proverbs in your language?

1 Time flies when you're having fun.
2 Time waits for no man.
3 So many things, so little time.
4 Life is short and time is swift.

80 Unit 7 Time

Speaking

1 Work in pairs and choose the five most important inventions from the list. Then rank them from 1 (most important) to 5 (least important).

Top Time-saving Inventions	
The hairdryer	The personal computer
The internet and email	The photocopier
The microwave oven	The plane
The mobile phone	The washing machine

Useful phrases

- I think …
- Why do you think so?
- Because … used to take a very long time.
- I agree / disagree.

2 Compare your list with another pair. Do you agree?

3 Can you think of other things that save time?

A Tale of Two Cities

It was the best of times, it was the worst of times, it was the age of wisdom, it was the age of foolishness, […] it was the spring of hope, it was the winter of despair, we had everything before us, we had nothing before us …

A Tale of Two Cities is a romantic adventure set in London and Paris. It happens in the years just before the French Revolution, a time of great changes in Europe.

A Tale of Two Cities is a historical novel. The story is invented, but the background is based on real events.

Actor Sir John Martin-Harvey playing Sidney Carton, the main character in the story (1926).

Glossary

foolishness (*noun*) – stupid behaviour
wisdom (*noun*) – knowledge and experience

Reading and Speaking

1 🔊 2.30 Read and listen to the first lines of *A Tale of Two Cities*.

2 Work in pairs. Some people say that the first line of the extract could be about the times we live in now. Do you agree? Are we living in the best of times and the worst of times?

3 Complete the sentences with your own ideas.

It is the best of times because …
It is the worst of times because …

4 Compare your ideas with another pair.

Charles Dickens
(1812–1870)
Considered one of the greatest English novelists in history, Dickens came from a very poor family. His books often talk about the situation of poor people in Victorian England.

Time Unit 7

UNIT 7 Time & Money

Part 3

Vocabulary
Money, verb phrases

Reading
A lifetime of financial concerns

Grammar
Present perfect with yet & already

Pronunciation
/ʌ/

Vocabulary

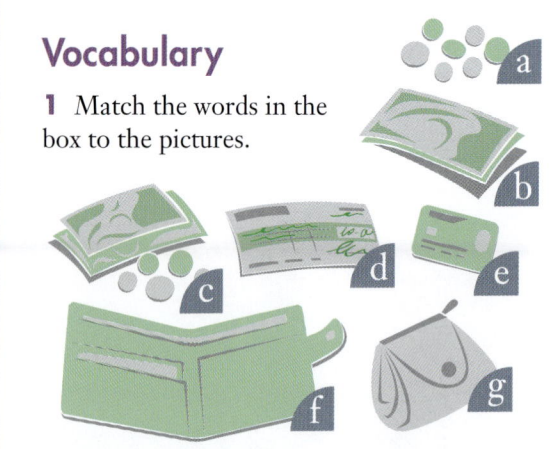

1 Match the words in the box to the pictures.

```
cash    cheque   coins
credit card   notes   purse   wallet
```

2 Cross out the option that is not possible.

1 You earn
   a a salary
   b money
   c the lottery.
2 You can spend money
   a on clothes
   b on food
   c in the bank.
3 You can take out a loan
   a from a bank
   b from your wallet
   c for a car.
4 You owe money
   a to a friend
   b to the bank
   c for your wallet.
5 People pay
   a electricity bills
   b water bills
   c money bills.

3 Look at the questions about money. Which questions would you **not** normally ask someone you don't know very well?

1 How much do you earn?
2 Where's the nearest cash machine?
3 Can you lend me some money?
4 How much did your jacket cost?
5 How much do you spend every week on food?
6 Do you have change for a five (dollar/euro/pound) note?
7 How much cash do you have with you now?
8 Do you owe a lot of money?

4 Compare your answers with a partner.

Reading

1 Look at the title of the text on page 83. What do you think it is about?

2 Read the text and check your answer.

3 Read the text again and answer the questions.

1 How much does the child's toy cost?
2 Does the university graduate have a job?
3 When does the family man pay the bills?
4 Where do the young couple work?
5 What has the heir done with her money?
6 Do the retired couple have money problems?

4 What are common money concerns for people your age?

Grammar

*I've **already** saved €3.*
*I haven't started work **yet**.*

- use *already* to emphasise something has happened before now
- use *yet* to talk about something that has not happened, but will probably happen soon

1 Find examples of *yet* and *already* in the text and complete the rules.

We use *yet* and *already* with the _____ tense.
We use _____ in affirmative statements.
We use _____ in negatives and questions.

2 Work in pairs. Look at the *to do* list and make sentences with *yet* or *already*.

She has already done the shopping.
She hasn't paid the bills yet.

```
do the shopping ✓
pay the bills
call work about a day off
do English homework ✓
go to the bank ✓
phone parents
```

82 Unit 7 **Money**

3 Make your own *to do* list. Write down six things. Include …
- three things you haven't done yet, but would like to do this week.
- three things you have already done this week.

4 Compare your list with a partner. Ask questions.

A: *Have you done your homework yet?*
B: *Yes, I have.*
A: *Have you visited your parents yet?*
B: *No, I haven't.*
A: *When are you going to visit them?*

G Grammar focus – explanation & more practice of *yet* & *already* on page 144

Pronunciation

1 2.31 Listen and repeat the sound and words.

/ʌ/, sun, mother

2 2.32 Tick (✔) the words that have the /ʌ/ sound. Then listen and check your answers.

| brother | bus | buy |
| cost | home | money | some |

3 2.33 Read and listen to the poem below.

4 Work in pairs. Read the poem, one line each at a time.

Routine

More **work**.
　　　　Less **fun**.
More **money**.
　　　　More **buying**.
More **fun**.
　　　　Less **money**.
More **work**.
　　　　Less **fun**.
More **money**.
　　　　More **buying**.
More **fun**.
　　　　Less **money**.
More **work**.

Stuart Doggett

A lifetime of financial concerns

As we get older our money concerns change, but they don't go away…

The retired couple
'My wife and I stopped work last month. We haven't received any money from the government yet but we have our savings, and we've already paid for our house. When the money comes, we'll travel. We've always wanted to go to France. Maybe now we can.'

The university graduate
'I haven't started work yet and I owe $10,000. How am I going to pay this money back?'

The heir
'With the money my uncle left me, I've already paid for my house and a new car. I'm going to put the rest in a special bank account for my children.'

The family man
'Our situation has become more difficult since we had our second child. Everything is getting more and more expensive. We really don't look forward to the end of the month when we have to pay everything.'

The eight year old
'I've already saved €3. Two more and I can buy the toy I want!'

The young couple
'Our friends often ask us: "Have you bought a place yet?" Well, we've already visited three banks and none of them want to help us. It's crazy, houses are so expensive here. We're thinking of living outside the city centre, but that means we have to commute and we don't really want that.'

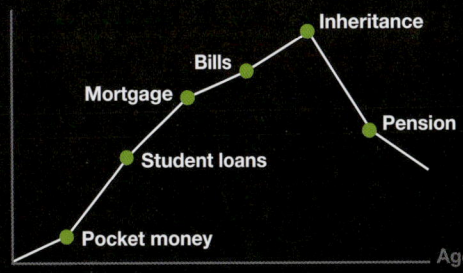

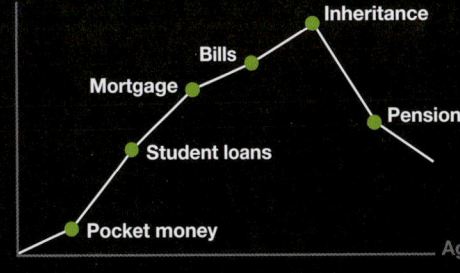

Financial concerns: Pocket money, Student loans, Mortgage, Bills, Inheritance, Pension — Age

Money Unit 7　83

Unit 7 Time & Money

Part 4

Speaking
Describing pictures

Reading
A different kind of bank

Speaking
A bank loan

Speaking

Look at the pictures of people meeting at a bank. Work in pairs and describe the similarities and differences between them.

Useful language

- formal clothes
- married couple
- outside
- group of women
- modern office
- traditional clothes

Useful phrases

- In this picture … but in this picture …
- In this picture they are wearing … but in this one they are wearing …
- This picture was probably taken in … while this one was taken …

Reading

1 2.34 Read and listen to *A different kind of bank*. Find two differences between a Grameen Bank and a normal bank.

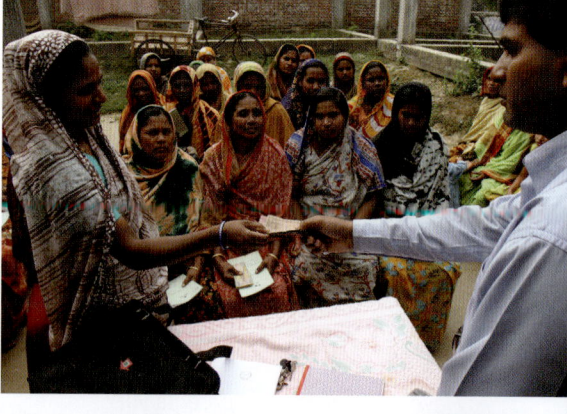

> I made a list of people who needed just a little bit of money. And when the list was complete, there were 42 names. The total amount of money they needed was $27. I was shocked.
> **Muhammad Yunus**

> This is not charity. This is business: business with a social objective, which is to help people get out of poverty.
> **Muhammad Yunus**

A different kind of bank

The Grameen Bank in Bangladesh is very different from a normal bank. In the words of its founder, Muhammad Yunus, **normal banks work on the principle 'the more you have, the more you can get. In other words, if you have little or nothing, you get nothing.'** The Grameen Bank system works on the principle that the person who has nothing is the first person who should get a loan from the bank.

The bank was started as a project in 1976 by Yunus. It gives people very small loans, called microcredit. In 1983 the Grameen Bank Project became an independent institution and the bank is now owned by its borrowers. There are more than seven million people who borrow from the Grameen Bank and 97% of them are women. It has more than 2,000 branches covering 79,000 villages. In normal banks, people go to the bank for a loan. In Grameen banks, the bank workers go and visit people in the villages. The bank often lends money to groups of women to start their own small businesses.

The Grameen bank system works very well in Bangladesh. Borrowers pay back more than 98% of the loans, and the bank has made a profit almost every year. It uses its profits to help with natural disasters.

In 2006 the Nobel committee gave Mohammad Yunus the Nobel Peace Prize for his work with the bank.

Glossary

branch (*noun*) – an office representing a large company
charity (*noun*) – an organisation that gives money and help to people who need it
founder (*noun*) – someone who starts an organisation
poverty (*noun*) – a situation where people do not have enough money to pay for basic needs

2 Read the text again and choose the correct answer.

1 The Grameen Bank thinks that … should get loans first.
   a rich people   b people with nothing
   c women
2 It lends … to people.
   a small amounts of money
   b large amounts of money
   c no money
3 Most of the people who borrow from the bank are …
   a women.   b poor.
   c both women and poor.
4 Grameen Bank workers meet the borrowers …
   a in their offices.   b in the capital city.
   c in their villages.
5 The bank gets back … of the money it lends.
   a a bit   b almost all   c all

3 What do you think of the Grameen bank? Is it a good idea?

Extend your vocabulary – *borrow* and *lend*

If we *borrow* something from someone, they give it to us and we agree to give it back.
I need to borrow some money from the bank.

If we *lend* something to someone, we give it to them and they agree to give it back to us.
The bank is going to lend me some money.

Complete the sentences with the correct form of *borrow* or *lend*.

1 My pen isn't working. Can I _____ yours?
2 She _____ him two thousand euros for the car. He hasn't paid it back yet.
3 I don't have enough money for the bus. Could you _____ me some?
4 We didn't have enough chairs, so we _____ some from the neighbour.

Speaking

1 Read the situation below.

> **Situation**
> The bank has lent your learning institution €12,000 to modernise the facilities. The director has asked you for suggestions on how to spend the money. What does your institution need?

2 Work in small groups and discuss what you are going to buy. Remember that your budget is €12,000. Write down your final list of items.

3 Present your plan to another group. Give reasons for your decisions.

Useful phrases

- We need …
- We don't need …
- … is more important than … because …
- I don't think … is as important as … because …
- I don't think … is very important because …
- We have decided to spend … on … because …

CD players
€150 each

Computers
€1,000 each

Electronic whiteboards
€1,000 each

Food and drink machine for students
€2,500

Modern desks and chairs
€ 1,500 per classroom

Nice chairs for the teachers
€150 each

Painting and decoration
€400 per classroom

Televisions with DVD players
€400 each

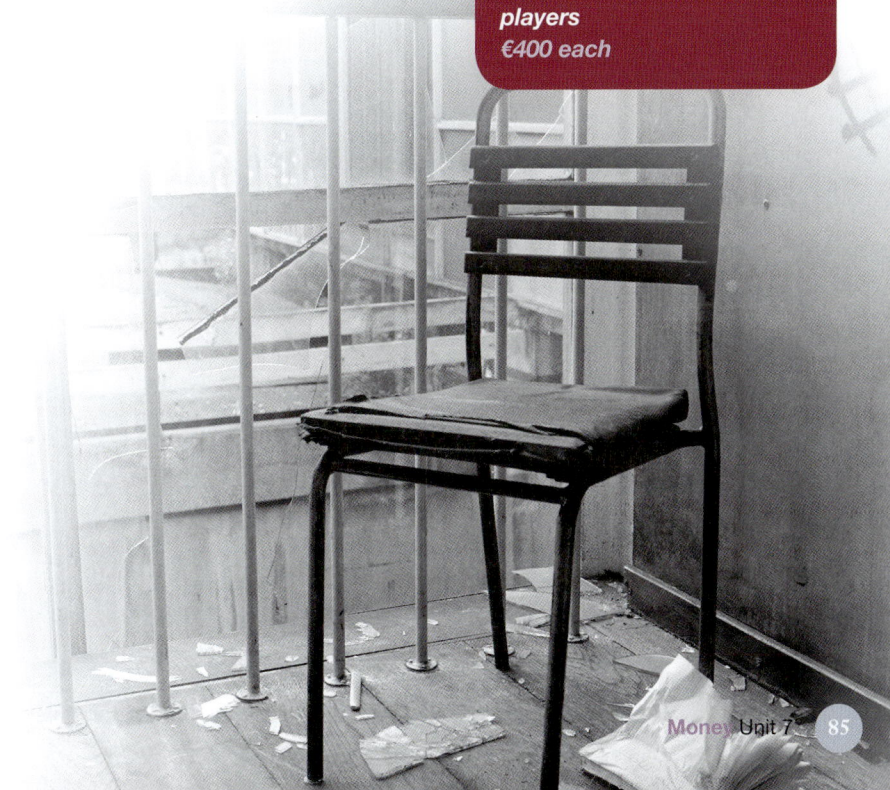

UNIT 7 Function globally shopping in a market

a b c d

Warm up

1 Look at the pictures of four different markets. Work in pairs and describe the similarities and differences between them.

Useful phrases

- This stall sells …
- I think this market is in …
- The stallholder is …

2 Which market could you see in your country?

Listening

1 2.35–2.37 Listen to three conversations. Match each one to a photo.

2 Listen again and answer the questions.
Conversation 1: What does the man want?
How much is the final price?
Conversation 2: What does the woman buy?
Conversation 3: What does the woman want?
Why is she sad at the end?

Language focus: shopping

1 Correct the mistakes in these sentences.
1 How much it is?
2 I can help you?
3 I just looking thanks.
4 Have you a red shirt?
5 You can to have it for a hundred and twenty-five.
6 I take it.
7 No, thanks. I leave it.
8 That very expensive.

2 2.38 Listen and check your answers. Then listen and repeat the phrases.

Speaking

Work in pairs and choose **one** of the tasks below.

A Choose one of the markets and roleplay a conversation. Use the new expressions you have learnt.

B Choose three things (eg your book, your pencil, your phone). You are going to try and *sell* them to your partner. Decide a price for each thing.

Try and sell your things to your partner. Use the new expressions you have learnt.

86 Unit 7 **Function globally**

Global English

The **English language** and the number **four** by David Crystal

If there's a number you should remember when thinking about the way the English language has changed over time, it is the number four.

The first boats carrying Angles, Saxons and Jutes from the north of Europe arrived in several parts of the British Isles in 449 AD. The different dialects they spoke gave us the earliest form of English – Old English, or Anglo-Saxon. Exactly 400 years later, King Alfred 'the Great' was born. He is especially famous in the history of English, because it was thanks to his planning that Old English literature survived.

In 1400, Chaucer died, leaving us the literary highlight of Middle English, *The Canterbury Tales*. Soon after, a major sound change began which affected many English vowel sounds. This 'Great Vowel Shift' is the main reason that Chaucer's language sounds so different from the English we use today.

In 1600, when Shakespeare was writing, roughly 4 million people spoke English in Britain. Today, around 400 years later, 400 million people speak English as a mother tongue, and four times as many speak it as a second or foreign language.

Glossary

Angle, Saxon, Jute (noun) – the names of Germanic peoples who lived in England

dialect (noun) – a way of speaking a language that is used only in a particular area or by a particular group

shift (noun) – a change in something

Timeline of the English Language

449 AD _____

787 AD **Viking raids** began in England – Scandinavian influence on English names for people and places

849 AD _____

1066 **Norman invasion** of England. The French language influences English in many ways.

1400 _____

1400s–1500s _____

1476 **First printing press** set up in England. Standard writing system starts to develop.

1600 _____

1600s English comes into contact with other languages through **colonisation**.

1800s Time of the **Industrial Revolution** and **British Empire**. Huge changes in English.

1884 New English Dictionary project begins – will become the **Oxford English Dictionary**.

late 1900s Rise of the internet and **globalisation**. English becomes world language.

2000 _____

Warm up

Look at the timeline for the English language. Tick (✔) the bold phrases that you have heard of before.

Reading

1 Read the text *The English language and the number four*. Find three reasons why the number four is important.

2 Read the text again and complete the timeline with information from the text.

Language focus

Choose the option with the same meaning as the underlined phrases.

1 <u>exactly 400</u> years later
   a 400   b 390–410

2 <u>roughly 4 million</u> people
   a 4 million   b 3.8–4.2 million

3 <u>around 400</u> years later
   a 400   b 395–405

4 400 million speak English as a mother-tongue, and <u>four times as many</u> speak it as a second or foreign language
   a 100 million b 1,600 million

Speaking

Work in pairs and discuss the questions.

- Can you think of any examples of how your language has changed? For example, a word or phrase that doesn't exist anymore.
- What other languages have an influence on your language? Can you give examples?
- Does your language have an influence on any other languages? Which ones?

Unit 7 Writing giving your opinion

Reading

1 Read Tayse's essay on *Life today is too fast and people don't have enough time for what is important*. Does she agree with the statement?

(1) _____.
People have too many things to do and spend all their time rushing from place to place. We travel by car and plane, communicate by email and mobile phone, and get information immediately on the internet. Even our food nowadays is often fast food.

(2) _____.
We worry about work and our obligations, and consequently become stressed and ill. We spend our time earning more money and buying more and more things, and so we lack time for what is important. We rarely spend time with friends and family or stop to relax or have fun.

(3) _____.
We should spend more time seeing our friends and family. We also need to think about relaxing and enjoying ourselves, even for a few hours a day. We need to find time to listen to music, read books for enjoyment, and enjoy our hobbies. We can't let life pass us by.

2 Read the essay again and put the sentences in the correct places. How do the sentences help us to understand each paragraph?

a I believe it is important to realise that there are other things in life as well as work and money.
b As a result of this, we save time but end up filling it with other things.
c It is certainly true that for many people, especially in big cities, life today is too fast.

3 Do you agree with Tayse's opinions?

Writing skills: organising your ideas

Look at Tayse's essay plan below. Put the points in each paragraph in the correct order.

1 Life today too fast
  a too many things to do – always rushing
  b life in big cities too fast
  c transport, communication, internet, food

2 Don't have enough time for what is important
  a no time for friends and family
  b earn money – buy things
  c worry about obligations – become stressed
  d save time but fill it with other things

3 Conclusion – what to do
  a spend more time with friends & family
  b can't let life pass us by
  c relax, have fun – music, reading, hobbies
  d need to realise other things are important

Language focus: giving your opinion

Complete these sentences from the text.

1 _____ realise that there are other things in life as well as work and money.
2 _____ spend more time seeing our friends and family.
3 _____ find time to listen to music.
4 _____ let life pass us by.

Preparing to write

1 Work in pairs and choose one of the statements below to write about. Do you agree with the statement?

- Schools and universities do not teach students enough about how to manage their time.
- The love of money is the root of all evil.

2 Write three paragraph headings and then write notes under each heading.

Saying what you think

- It is (certainly) true that …
- I (personally) believe that …
- It is my opinion / view that …

Writing

Write your essay. Use your notes and the useful phrases to help you.

Global review

Grammar

1 Complete the sentences with the correct word.
1. My birthday is _____ November 12th.
2. What are you doing _____ the weekend?
3. The best time to get married is _____ the spring.
4. I've lived in my house _____ six years.
5. I've studied French _____ last year.
6. I've had this purse _____ I was ten years old.

2 Put the words in the correct order.
1. yet / bill / paid / electricity / you / the / have?
2. gave / me / a / bank / loan / the.
3. saved / three / have / I / already / euros.
4. fun / flies / you're / time / having /when.

Vocabulary

1 Match the words on the left to the ones on the right.

jet	money
student	jam
pocket	watch
over	lag
traffic	loan
cash	time
wrist	machine

2 Put *owe*, *borrow* or *lend* in each gap.
1. Could you _____ me ten dollars, please?
2. I need to _____ some money from the bank.
3. How much do I _____ you for the tickets?

Speaking

1 Work in groups of three. Talk about yourselves using *for* and *since* and try to find three things that are the same for all of you.

I've known Maria **for** three years.
I've had my watch **since** January.
We've all studied English **for** two years.

2 Work in groups of three and discuss your English classes. Find three things you've already studied, and three things you haven't studied yet.

We've **already** studied the present perfect.
We haven't practised writing letters **yet**.

3 Work in pairs and ask each other these questions.
- What do you usually spend your money on?
- Do you save money? How? What for?
- How do you like to spend your free time?

Study skills

Managing your study time

1 Answer the questions about study time. Then discuss your answers with a partner.
1. When do you study best?
   a. In the morning.
   b. In the afternoon or evening.
   c. Late at night.
2. What do you do with homework?
   a. Do it straight away.
   b. Do it when you are ready.
   c. Do it at the last minute.
3. How do you study outside class?
   a. Just do your homework.
   b. Re-read the work done in class.
   c. Do other work as well.
4. When do you re-read your notes?
   a. Before meals.
   b. Travelling to school or work.
   c. Before going to sleep.

Top tips for study time

* Find the time when you work best, and study then.
* Re-read the work you have studied in class. Little and often is best, e.g. ten minutes a day.
* Use spare moments to re-read your class work, eg before meals, between classes, on the bus or waiting for an appointment.
* Decide what is most important.
* Make a work plan and follow it.
* Don't waste time thinking about work – do it straight away!

2 Make a study plan for next week. Use your answers to exercise 1 and the Top tips to help you.
- What will you do?
- When will you do it?

Home & Away

Part 1

Speaking
A tour of your home

Pronunciation
/h/

Listening
Famous homes

Grammar
Passive voice

Reading & Writing
Bram Stoker's Dracula

Speaking

Draw an outline of the rooms in your house or flat. Then work in pairs and take your partner on a *tour* of your home.

Useful language

- balcony
- bedroom
- front door
- kitchen
- study
- bathroom
- dining room
- hall
- living room
- toilet

Useful phrases

- This is the …
- Over here there's a …

Pronunciation

1 2.39 Listen and repeat the sound and the word.

/h/, home

2 2.40 Listen to the sentences. Underline the words with the /h/ sound.

Home is where … the heart is.
happy memories are.
you hang your hat.
the hard drive is.
your hopes are.

3 Listen again and repeat the sentences. Which one do you like the best?

Listening

1 Look at the pictures of three famous homes. Where are they? Who do you think lived there? Use the words in the box to help you guess.

| castle | Dracula | film set | ghost |
| haunted | prince | prisoner | tower |

2 2.41–2.43 Listen to people talking about these homes and check your answers.

3 Listen again. Are the statements true (*T*) or false (*F*)?

Conversation 1:
a The tower was built more than 900 years ago.
b The young princes were put in the tower by their uncle Richard III.

Conversation 2:
a The house was used in a film.
b The house is never open.

Conversation 3:
a The castle is still occupied by the government.
b Dracula never saw the castle.

4 Are there any famous homes in your town? Where are they? Who lived there?

Extend your vocabulary – *house* and *home*

A *house* is a building that people live in.
She lives in that big house.
Someone's *home* is the place where they live.
That flat is the home of a large family.

Complete the sentences with *house* or *home*.
1 I'm going _____ after class.
2 Please do exercise 3 for _____ work.
3 See that big red _____ over there? My father lives there.
4 I'll do the shopping and cleaning, but you do the other _____ work.
5 Hi, I'm not at _____ at the moment. Please leave a message.

90 Unit 8 **Home**

Grammar

*People say the tower **is haunted**.*
*The castle **was returned** to its owners.*

- we use the passive voice when we want to focus on the action, not the person who does the action
- we also use the passive voice when we do not know who does the action or it is not important

1 Read the sentences from the listening and decide if they are active (*A*) or passive (*P*).

1. The Tower of London was built in 1078.
2. Their uncle put them in the tower.
3. It was used in the film *Psycho*.
4. People believe that Vlad Tepes – the original Dracula – lived here.
5. It is visited every year by thousands of people.

2 Complete the texts with the correct form of *to be*.

Official residences around the world

The **Palacio de la Moncloa** is the official residence of the Spanish prime minister in Madrid. It *was / is* destroyed during the Spanish Civil War, but it *was / is* rebuilt afterwards.

Abdeen Palace, in central Cairo, *is / was* built in 1874 for the Egyptian royal family. Today it *is / was* used as an official residence for the president and a museum.

The Lodge, located in Canberra, Australia, *is / was* built in 1926. It *was / is* meant to be a temporary home for the Australian prime minister. Now it is the official one.

The official residence of the president of Ukraine is **Mariyinsky Palace** in Kiev. It *is / was* constructed in the 18th century and *is / was* used as military headquarters between 1917 and 1920.

The **Zhongnanhai** is a group of buildings in Beijing, China. It *is / was* used as an official residence of the head of state in the past. Today, when foreign politicians come to visit, they *were / are* welcomed there.

G **Grammar focus** – explanation & more practice of the passive on page 146

Bram Stoker's Dracula

As Jonathan Harker approaches the castle doors, they open. An old man, carrying a lamp, enters the room.

Dracula: Welcome to my home.

Harker: Count Dracula?

Dracula: I am Dracula, and I bid you welcome, Mr Harker, to my house. Come in.

Dracula: You will, I trust, excuse me that I do not join you. But I have already dined and I never drink ... wine.

The novel *Dracula* was written in 1897 by the Irish novelist Bram Stoker. There have been many adaptations of the novel for film. The 1992 film *Bram Stoker's Dracula* was directed by Francis Ford Coppola.

Reading and Writing

1 Read the scene from the film *Bram Stoker's Dracula*.

2 Work in pairs and write the next three lines of the dialogue. Then present your scene to another pair.

Language note: *I bid you welcome* is a formal, literary way of saying welcome.

Home Unit 8

Home & Away

UNIT 8

Part 2

Vocabulary & Speaking
Animals

Reading
The cat came back

Vocabulary
Prepositions of movement

Vocabulary and Speaking

1 Look at the pictures of different animals. Would you keep any of these animals in your home? Which ones?

| budgie | cat | dog | goldfish | hamster |
| horse | mouse | rabbit | snake | spider |

2 Which of these animals have …

a tail?   eight legs?   fur?
big ears?   fins?   wings?

3 Work in pairs and ask each other these questions.

- Did you have a pet as a child? What was it?
- Are you afraid of any of these animals?

Reading

1 Do you prefer cats or dogs? Why? Tell a partner.

I prefer … because they are friendlier / more intelligent / more interesting.
I don't like cats or dogs.

2 Read the introduction to *The cat came back* on page 93 and discuss the questions in pairs.

- Do cats have any special meaning in your country?
- Do many people keep them as pets? What is the most common pet?
- In English, people sometimes say that cats have nine lives. Does this expression exist in your language?

3 Quickly read the rest of the text and choose the best subtitle.

a True stories of cats who lived in different countries.
b True stories of cats who travelled a long distance to come home.
c True stories of cats who loved their owners.
d True stories of cats who travelled a long distance to leave home.

4 🔊 2.44 Read and listen to the text and complete the sentences with the names of the cats.

1 _____ lived in the USA.
2 _____ came home after about two months.
3 _____ and _____ came back home after a week.
4 _____ went to his owners' second home.
5 _____ was happy but very dirty.

5 Find words in the text with these meanings.

1 so important that you should not criticise it (introduction)
2 the official line that separates two countries (paragraph 1)
3 very dirty (paragraph 2)
4 the sound a cat makes when it's happy (paragraph 2)

6 Which story do you think is the most surprising? Do you know any unusual pet stories?

92 Unit 8 Home

The cat came back

Archaeologists estimate that humans and cats have lived together for more than 9,000 years. In Ancient Egypt, cats were considered sacred animals and protectors of the home. Today there are an estimated 500 million domestic cats in the world, making cats one of the most common animals in the home. It's common to say that cats have nine lives because of their strange ability to survive, as the following true stories show.

Minosch – travelled 2,400 km through Germany. In 1981 Mehmet Tune, a Turkish man living in Germany, went to Turkey with his cat and family for a holiday. At the Turkish border Minosch disappeared. Sixty-one days later, back in northern Germany, the family heard a noise at the door. It was Minosch.

Howie – walked 1,900 km across Australia. In 1978 this three-year-old cat walked home from the Gold Coast in Queensland, Australia, to Adelaide. The trip took a year. Kirsten Hicks, the cat's owner, said that although he was filthy and bleeding, Howie was actually purring.

Ernie – travelled 965 km to Texas. In September 1994, Chris and Jennifer Trevino's cat Ernie jumped out of a pick-up truck while it was travelling down the motorway. The cat was 965 km away from home. A week later, Ernie walked back into the Trevino family home in Victoria, Texas.

Gringo – travelled 780 km down to the French Riviera. The Servos family lost their pet cat Gringo from their home in northern France in December 1982. The following July they learnt that the cat was in the south of France. Gringo had travelled through France and arrived at the Servos's summer home a week later. The neighbours took care of him until the Servos family arrived.

Vocabulary

1 Look at the pictures and complete the sentences with the correct prepositions from the box.

across	across
along	down	in
into	out of	past
through	up

2 🔊 2.45 Listen and check your answers. Then cover the sentences and try to retell the story.

1 Ernie jumped _____ the truck and walked _____ the highway.

2 He went _____ a bridge, and _____ some fields.

3 He walked _____ the river, but fell _____ by accident.

4 He ran _____ some sleeping dogs.

5 He climbed _____ a tree to sleep and climbed _____ again the next morning.

6 He walked _____ the family home one week later.

Home Unit 8

UNIT 8 Home & Away

Part 3

Reading
Travel guidebooks

Listening
Conversations with travel guides

Grammar
First conditional

Reading & Speaking
The Beach

Reading

Read *A quick guide to the world's most famous guidebooks* and complete the sentences with the names of the guidebooks.

1 _____ became famous for its restaurant reviews.
2 _____ was written by a soldier.
3 _____ was the first modern guidebook.
4 _____ and _____ were written for people without a lot of money.

Which of these guidebooks did you know about already?

Listening

1 🔊 2.46–2.48 Listen to three conversations between tourists and travel guides / agents. Choose the correct situation for each one. There is one place you don't need.

| beach | city centre | market | travel office |

2 Listen again and choose the correct answers.

Conversation 1: The man wants to travel …
 a to the USA.   b this month.
 c next month.

Conversation 2: The tower is …
 a the newest building in the city.
 b the tallest building in the city.
 c the oldest building in the city.

Conversation 3: The guide persuades the man to …
 a buy a carpet.   b have lunch.
 c visit the city.

Extend your vocabulary – words that mean *trip*

A *trip* is when we go somewhere and come back again.
A *drive* is a trip in a car. A *flight* is a trip in a plane.
A *journey* is a long trip from one place to another.
A *tour* is a trip to a place where there are interesting things to see.
A *ride* is a short trip in a car or bus or on a bicycle or motorcycle.

Replace the underlined words with other words that mean *trip*.

1 I went for a <u>trip</u> in my brother's new car.
2 They were very tired and had jet lag after the third <u>plane trip</u>.
3 He took me for a <u>trip</u> in his new Volkswagen.
4 She's saving money for her next <u>trip</u> across Europe.

A quick guide to the world's most famous guidebooks

Baedeker's: these were the first modern travel guidebooks and were published in Germany in 1835.

Michelin: the first guide to travelling through France was written by André Michelin in 1900. The Michelin stars are one of the most famous systems for reviewing restaurants in the world.

Frommer's: the book *Europe on $5 a day* was written in 1957 by Arthur Frommer, an American soldier, and was one of the first budget travel guides.

Lonely Planet: the *Lonely Planet* guidebooks were started by Tony and Maureen Wheeler in 1973. They were originally written for budget travel in Asia, but now cover almost every country in the world.

94 Unit 8 *Away*

The Beach

In *The Beach*, the main character Richard finds a secret community of travellers in Thailand. They live on a perfect beach, a place that is not in any guidebooks. Here Sal, a woman who lives there, explains the idea behind the secret community to Richard.

'Of course this is more than a beach resort. But at the same time, it is just a beach resort. We come here to relax by a beautiful beach, but it isn't a beach resort, because we're trying to get away from beach resorts. Or we're trying to make a place that won't turn into a beach resort. See?'

'No.'

Sal shrugged. 'You will see, Richard. It really isn't that complicated.'

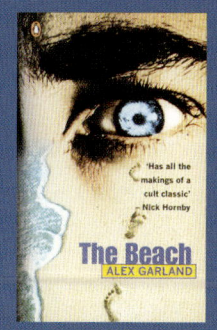

Grammar

*If you **go** up the tower, you **won't** regret it.*
*If you **buy** one of these carpets now, I **can** get a good price for you.*
*I'll ask if you **like**.*

- use the first conditional to talk about a possible future situation
- use the present simple in the *if* clause
- use *will*, *can* or *might* plus verb in the main clause
- the *if* clause can be the first or second clause in the sentence

1 Complete the sentences from the listening with the correct phrase.
1 If you *travel / will travel* this month, *you'll / you* get an extra 20% discount.
2 If you *will go / go* up the tower, you *won't / don't* regret it.
3 *We'll / We* go there later if you *will want / want*.
4 If you *buy / will buy* two, she *will give / gives* you a big discount.

2 What is the difference between these sentences?
a If I go to London, I'll buy an English guidebook.
b If I go to London, I might buy an English guidebook.
c If I go to London, I can buy an English guidebook.

3 Work in pairs. Read the situations and complete the sentences with your own ideas.
1 You want to go somewhere this weekend. (sunny or raining?)
   If it's sunny, we'll …
2 You have won a big prize (a trip for two or money?)
   If we win the trip for two, we …
3 Your friend is going to have a baby and you want to buy a present. (boy or girl?)
   If it's a boy …

G **Grammar focus** – explanation & more practice of the first conditional on page 146

Reading and Speaking

1 Check you understand the phrase *beach resort*. Are there any beach resorts in your country? Do you like them?

2 2.49 Read and listen to the text. Then work in pairs and discuss the questions.
- What do Sal and the others want to avoid? Why?
- Do you often visit places that are popular with tourists?
- Are there any places in your country that have too much tourism? Where?

Alex Garland (1970–) is an English writer of novels and films. He wrote his first novel *The Beach* in 1996 when he was 26 years old and it became a classic. It was made into a film in 2000.

UNIT 8 Home & Away

Part 4

Speaking
Describing photos

Vocabulary
Adjectives & prepositions

Reading
New kinds of tourism

Grammar
Second conditional

Pronunciation & Speaking
Sentence stress

Speaking

Work in pairs. Look at the pictures below and describe them. How do you think they are connected?

Useful language

- ancient
- disaster area
- operating theatre
- castle
- kitchen
- storm

Useful phrases

- It looks a bit like …
- This picture shows … while this one shows …
- This picture looks nicer / more interesting / more boring than …

Vocabulary

1 Complete the sentences with the correct prepositions.

| about | at | in | of | of | with |

1 I'm interested _____ historical and cultural places.
2 I'm bored _____ beach holidays; we go to the beach every year.
3 I'm worried _____ the situation and I want to help.
4 I'm fond _____ sand, sea and sun.
5 I'm not good _____ cooking, but I want to learn.
6 I'm a bit afraid _____ old castles and places like that.

2 Match the sentences in exercise 1 to the pictures from the speaking activity. More than one answer may be possible.

3 Complete the sentences in exercise 1 with your own ideas.

Reading

1 Read the text *New kinds of tourism* on page 97. Which kind of tourism does each picture show?

2 Read the text again and put the sentences in the correct places in the text.

a This kind of tourism involves going to a different country for health care and at the same time enjoying more typical tourist attractions.
b New Zealand has benefited from this kind of tourism since the film *The Lord of the Rings* was made there.
c The increase in the number of tourists also means an increase in the kinds of tourism now available.
d Cooking holidays are growing in popularity, especially in countries like Italy and France.
e This kind of tourism is not very popular with local residents for obvious reasons.

3 What is your opinion of these different kinds of tourism? Write a number for each one. 1 = very acceptable, 5 = completely unacceptable

Then compare your ideas with a partner.
I think … is very acceptable.
I have some problems with …
I think … is unacceptable.

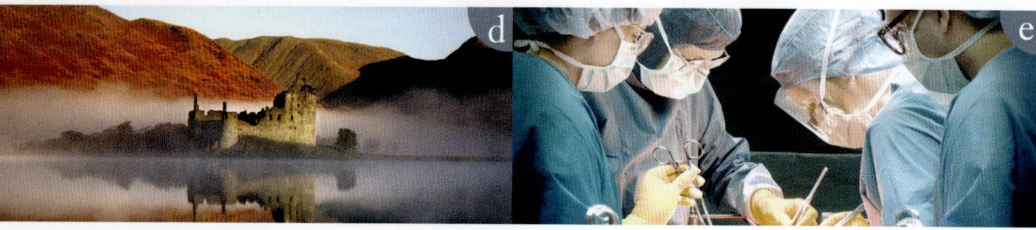

New kinds of tourism

Would you do it if you had the chance?

People are travelling more than ever before. The World Tourism Organisation (UNWTO) predicts that by 2020 the number of international travellers will be more than 1.6 billion people per year (see chart). _____ Here are four different kinds of tourism that have appeared recently.

Medical tourism

Medical tourism can be for a variety of things, from operations to visits to the dentist or even cosmetic surgery. ___a___ A few of the popular countries offering medical tourism are India, Cuba, Thailand, Argentina and Jordan. In Kenya they even offer medical safaris.

Culinary tourism

Nearly all tourists eat in restaurants, and dining is one of the top three tourist activities. But if you were in a country famous for its food, would you learn how to cook it? Welcome to the more extreme form of culinary tourism, where people go to another country to learn how to prepare its food. _____

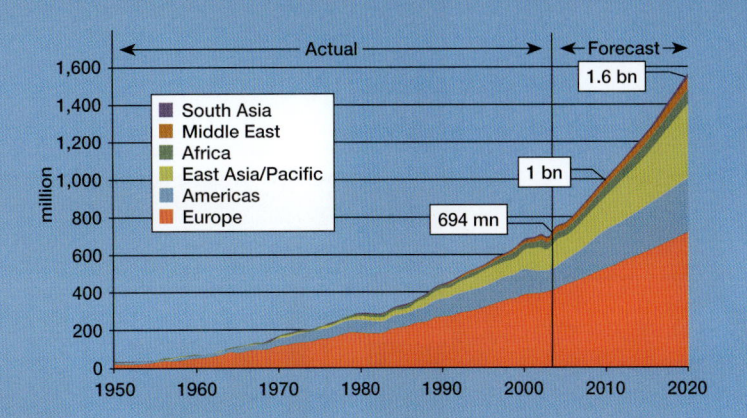

Disaster tourism

Disaster tourism involves visiting the site of a disaster. Examples include tours to New Orleans after Hurricane Katrina, to parts of Thailand after the tsunami or tourist visits to ground zero in New York. _____

Literary tourism

Another growing area of tourism is literary tourism. This is a kind of cultural tourism and there are several types. It can be connected to the life of an author, for example visiting the author's home or favourite places, or connected to the lives of characters in a story. It can also be a visit to a place where a film was made. _____

Glossary

cosmetic surgery (*noun*) – medical operations that improve someone's appearance

ground zero (*noun*) – a place where a lot of people have been killed

health care (*noun*) – the services that look after people's health

safari (*noun*) – a journey, especially in Africa, to see wild animals in their natural environment

tsunami (*noun*) – a very large wave that is caused by an earthquake under the sea

Grammar

1 Look at sentences 1–3 and answer questions a–c below.

1 *If you were in a country famous for its food, would you learn how to cook it?*
2 *If I went to Morocco, I would visit* the market in Medina.
3 We *wouldn't visit* the disaster area *if we were in New Orleans*.

a What tense are the verbs in the underlined parts of the sentences?
b What form of the verb follows *would* in the other part of the sentences?
c Are these real or unreal situations?

2 Which sentence in each pair is about an unreal situation?

1 a We'll go if we have the money.
  b We'd go if we had the money.
2 a Would you visit there if you could?
  b Will you visit there if you can?
3 a I'd never visit a disaster zone.
  b I'll never visit a disaster zone.

Grammar focus – explanation & more practice of the second conditional on page 146

Pronunciation and Speaking

1 🔊 **2.50** Look at this question. Only the stressed words are written. Listen and write the missing words.

_____ you _____ go anywhere _____ _____ world, where _____ _____ go?

2 Listen again and repeat the question. Then work in pairs and ask each other.

3 Work in pairs and ask each other the questions in the box. Pay attention to the stressed words.

Language note: *would you* is often pronounced /wʊdjuː/ or /wʊdjə/ in fast connected speech.

- If you could work or study in another country, would you do it? What country would you prefer?
- If some foreign friends visited you for one day and wanted to see some sights, where would you take them?
- What would you do if your son or daughter told you they wanted to travel on their own?
- If you went to England, would you buy souvenirs? What would you buy? Who for?

Away Unit 8   97

Function globally speaking on the telephone

Warm up

Work in pairs. Roleplay a short phone conversation for each situation.

Situations
1 A: phone B. You can't go to work today. Say why.
2 B: phone A. You have a problem in your kitchen. You want A to come and fix it.
3 A: phone B. You would like to reserve a room in B's hotel for two nights.
4 B: phone A. Tell A about a fantastic holiday you have just returned from.

Listening

2.51–2.54 Listen to four short phone conversations. What is the man trying to do? What happens at the end?

Language focus: telephone English

1 Put the words in the correct order to make useful phrases.

1 about calling the English learning holiday I'm.
2 Mrs Knight can speak to I?
3 please a moment, just.
4 call back I'll.
5 a message I can take?
6 Greenway hello, Holidays.
7 Pablo Alonso is hello, this.
8 you put I'll through.

2 2.55 Listen and check your answers. Then listen and repeat the phrases.

3 Look at sentences 1–8 in exercise 1 and match them to the functions a–h below.

Which phrase do you use …
a when you answer the phone?
b to say who you are?
c to say the purpose of your call?
d to politely ask the other person to wait?
e to connect one caller to another?
f to ask to speak to someone?
g to ask if the other person wants to leave a message?
h to say you will call again later?

Speaking

Work in pairs and choose **one** of the tasks below.

A Repeat the warm up activity using the new expressions you have learnt.

B Prepare a phone conversation. Use the diagram below to help you. Then practise your conversation.

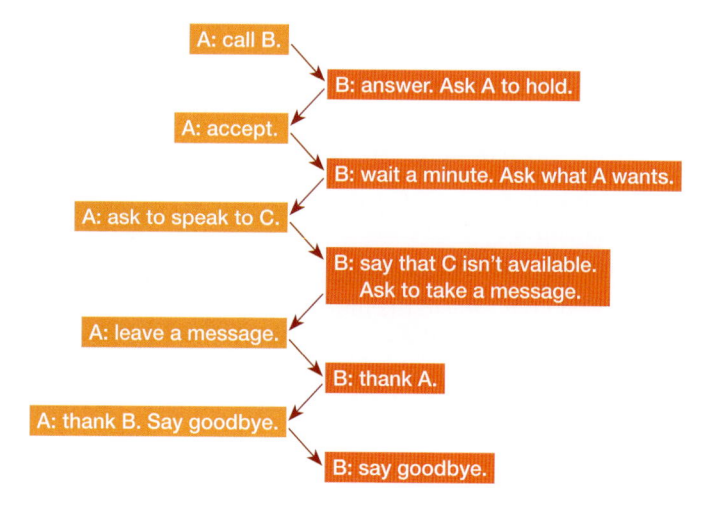

A: call B.
B: answer. Ask A to hold.
A: accept.
B: wait a minute. Ask what A wants.
A: ask to speak to C.
B: say that C isn't available. Ask to take a message.
A: leave a message.
B: thank A.
A: thank B. Say goodbye.
B: say goodbye.

Unit 8 **Function globally**

Global voices

cottage   terraced houses

block of flats

Warm up

1 Look at the pictures of different homes. Work in pairs and describe the similarities and differences between them.

2 Are any of the pictures similar to homes in your country?

Listening

🔊 2.56–260 Listen and cross out the topic the speaker **doesn't** mention.

1 David, Georgia
 a blocks of flats b houses in the villages c house prices
2 Elena, Russia
 a big houses b house prices c rooms in a house
3 Valeria, Bolivia
 a blocks of flats b coloured houses c homes in Oxford
4 Katie, Northern Ireland
 a terraced houses b blocks of flats c varied homes
5 Bea, England
 a house prices b living rooms c house mates

David, Georgia   Elena, Russia
Valeria, Bolivia   Katie, Northern Ireland   Bea, England

Language focus: adverbs of degree

1 Put the adverbs of degree into three groups.

+	++	+++
___	___	___
___	___	___

a bit   extremely   fairly   quite   slightly   very

2 Match the speakers 1–5 to the summaries a–e. Then listen again and check your answers.

1 David, Georgia ___
2 Elena, Russia ___
3 Valeria, Bolivia ___
4 Katie, Northern Ireland ___
5 Bea, England ___

a The homes in my country are quite varied. They have different pretty colours.
b Homes in my country are very big; in the cities there are blocks of flats, and in the country there are more houses.
c In my country many young people share a big house together; homes are quite large.
d Flats in my country are extremely expensive, much more expensive than flats in Great Britain.
e Terraced houses in my city are fairly typical. They have two rooms upstairs and two rooms downstairs.

3 Which sentences in exercise 2 are true for your country?

Speaking

1 Choose **one** of the topics below. Make some notes using the questions to help you.

- Homes in your country and homes in Great Britain / USA. Different? How?
- An extremely big house you have visited. Whose? Where? What's it like?
- A part of your city where the buildings are quite ugly. Where? What do they look like?
- A part of your country where homes are fairly cheap. Where? How much? Why?

2 Work in pairs and tell each other about your topic.

I'm going to tell you about an extremely big house I've visited. It's a friend's house, and it is outside the town. It has many bedrooms, and a very large living room …

Writing a description of a town

Reading

Read Aneta's description of her town and answer the questions.
1. What are the town's main attractions?
2. What does Aneta like and dislike about the town?
3. Would you like to visit the town? Why?

Hi Mariko

How are you? I hope you are well. I'm so glad you are coming to stay with me next month. Will be great to see you again.

Let me tell you a bit about my town. Is called Rajec and is in the north of Slovakia, near the Mala Fatra mountains. Is not a large town (are about 7,000 inhabitants) but is very old and beautiful. The main attraction of the town is the 16th-century Town Hall. Is also a medieval square in the centre of the town, as well as lots of historical buildings. Outside the town are also thermal baths, and a golf course and tennis courts.

The worst thing about Rajec is that is a bit quiet and isn't much to do at night. Is no cinema, and are not many bars and restaurants. But what I like best is the countryside around the town. Is wonderful to go walking there in the summer. Are mountains nearby, as well as a small lake.

Anyway, that's all for now. I'm looking forward to seeing you soon.

Love,

Aneta

Language focus: *it* and *there*

1. Aneta has forgotten to use *it* seven times and *there* seven times. Write the words in the correct places in her description.

   It will be great to see you again.

2. Complete the rules using *it* or *there*.
   a. Use _____ to talk about something for the first time.
      _____ is an old Town Hall. _____ aren't many bars.
   b. Use _____ to talk about something you have already mentioned.
      _____ is very old. _____ is near the mountains.

Writing skills: giving more information

Make your writing more interesting by giving more information about places.

Put the clauses with *where* in the best place in the email.
1. …, where people go skiing in the winter
2. …, where you can go for a day trip
3. …, where you can go fishing
4. …, where you can enjoy the natural hot water all year round

Preparing to write

Work in pairs and ask each other the questions. Use the useful phrases below to help you.
1. What's your town called?
2. What sort of town is it?
3. Where is it exactly?
4. What is it like?
5. What are the main attractions?
6. What can you do there?
7. What is the worst thing about the town?
8. What do you like best about the town?

Describing a town

- It's a small / medium-sized / large town / city / village.
- It's historical / modern / touristy / a bit quiet / quite lively.
- It's in the north / in the south-east / in the centre of …
- It's on the coast / near the capital city.
- There are lots of shops / no historical buildings.
- There's a medieval castle / no shopping centre.
- There's a lot / not much / nothing to do (at night).

Writing

Write an email like Aneta's to describe your town to a friend. Use your answers from above to help you.

Global review

Grammar

Complete the sentences with the correct words.
1 The Tower of London *was built / was build / built* in 1078.
2 Every year, Dracula's Castle *visited / visit / is visited* by thousands of tourists.
3 People *do not permit / is not permitted / are not permitted* to take photographs too close to 10 Downing Street.
4 I'm bored *at / with / on* my job so I'm going to leave.
5 If you *don't / won't / wouldn't* hurry, you'll miss the bus.
6 I would visit Brazil if I *have / had / would have* enough money.
7 You'll never pass the exam if you *don't / won't / didn't* study.
8 You *will / can / could* see lions if you went on safari.

Vocabulary

1 Read the definitions and complete the words.
1 an animal with a very long neck — g _____
2 the biggest animal in the world — w _____
3 an insect that makes honey — b _____
4 a book that tells you about places to visit — g _____
5 something you pack before you travel — s _____

2 Complete the directions using the correct prepositions.
Go (1) _____ the road,
(2) _____ the bridge and
(3) _____ the church.

Speaking

1 Work in pairs and ask each other the questions.
- If you could live anywhere in the world, where would you live, and why? What would your house be like?
- Where would you go if you could travel anywhere in the world? What would you do there? What could you see?

2 Work in pairs. You are going on holiday together. Discuss and decide where you are going.

A: you want to go to a tropical beach. Think of some reasons why.
B: you want to go to a city. Think of some reasons why.

Useful phrases

- A: If we go to Hawaii, we can …
- B: Yes, but … is boring. If we go to …, we can …

Study skills

Learning words with prepositions

1 Work in pairs. Can you remember which prepositions were used in these sentences?
1 Hi, I'm not _____ home _____ the moment.
2 The castle is known _____ Dracula's Castle.
3 If you were in a country famous _____ its food, would you learn how to cook it?
4 You are going _____ a three-day trip.

> When you learn new words, it is a good idea to learn them with the preposition they are used with.
>
> interested **in**   **at** home   go **on** a trip

2 Look up these adjectives in your dictionary. Write the preposition they are used with and an example sentence from the dictionary.

Similar *to*
Their situation is very similar to ours.

1 different _____
   _____
2 married _____
   _____
3 related _____
   _____
4 keen _____
   _____

3 Use a dictionary to find out whether these words are used with *to*, *for* or *on*.
1 go _____ holiday
2 go _____ a drive
3 go _____ the cinema
4 go _____ a drink
5 go _____ safari
6 go _____ a picnic
7 go _____ a cruise
8 go _____ a concert
9 go _____ lunch
10 go _____ a tour

UNIT 9 Health & Fitness

Part 1

Speaking & Listening
The common cold

Vocabulary
Feeling ill

Pronunciation
Ch & gh

Listening
Cures for the common cold

Grammar
Modal verbs of advice

Writing
A sick note

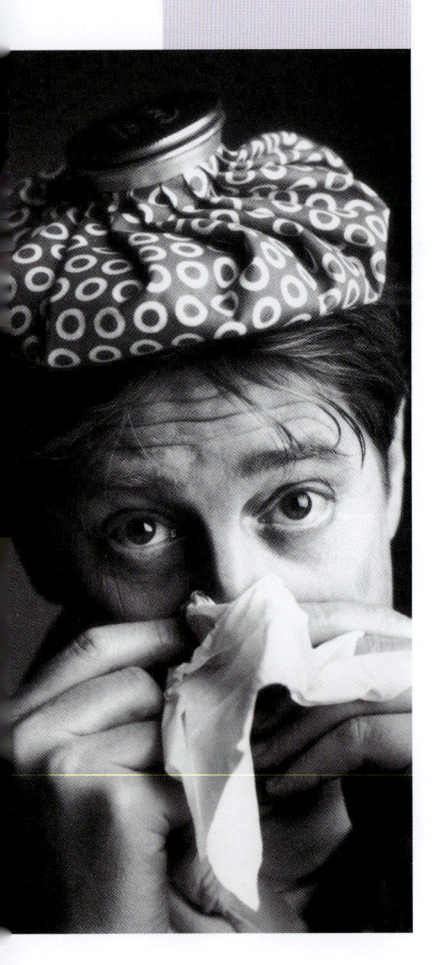

Speaking and Listening

1 Work in pairs and ask each other the questions.
- How often do you get a cold?
- Have you had a cold yet this year?
- Do you ever take time off work or school with a cold?

2 Try to complete the information about the common cold with the numbers in the box. There are two numbers you don't need.

| 24–48 hours | 2 months | 2–5 | 50 |
| 200+ | 2–3 years | $3.5 billion | 6–10 |

In numbers … the common cold

- the number of viruses that cause the common cold
- the average number of colds an adult gets every year
- the average number of colds a child or baby gets every year
- the average time you have a cold before you feel the symptoms
- the average time in your life you will have a cold
- the cost of the common cold in the US every year (from lost time at work and school)

3 2.61 Listen and check your answers.

Vocabulary

1 Complete the sentences with the correct word.
1. *What's / How's* the matter?
2. I *feel / have* tired.
3. I've *got / feel* a headache.
4. I've got a *hurt / sore* throat.
5. My back *hurts / is hurts*.
6. I have a *blocked / blocking* nose.
7. *I'm / I've* always sneezing.

Language note: when you talk about feeling ill you can use *I have* or *I've got*.

2 Replace the underlined words in exercise 1 with the words in the box. There may be more than one possible answer.

cough	coughing	fever
head	leg	sick
stomach ache	toothache	wrong

3 Work in pairs. A: turn to page 127. B: turn to page 129.

Pronunciation

1 2.62 Listen to the groups of words. Which word has a different *ch* or *gh* sound?
1. cheap   chicken   choose   machine
2. character   catch   technique   headache
3. tough   enough   ought   cough

2 Write the words from exercise 1 in the correct columns.

/f/	/k/	/tʃ/	/ʃ/	silent

3 2.63 Listen and repeat the sentences. Pay attention to the *ch* and *gh* sounds.
1. I've had enough of this cough.
2. I think I caught it from Charles.
3. He's had a headache for ages.

4 2.64 Read and listen to the poem below. How many different pronunciations of *ough* are there?

I take it you already know
Of tough and bough and cough and dough.
Others may stumble but not you,
On hiccough, thorough, slough and through.
…
A dreadful language? Man alive,
I'd mastered it when I was five.

5 Try to read the poem aloud.

Listening

1 Read the quote about the common cold. What advice would you give to someone with a cold?

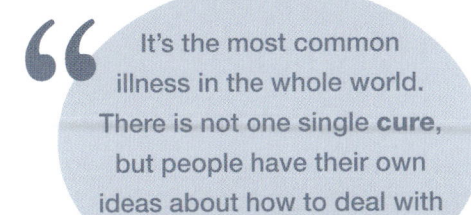

> *It's the most common illness in the whole world. There is not one single **cure**, but people have their own ideas about how to deal with **the common cold**.*

2 🔊 **2.65** Listen to the different people answering the same question. List the pictures above in the order that you hear them: eg b, …

3 Choose one of the verbs in the box. Listen again and make notes on the advice you hear with that verb.

| breathe | drink | eat |
| go | stay | take | wash |

4 Compare your notes with a partner. Then check the audioscript on page 157.

Grammar

*You **should** eat garlic.*
*You **shouldn't** do any exercise.*
*You really **ought to** wash your hands regularly.*
*You **must** stay in bed.*

- use *should* to give advice and make suggestions
- we can also use *ought to*, but *should* is more common
- *must* is similar to *should* but is stronger

1 Use the pictures and your own ideas to give advice to someone with a cold.

I think you should …
I don't think you should …

2 Make new sentences with the words in brackets.

Can't sleep at night? Advice for insomniacs …

Drinking coffee before bed is a very bad idea. (*mustn't*)
You mustn't drink coffee before bed.

1 Try taking a warm bath before bed. (*should*)
2 Sleep on a good bed. (*should*)
3 It's a good idea to see a doctor if the problem continues. (*ought to*)
4 Smoking before you go to bed isn't a good idea. (*shouldn't*)
5 Try to get some exercise during the day. (*should*)

G **Grammar focus** – explanation & more practice of modal verbs on page 148

Writing

1 Read the three situations and choose **one**.

Situations
1 You have been invited to a party tonight, but you don't feel well. Write a note to your friend. Explain the situation and apologise.
2 You have a special exam tonight but you don't feel well. Write a note to your professor. Explain the situation and ask if you can do the exam another time.
3 You don't feel well today and you can't go to work. Write a note to your co-worker. Explain the situation and ask them to change shifts with you.

2 Work in pairs and swap your sick notes. Write a short reply and give the person some advice.

Useful language

- I'm sorry but I can't …
- I'm sorry but I won't be able to …
- I'm not feeling very well.
- I've got …
- I think I've got …
- Sorry to hear that you're not feeling well.
- Don't worry, we / you can …
- Get better soon.

Health Unit 9

UNIT 9 Health & Fitness

Part 2

Vocabulary
Medical treatment

Pronunciation
Word stress

Reading
Milestones of modern medicine

Grammar
Could / couldn't, had to / didn't have to

Vocabulary

1 Complete the questions with the correct form of the verbs.

Have you ever …
_____ an operation?
_____ in a hospital overnight?
_____ a bone?
    break   have   stay

Do you …
_____ a check-up with your doctor?
_____ the dentist? How often?
_____ any pills?
    go for   take   visit

Are you afraid of …
_____ injections?
_____ to hospital?
_____ ill?
    become   go   have

2 Choose one question from each box. Work in pairs and ask each other the questions.

Pronunciation

1 Put these words into groups with the same number of syllables. Then mark the stressed syllable.

alcohol	Arabic	hospital
medical	operation	originally
pharmacy	preservation	translation

2 🔊 2.66 Listen and follow *Arab influences on medicine* to check your answers. What do you notice about the last syllable of the words?

3 🔊 2.67 Listen and repeat the words from exercise 1.

Avicenna, Prince of Physicians (980–1037)

Arab influences on MEDICINE

The world of **medicine** was influenced greatly by the Arab world.

The first **pharmacies** and **medical** schools were developed in Damascus, Cairo and Cordoba.

The Arabs were also the first to use **alcohol** to treat illnesses. The word **alcohol** is **originally** an **Arabic** word.

In 977 one of the biggest **hospitals** in the world was founded in Baghdad. More than 20 doctors performed **operations** there.

The world of **Arab medicine** is also responsible for the **translation** and **preservation** of important **medical** works by Ancient Greeks, such as Hippocrates.

4 Work in pairs and practise reading the text. Each person reads one line each. Pay attention to the word stress.

Reading

1 The words in the box are from a text called *Milestones of modern medicine*. Check you understand what they mean.

| anaesthesia | antibiotics |
| disease | DNA | vaccines |

2 What do you think the text is about? Choose one answer.
a important discoveries in medicine
b the most serious diseases in medicine
c a competition between doctors

3 🔊 2.68 Read and listen to the text on page 105 and check your prediction.

4 Read the text again and complete the sentences with the names of the milestones.
1 _____ helped identify many diseases.
2 _____ reduced deaths from dirty water.
3 _____ reduced deaths by infection.
4 _____ helped doctors with operations.
5 _____ was invented to treat rabies.
6 _____ were discovered by accident.

5 The *British Medical Journal* asked doctors to vote for the most important milestone. Which do you think won?

104 Unit 9 **Health**

Grammar

Doctors could treat infections properly.
Doctors didn't have to wash their hands.
Patients had to be awake during operations.

- use *could* and *couldn't* to talk about things that were or were not possible in the past
- use *had to* and *didn't have to* to talk about obligation or no obligation in the past
- the past form of *must* is *had to*

1 Complete the texts with *had to*, *didn't have to* or *could*.

The X-ray
Before 1900 if doctors wanted to know what was inside a person's body they _____ open it. In 1895 a German professor called Wilhelm Röntgen was experimenting with vacuum tubes. He discovered that he _____ see the bones inside his hand. He won the Nobel Prize for Physics in 1901.

Risks of smoking
In the past tobacco companies _____ put a warning on cigarettes. Doctors did not know that smoking _____ cause cancer. People began to realise that smoking kills after two important medical studies in the 1950s.

2 Work in pairs. Look at the words in the box and say what people *could*, *couldn't* or *had to* do before these inventions.

ambulance	anaesthesia
eye glasses	microscope
thermometer	wheelchair

G **Grammar focus** – explanation & more practice of *could* & *had to* on page 148

Milestones of MODERN MEDICINE

In 2007 the *British Medical Journal* asked doctors and nurses from around the world what the most important discoveries in modern medicine were. Here are some of the finalists.

Anaesthesia Before anaesthesia patients had to be awake during operations. At the end of the 1800s, drugs were developed that stopped the feeling of pain. Operations became much easier for doctors and much less painful for patients.

Antibiotics In 1928 Alexander Fleming accidentally discovered that penicillin kills bacteria. This had an enormous impact on medicine. Doctors could treat infections properly. Antibiotics were first produced on a massive scale during World War 2.

DNA The structure of DNA was discovered in the 1950s by two scientists, James Watson and Francis Crick. Crick was a British physicist and Watson, who was American, studied ornithology (birds). The discovery of DNA has helped to identify many diseases and has changed modern medicine.

Germ theory Before 1847 doctors didn't have to wash their hands before an operation. Ignaz Semmelweis, a doctor from Vienna, realised that women in labour could be dying from infections passed on by the hands of their doctors. This became the germ theory of disease. At the end of the 19th century, infection caused 30% of deaths. By the end of the 20th century it caused less than 4%.

Sanitation As cities grew in the 1800s, so did pollution. Dirty water caused many diseases. This turned attention to water systems and sanitation was born. Clean water helped death rates fall by the beginning of the last century.

Vaccines Louis Pasteur created the first vaccine for rabies in 1885. Vaccines have saved millions of lives over the last century and will continue to do so for years to come.

Glossary
bacteria (*noun*) – very small living things. Some types of bacteria cause diseases
identify (*verb*) – to recognise something and to understand what it is
infection (*noun*) – a disease that is caused by bacteria or by a virus
labour (*noun*) – the process by which a baby is pushed from its mother's body when it is being born
rabies (*noun*) – a serious disease passed from animals to humans
sanitation (*noun*) – conditions and processes relating to the water supply and human waste

Health Unit 9

UNIT 9 Health & Fitness

Part 3

Vocabulary
Sport

Reading
Olympic ...

Grammar
Past perfect

Speaking
Sports questionnaire

Vocabulary

1 Look at pictures a–i. What sports do they go with?

2 Look at the examples and complete the table with the names of sports from exercise 1.

play	go	do
squash	jogging	aerobics
		yoga

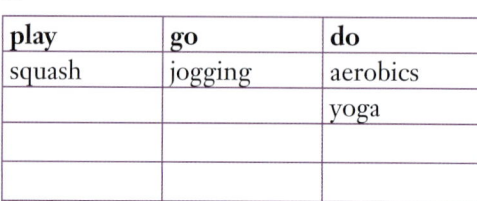

3 Read the clues. What sport is it?

> This is a team sport. You play this sport outside. There are eleven players in the team. You have to pass the ball to other players with your foot. You have to kick the ball into the goal to get a point. You mustn't touch the ball with your hands.

4 Work in pairs. Choose a sport from this page and write some clues for it. Use the words in the box to help you.

| dive | goal | hit | hole | individual |
| kick | ride | run | throw | wear |

a — judogi with black belt
b — 1966 Brazil World Cup kit
c — Olympic swimsuit
d — ball
e — gloves
f — clubs
g — helmet
h — net
i — pair of skis

Reading

1 Do you watch the Olympic Games? Do you know when the next Olympic Games are? Do you know where they are? Tell a partner.

2 Quickly read the texts about the Olympics on page 107. What is the best way to complete the title?

a winners
b dreams
c losers
d records

3 Read the texts again. What do you think happened next? Write a sentence in each gap. Then compare your ideas with a partner.

4 Turn to page 130 to check your answers.

5 Do you know any interesting sport stories?

Extend your vocabulary – *win* and *beat*

We *win* a game, competition, election or prize.
She won the gold medal.
We *beat* someone in a game, competition or election.
He beat the other runners in the event.

Complete the sentences with the correct word.

1 She always *beats* / *wins* me at tennis.
2 He *beat* / *won* his first race when he was twelve years old.
3 Russia *beat* / *won* the USA for the gold medal.
4 I don't think I can *beat* / *win* him. He's too good.
5 We were *beaten* / *won*. The other team was better.

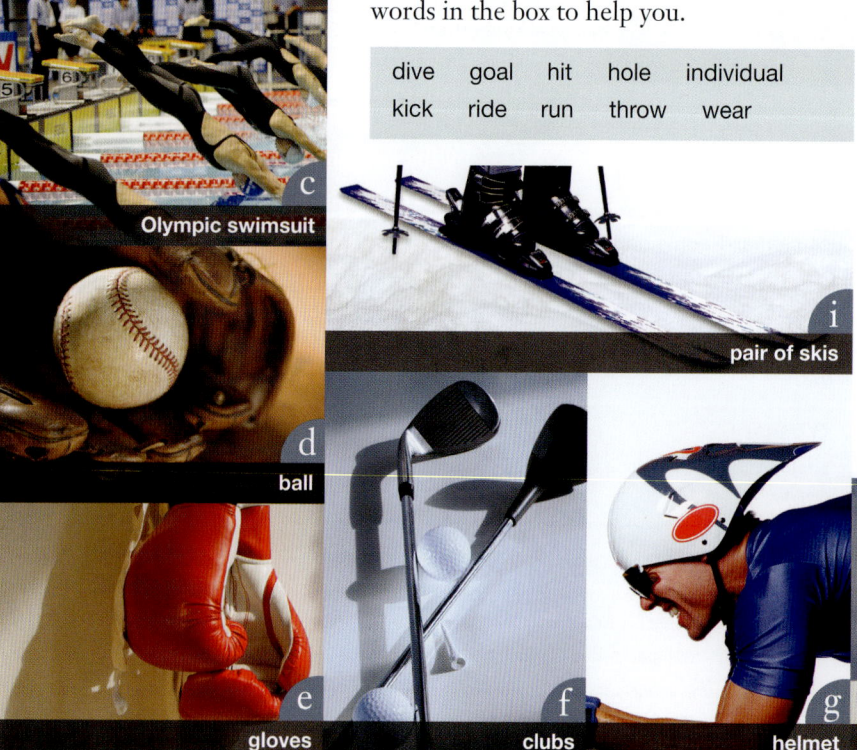

Unit 9 Fitness

Grammar

*Ramzan **continued** but the other swimmers **had stopped**.*
*He **didn't win** the race because the officials **had helped** him.*

- use the past perfect to talk about an event in the past that happened before another event or before a specific time in the past

1 Complete the texts with the correct words.

| couldn't go | had lost | told |

1992 Olympics, Barcelona, Spain
A few minutes before his fight, Iranian boxer Ali Kazemi suddenly _____ the judges that he _____ in the ring. He _____ his gloves!

| had fallen | had thrown | lost |

1956 Olympics, Melbourne, Australia
Soviet rower Vyacheslav Ivanov only had his gold medal for a few minutes before he _____ it. He was so happy he _____ the medal into the air and it _____ into the lake.

2 Write reasons why these things might have happened. Then share your ideas with a partner.

The athlete stopped running and started crying.
Maybe she had lost the race. Maybe she had hurt her leg. Maybe she had won.

1 The football match was cancelled at the last minute.
2 The number one tennis player lost the first match of the tournament.
3 An important basketball player could not play in a game.

G **Grammar focus** – explanation & more practice of the past perfect on page 148

Olympic

They are the world's fittest people. But even Olympic athletes have had their share of difficult, heart-breaking or just plain embarrassing moments …

Short cut – 1904 Olympics, St Louis, USA American Fred Lorz crossed the finish line of the Olympic marathon with a time of 3 hours and 13 minutes. He had beaten the second runner by 15 minutes. Lorz looked happy and fresh, and smiled for the photographers. Just before they gave him the gold medal, the race officials arrived to make a complaint. They took away the medal, and Lorz was banned from races for a year.

A helping hand – 1908 Olympics, London, England The Italian Dorando Pietri was one of the unluckiest marathon runners. When he arrived in the stadium, he was very tired. The people were cheering, but Pietri couldn't continue. He fell down and got up again four times. Finally, around seven metres from the finish line, he fell down again and didn't move. Worried officials ran over and picked him up. He crossed the finish line and won the gold medal. But a few hours later the Olympic committee had to take it away from him again. They said he couldn't be the winner because _____

The extra distance – 1952 Olympics, Helsinki, Finland Pakistani swimmer Mohammed Ramzan made history in the 1,500-metre swimming event. When all the other swimmers had finished, Ramzan continued going. He swam an extra 100 metres. _____

A new Olympic record – 2000 Olympics, Sydney, Australia Eric Moussambani of Equatorial Guinea became one of the most loved athletes of the 2000 games. His race was the 100-metre freestyle swim. He jumped into the pool and started swimming. After the first 50 metres he was very tired. He went more and more slowly and almost stopped in the middle of the pool. The officials worried that he was drowning. But Moussambani continued and finally finished the race with a time of 1 minute and 52 seconds, the slowest in the history of the Olympics. Still, Moussambani was happy. _____

Speaking

1 Look at the sports questionnaire and write one more question.

2 Ask other students the questions. If someone answers *yes*, write their name and ask the follow-up question.

A: *Do you play a sport?*
B: *Yes, I do.*
A: *Which sport?*
B: *Volleyball.*

Glossary

ban (verb) – to say officially that someone is not allowed to do something
drown (verb) – to sink under water and die
embarrassing (adjective) – making you feel nervous, ashamed or stupid
official (noun) – someone with an important position in an organisation

Find someone who …

plays a sport.	Which sport?
watches a sport on television.	Which sport?
is a fan of a team.	What team?
has been to a football match.	When?
hates sports.	Why?
used to play a team sport.	When? What sport?
doesn't do any sport.	Why not?

Fitness **Unit 9**

UNIT 9 Health & Fitness

Part 4

Speaking
A visit to the doctor

Reading & Listening
At the doctor's

Grammar
Reported statements

Vocabulary
Say, tell and ask

Speaking
Fitness questionnaire

Speaking

1 Look at the pictures. What do you think is happening?

2 Work in pairs. Choose one of the pictures and prepare a short dialogue to go with it.

3 Present your dialogue to another pair.

Reading and Listening

1 🔊 2.69 Read and listen to the dialogue between a doctor and his patient. What is the good news and the bad news?

2 Cover the dialogue and try to remember. What did the doctor say …

1 about red meat?   4 about exercise?
2 about salt?   5 about work?
3 about coffee?

3 🔊 2.70 Listen to Mr Cartwright talking to his wife about his doctor's appointment. What information is the same and what is different?

D = Doctor   **P** = Patient

D: Ah yes. Mr Cartwright. Please sit down. How are you feeling?
P: I'm fine, thanks.
D: I have the results of your tests.
P: Oh good!
D: Hm.
P: What's the matter?
D: Well, there's good news and bad news. Good news and bad news.
P: Give me the bad news first.
D: The bad news is, well, you aren't very fit. And you need to change your eating habits.
P: Do you mean a diet?

D: I'm afraid so, Mr Cartwright. I'm afraid so.
P: I see.
D: You can't eat any more red meat. It's really not good for your heart.
P: Oh.
D: You also have to stop putting salt on your food.
P: Er. No meat, no salt.
D: That's right. The other thing is coffee. Do you drink coffee?
P: Um, yes. Four or five cups a day actually.
D: Yes, well, only one cup of coffee a day from now on. One cup of coffee. And no sugar in the coffee, either.

P: Is that all?
D: No. You also need to do exercise. I have a daily exercise plan for you here.
P: Every day?
D: That's right, Mr Cartwright. Daily means every day.
P: What's the good news, doctor?
D: The good news is that you are healthy enough to go back to work. You can start again tomorrow!
P: Oh.

Grammar

'You are healthy.' She **said** I **was** healthy.
'You can eat some red meat.' She **said** I **could** eat some red meat.

- use reported speech to say what another person said
- in reported speech, the verb often goes one tense *back*
  present simple → past simple
  present continuous → past continuous
  present perfect → past perfect
  past simple → past perfect
- other words such as pronouns can also change in reported speech

1 Change the sentences to direct speech. Then check your answers in the conversation on page 108.

The doctor told me she had the test results.
'I have the test results.'
1 I said I was fine.
2 She said that I wasn't very fit.
3 She told me that I couldn't eat any more red meat.
4 She told me that I also needed to do some exercise.

2 Change these sentences to reported speech. Then decide who said each one: the doctor or the patient.

'I've felt very ill for the last five days.'
The patient said he'd felt very ill for the last five days.
1 'You don't have a fever.'
2 'I've ordered some more tests.'
3 'I'm not feeling very well at the moment.'
4 'Going to work isn't a good idea.'
5 'I can give you a sick note.'
6 'I have a bad headache.'

G **Grammar focus** – explanation & more practice of reported statements on page 148

Vocabulary

1 Complete the story with *say*, *tell* or *ask*.

I went to the doctor last week.
He _____ me 'How do you feel?'
I _____ him I didn't feel very well.
He gave me some pills.
First, he _____ me I should take one green pill with a glass of water when I got up.
Then he _____ 'Take one red pill with a glass of water after lunch.'
Finally, he _____ that I should take a blue pill with a glass of water before bed.
I _____ the doctor 'What's the matter with me?'
He _____ me that I wasn't drinking enough water.

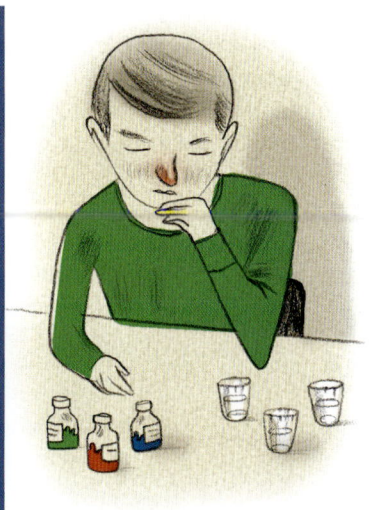

2 🔊 **2.71** Listen and check your answers.

3 Complete the rules with *say*, *tell* or *ask*.
a _____ always takes an object such as *me, him, her, the people*.
b _____ never takes an object.
c _____ can take an object, but doesn't have to.

Speaking

1 Choose **four** of these questions. Then work in pairs and discuss the questions.
- Do you do any exercise?
- Do you prefer to exercise alone or with friends?
- Did you do a sport when you were younger? Which one?
- What are the best ways to keep fit?
- Do you have a family doctor? What's their name? How long have you been a patient?
- What food do you think is the healthiest?
- Do children in your country get enough exercise?

2 Work with a new partner. Report two things you learnt from your first partner. Use *said* or *told* plus reported speech.

Function globally describing illness

Warm up

Read the label. Find words or phrases with these meanings.
1 takes away pain for a short period of time (4 words)
2 a woman who is going to have a baby (1 word)
3 ask (1 word)
4 don't let children touch this (6 words)
5 might make you feel tired or sleepy (3 words)

How to read a drug label

Active ingredient
Acetaminophen 500g

Active ingredient tells you what chemicals are in the medicine.

Uses
Temporarily relieves minor pains due to
- headache
- backache
- the common cold
- toothache

Uses or Indications tell you what to use the medicine for.

Warnings
Do not use with alcohol. If you are pregnant, consult a doctor before use. Keep out of reach of children. May cause drowsiness.

This section tells you things you shouldn't do or take with this medicine.

Directions
Adults and children 12 years and older. Take two tablets every four to six hours as needed. Do not take more than 8 tablets in 24 hours.

This section tells you the recommended dosage – how much you should take and how often.

Listening

🔊 **2.72** Listen to a conversation in a pharmacy. What is the man's problem? What does he buy?

cough syrup    tablets 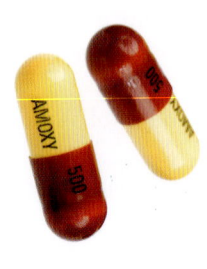   antibiotics

Language focus: talking about illness

Listen to the conversation again and complete the phrases with one or more words.

1 I _____ for a sore throat.
2 We _____ this syrup or these tablets.
3 _____ better?
4 How many _____?
5 How often _____?
6 _____ before mealtimes.
7 _____ allergic to any _____?
8 I'm afraid _____ a prescription for that.
9 You _____ a doctor if _____.

Speaking

Work in pairs and choose **one** of the tasks below.

A Look at the audioscript on page 157 and practise the conversation. Then create a similar conversation with different information.

B Roleplay a visit to the pharmacy. Use the new expressions you have learnt.

> A: you are visiting another country. You don't feel well. Think of your symptoms.
> B: you work in a pharmacy. Listen to A and suggest something for the problem.

Global English

Sports English
by David Crystal

Sports commentary is very familiar these days but it only arrived with the start of radio and television broadcasting. The term *sports announcer* was first used in 1923, soon followed by *sporting commentator* in the UK and *sportscaster* in the US. The modern British term, *sports commentator*, dates from the 1930s.

5 Sports commentating sounds easy, but it's difficult to do well, especially on radio, where a long silence can mean disaster. Detailed knowledge of the sport, keen observational skills, the ability to **think on your feet**, and above-average linguistic skills are essential. To make the job easier, commentators can use 'tricks of the trade' such
10 as formulaic expressions. In horse racing there are certain things commentators always say at particular moments such as *They're off!*, *in the lead*, and *into the straight they come*. This means there is less for them to remember and it helps with fluency.

Each sport has its own style, reflecting the atmosphere and
15 momentum, from the wild excitement of football (*It's a GO-O-O-AL*) to the quiet tones of snooker. There's distinctive grammar and vocabulary too. Commentaries are the perfect place to find the English present tense, both simple and continuous (*he's looking for a chance ... he scores ...*), and incomplete sentences (*Beckham to Kaka ... back to Beckham ...*).

20 But if you're looking for new vocabulary, you'll find more in the keep-fit disciplines, such as yoga (with its hundreds of words taken from Sanskrit), Pilates (with its unusual pronunciation taken from the name of its founder, Joseph Pilates, 'puh-lah-teez'), and the combination of yoga and Pilates *yogalates*. And that's just **the tip of the iceberg** of new linguistic blends. If
25 you're into *exertainment* (exercise + entertainment) you'll know about the many kinds of *exergaming* (exercise + gaming). The neologisms keep your tongue linguistically fit too.

Glossary

above-average (*adjective*) – good, better than normal
discipline (*noun*) – a subject or sport
formulaic expression (*noun*) – an expression that has been used lots of times before
keen (*adjective*) – very strong
linguistic blend (*noun*) – a mixture of two or more words
neologism (*noun*) – a new word or expression, or an existing word with a new meaning
sports commentator (*noun*) – a person whose job is to give a description of a sporting event on television or radio as it happens.

Warm up

Read the definition of *sports commentator*. Are there any well-known sports commentators in your country? What are they famous for?

Reading

1 Read the text *Sports English*. Tick (✔) the topics that are mentioned. There are two topics you do not need.

a different words for sport
b sports commentary
c style of speaking
d winners and losers
e English grammar
f new vocabulary

2 Read the text again and find examples of ...

a something you need to be a good sports commentator.
b a 'formulaic expression' that helps commentators sound more fluent.
c an example of an incomplete sentence used in sports.
d a 'keep-fit' sport.
e a neologism.

Language focus

1 Look at the expressions in **bold** in the text. Answer the questions below.

1 If you *think on your feet*, you ...
   a are a very quick runner.
   b have good ideas and make decisions quickly.
   c get nervous in a difficult situation.
2 If we say something is *the tip of the iceberg*, it means ...
   a there is a lot more of it that you can't see.
   b there is only a little bit of it.
   c it is a very dangerous thing.

2 Put each of the expressions into an example of your own. Tell a partner.

Speaking

Work in pairs and ask each other the questions.

- Do you enjoy listening to commentators?
- What sports do you like to watch?
- Do you do any *exergaming*?

Writing an online post

Reading

1 Read the question from an online forum. Then read Darina's response and tick (✔) the suggestions she makes.

take exercise at home	go for a walk
go on a diet	have an exercise plan
join a gym	spend a long time exercising
take up a new hobby/sport	walk or cycle to work

Dear Darina
Health & Fitness Expert

I need to get fit but I work full time and don't have a lot of time to take exercise. Can anyone out there help please?
Carla

Good question Carla. I had the same problem but I found some solutions. If you don't have much time, just try to be more active in your daily life. You could walk or cycle to work instead of taking the bus or driving. If you take a bus, why not get off one stop early and walk a bit longer? And try to go for a walk in your lunch break instead of sitting inside in front of a computer. It will make you feel a lot better!

If you have free time in the evening, consider joining an evening class. You could take up yoga, martial arts or dancing. That way you will meet people and have fun too! Alternatively, you could buy exercise equipment, a rowing machine or an exercise bike, and use it while you watch TV.

Most importantly, you should have a clear plan and stick to it. And you should exercise for a short time, but regularly. Hope this helps. Good luck and don't give up!

2 Do you do any of the things that Darina suggests? Which do you think is the best suggestion?

Writing skills: giving examples

We use *for example*, *for instance* or *like* to give examples.

1 Find three places in Darina's answer where she could use one of these phrases. Where would you put a comma?

2 Complete the sentences with the correct phrase.
1 Try not to use your car so much. You could walk or cycle to the supermarket, _____.
2 Why not take up a sport _____ tennis or swimming?
3 Consider getting up an hour early to take exercise. _____, you could go jogging, or go for a swim.

Language focus: giving advice

1 Look at Darina's response again and underline the phrases she uses to give advice.

2 Correct the sentences below.
1 Why you don't see a doctor?
2 Consider to go for a long walk.
3 You could starting a sport.
4 Just try be positive.
5 You should to watch less TV.

Preparing to write

1 Work in pairs and choose one of the problems below. Think of some solutions.

2 Work with another pair who chose the same problem. Did they think of the same solutions as you?
- I feel tired all the time.
- I'm having problems getting to sleep at night.
- My seven-year-old son loves fast food and unhealthy snacks. How can I get him to have a more healthy diet?

Writing

Write an online response like Darina's to give advice. Use your notes and the useful phrases below to help you.

Suggesting alternatives

- Instead of …, you could …
- Don't …; … instead!
- Alternatively, you could …
- Most importantly, you should …

Unit 9 Writing

Global review

Grammar

1 Put *had to*, *didn't have to*, *could* or *couldn't* in the gaps.

1 I broke my leg so I _____ stay in hospital for six weeks, and I _____ walk for two months.
2 I _____ have an X-ray because I hadn't broken any bones.

2 Complete the sentences with the past simple or past perfect form of the verbs in brackets.

1 Before the world _____ (develop) modern medicine, the Arabs _____ (found) many hospitals.
2 I _____ (feel) sick because I _____ (eat) too much chocolate.

3 Complete the sentences to report the conversation.

1 A: You're working too hard and you don't take enough exercise.
   The doctor told me I _____.
2 B: I'll give up my job and take up jogging.
   I said I _____.

Vocabulary

Complete the sentences with the correct word.

| beat | feel | have | have | hurts |
| matter | see | sore | take | won |

1 You look ill – what's the _____?
2 I _____ sick.
3 I've got a _____ throat.
4 You should _____ a doctor.
5 I have to _____ an operation.
6 I _____ a fever.
7 My back _____.
8 You should _____ two aspirin.
9 He _____ me at table tennis.
10 Manchester United _____ the football match.

Speaking and Writing

1 Work in pairs. Tell each other about a race, match or sporting event you have seen. Then work in a new pair and report what your partner told you.

2 Work in groups of four. Write down a real or invented problem. Then swap your papers and write advice using *should*, *shouldn't*, *must* or *mustn't*. Who gave you the best advice?

Study skills

Using your dictionary: exploring collocations

> Collocations are words which are often used together.
>
> catch a cold   a sore throat
> (not ~~take~~ a cold)   (not a ~~hurt~~ throat)

1 Look at these entries in the *Macmillan Essential Dictionary*. Notice how the dictionary gives information about collocations.

> **health** (*noun*)
> 1 the condition of your body, especially whether or not you are ill: *His health improved once he stopped working. She's had serious **health problems**. Lola is 85 and still **in very good health**. My father has been **in poor health** for some time.*

> *Adverbs often used with ill*
> **critically, dangerously, desperately, gravely, seriously, severely** + ill: used for saying that someone is very ill

2 Work in pairs. Try to guess which verb is **not** used with each noun below. Then check in a dictionary.

1 a get   b do   c make   d take   … exercise
2 a keep   b build   c get   d be   … fit
3 a call   b see   c order   d send for   … a doctor
4 a cause   b feel   c make   d relieve   … pain

3 Complete the sentences with the correct option. Then check your answers in a dictionary.

1 I have a *strong / heavy* cold today.
2 He was *strongly / violently* sick last night.
3 I had a *heavy / splitting* headache yesterday.
4 She is a *heavy / strong* smoker.

4 Use your dictionary to answer the questions.

1 You can *catch a cold*. What else can you *catch*? _____
2 You can have a *healthy diet*. What other adjectives go with *diet*? _____
3 You can have a *sore throat*. What else can be *sore*? _____
4 You can *recover from an illness*. What else can you *recover from*? _____

> Remember to record collocations, not just words, in your vocabulary notebook.

UNIT 10 New & Old

Part 1

Reading & Listening
Brave New Words

Vocabulary
New words in context

Grammar
Defining relative clauses

Writing
Definitions game

Reading and Listening

1 Look at the book cover and read the introduction to *Brave New Words* on page 115. What do you think the book is about?

2 2.73 Listen to an interview with the author of the book. Number the topics in the order you hear them.

abbreviations ___
borrowing words ___
combining parts of words ___
combining words ___
giving new meanings to words ___

3 Listen again and match the example words to the categories in exercise 2.

brunch   DVD   mouse
text messages   tsunami
virus   windows

4 Can you think of any new words in your language? What are they? What do they mean?

Vocabulary

1 Work in pairs. Look at the pictures below and read the captions. Try to guess the meanings of the words in bold.

Useful language

- Maybe it means …   • It could be a kind of …

2 Match the words in exercise 1 to the definitions below. There are two definitions you don't need.

a kind of car that produces carbon ___
the amount of greenhouse gases that an activity produces ___
a Japanese love story which is written for women ___
to search for something on the internet using the search engine Google ___
a number game from Japan which is now popular in English newspapers ___

3 Work in pairs and ask each other the questions.

- Do you ever google information on the web?
- Have you ever googled your own name?
- Have you ever done a sudoku puzzle?
- What are some ways of reducing your carbon footprint?

a. John tried to **google** information about Kenya for his next holiday.

b. His **carbon footprint** is bigger than yours.

c. Susan missed her stop because she was trying to finish her **sudoku**.

Brave New Words

The English language is a dynamic phenomenon. Like your mobile phone or the grass in the garden, it is continually changing, constantly acquiring new characteristics. Many of these changes occur because of the way we live. As the world changes we need to find different ways of describing it, to fill the gaps in our vocabulary for new ideas.

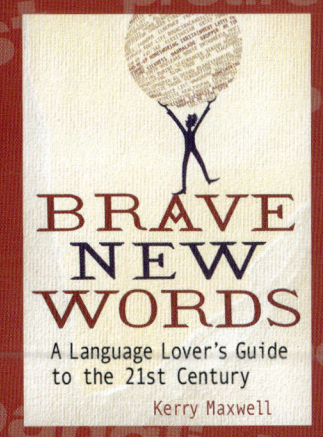

Some of these words will stay in our vocabulary, others won't. Only time will tell. But the ways we make new words will continue, and will create many more new expressions in years to come.

Kerry Maxwell

Kerry Maxwell is a lexicographer – a person who writes dictionaries. She has worked on many dictionary projects, including the *Macmillan English Dictionary*. She lives in England.

Grammar

Kerry Maxwell is someone **who** has written books about new words in English.
Tsunami is a Japanese word **which** has become used very frequently in English.
Brunch is a meal **that** people can have at 11 o'clock in the morning.

- use relative clauses to give information about something or somebody
- if we are talking about a person, we use *who* or *that*
- if we are talking about an object, we use *which* or *that*

1 Complete the definitions with *who* or *which*.

1 An *emoticon* is …
   a a symbol _____ is used in email messages to show emotion.
   b a strong emotion _____ people have about computers.
   c a person _____ doesn't show their emotions.

2 An *internaut* is …
   a a person _____ works for a short time in an office.
   b a game _____ people play on the internet.
   c a person _____ spends a lot of time on the internet.

3 *Hinglish* is …
   a a person _____ comes from the country Hingland.
   b a language _____ is a mixture of English and Hindi.
   c clothing from India _____ you wear on your head.

2 Work in pairs. What is the correct definition of each word?

G **Grammar focus** – explanation & more practice of defining clauses on page 150

Writing

Work in pairs and choose one of the boxes. You are going to write definitions for some new words.

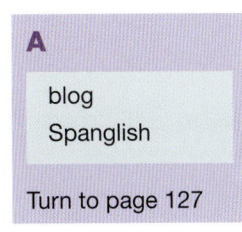

A	B
blog Spanglish	metrosexual spam
Turn to page 127	Turn to page 129

New Unit 10 115

UNIT 10 New & Old

Part 2

Vocabulary
Places

Reading
New places in a new world

Grammar
Definite article (the)

Speaking
Famous quotes

Vocabulary

1 Put the words in order from small to large. Use your dictionary to help you.

| capital | city | continent | country |
| planet | state / province | town | village |

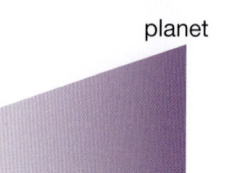

planet

2 Circle the word that does not belong in each group of words.

1 Africa — Asia — Armenia
2 Dallas — Italy — Frankfurt
3 Mars — Jupiter — Singapore
4 California — Canada — Washington
5 Tokyo — Liverpool — Paris

3 Choose a word from exercise 1 and write down some examples. Then include a word that does not belong. Work in pairs and tell each other your words. Say the odd one out.

Reading

1 Work in pairs. How many places in North America can you write down in one minute? Compare your list with another pair.

2 Read *New places in a new world* on page 117 and write the names in the correct places.

| New Jersey | New Mexico | New Orleans |
| Newfoundland | New World | New York |

3 Read the text again and complete the sentences with the same place names.

1 _____ is not part of the US.
2 _____ is very big and dry.
3 _____ was nearly destroyed.
4 _____ has many people who travel somewhere else for work or school.
5 _____ was a Dutch colony.
6 _____ was visited by Vikings.

4 Find words in the text with these meanings.

1 a place where something is born
2 to start a city or organisation
3 very special or unusual
4 to travel regularly to and from work

5 Do you know any other place names that begin with the word *New*? What are they?

Extend your vocabulary – words that mean *new*

New is a very general word. We sometimes use words with more specific meanings that sound more natural in a particular context.

equipment, computers	advanced, cutting-edge, modern
ideas	innovative, fresh
films, books	latest, recent
something just bought and never used	brand new

Replace the word *new* in the dialogues with a more suitable word or phrase.

1 A: Is that your car?
   B: Yes, it's *new*. I bought it yesterday.
2 A: Did you speak to Jeffrey about the project?
   B: Yes, I did. It was very helpful. He has a lot of *new* ideas.
3 A: What did you see?
   B: The *new* Tarantino film. It was OK.

116 Unit 10 **New**

New places in a new world

In the 15th century Pietro Martyr d'Anghiera, an Italian historian, was the first person to give the continent of America the name De Orbo Novo, which means the _____. The prefix *New* for cities and regions of North America has since become very popular. Here we collect a few *new* places to live.

Nicknamed the Big Apple, _____ is located in the American state of the same name. It's probably the most famous city in North America. Founded on Manhattan Island in the 17th century by the Dutch, it was originally called New Amsterdam.

_____ is a province in Canada. The province is in the east of the country, and the newest one to join Canada – it joined in 1949. Because of its position it was one of the first parts of North America that European voyagers discovered. The Vikings arrived here in AD 1000.

One of the largest states in the United States of America, _____ is in the south-west of the country. It is a very dry state, and is covered in mountains and desert. The state was one of the original Wild West states, and the population is unique for its Spanish, American and Native American mix.

Capital of the state of Louisiana in the south, _____ is famous for its multicultural history and nightlife. It is the birthplace of jazz. The city went through a dark period in its history in 2005 when it was almost destroyed by Hurricane Katrina.

Located in the north-east, _____ is one of the original 13 states of the USA. Because it's so close to New York, people sometimes call it the bedroom state as hundreds of thousands of its people commute to and from the city for work or school every day.

Grammar

1 Look at the highlighted examples of *the* in the text and match them to the rules a–d below.

We use *the* when …
a   there is only one of this person or thing.
b   this person or thing has been referred to before, in the text.
c   it is part of a name.
d   it is in a superlative phrase.

2 Choose the correct words to complete the texts.

New England is *a / the* region of *the / -* United States. It consists of *the / -* six states: Maine, New Hampshire, Vermont, Massachusetts, Rhode Island and Connecticut. New England was one of *a / the* first places *an / -* English people lived in America in 1620.

New Zealand is *a / the* country in the Pacific Ocean. It consists of two islands, *a / the* North Island and *a / the* South Island.

New Guinea is *an / the* island in the Pacific Ocean. It is *the / -* second largest island in *the / -* world. *An / The* island is divided into two parts – *the / an* Indonesian provinces of Papua and West Papua and *the / -* country of Papua New Guinea.

G Grammar focus – explanation & more practice of *the* on page 150

Speaking

1 Work in pairs. Read the incomplete quotes about America and try to finish them with your own ideas. Then work with another pair and share your ideas.

2 Which are the best quotes? Are they positive, negative or neutral about America?

3 Read the original quotes and find out who said them on page 130.

I think the most un-American thing you can say is …

All great change in America begins at the …

America is a …

England and America are two countries separated by a …

There is not a black America and a white America and Latino America and Asian America – there's …

New Unit 10   117

UNIT 10 New & Old

Part 3

Vocabulary & Speaking
Transport

Pronunciation
Consonant clusters

Reading
Old but loved: the Trabant

Grammar
Verb form review

Speaking
Driving questionnaire

Vocabulary and Speaking

1 What different forms of transport can you see in the pictures?

2 Which of these forms of transport …
1 have **wheels**?
2 go on **tracks**?
3 have **wings**?
4 have an **engine**?

3 Tick (✔) the correct collocations to complete the chart.

	drive	ride	get on / get off	get in / get out of
a car				
a bus				
a motorbike				
a bicycle				
the underground				
a plane				

4 Work in pairs and ask each other the questions.
- Which of the forms of transport have you used?
- Which do you prefer?
- Are there any forms of transport that you never use?

Pronunciation

1 🔊 **2.74** Listen and repeat the consonant clusters and words.

/pl/, plane
/tr/, tracks
/st/, stop
/str/, street

2 🔊 **2.75** Listen and repeat the sentences.
1 The driver tried to drive the train off the tracks.
2 There are still school students at the bus stop.
3 The station is straight down this street.
4 Please don't play with the plastic planes.

Reading

1 You are going to read an article about an old car called the *Trabant*. Which of these words do you expect to see?

cheap	communist	fans	fly
Germany	jokes	nostalgic	
pollution	smoke	speed	

2 🔊 **2.76** Read and listen to *Old but loved: the Trabant* on page 119 and check your answers.

3 Read the text again and find …
1 three reasons why the Trabant isn't a very good car.
2 three reasons that show the Trabant is still popular.

4 Work in pairs and discuss the questions.
- Have you ever seen a Trabant?
- Are there any objects that make you nostalgic for the past? Which ones?

Unit 10 Old

Old but loved: the Trabant

They're old, they're slow and they're noisy and smelly. So why are Trabants still popular?

They are still driving on Germany's roads, and have been in many popular films and music videos. The Trabant was East Germany's answer to the Volkswagen during communist times, and more than three million models were made before the fall of the Berlin Wall in 1989.

The name *Trabant* means *fellow traveller*. The first cars appeared in 1957. They were made from duroplast, a material made from recycled cotton from Russia. The Trabant needed 20 seconds to go from 0 to 100km per hour, and had a maximum speed of 112km per hour. The engine of the Trabant was special in two ways – it made a lot of noise and smoke and it produced a lot of pollution. Experts estimate that the Trabant produced five times more carbon monoxide than modern European cars.

Trabants – also called *Trabis* – have now become collectors' items, and have many fan clubs across Eastern and Western Europe. People say that the Trabi makes them nostalgic for old times. Even the smell of Trabi exhaust smoke is popular, and has been sold on the internet. Fan clubs celebrated the 50th anniversary of the Trabant in 2007, and many say there are going to be celebrations for the 75th anniversary in 2032. There are many jokes about the Trabant, but if this kind of popularity continues the Trabi will have the last laugh.

Q: How do you double the value of a Trabant?
A: Put petrol in it.

Q: Why is a Trabant the longest car?
A: There's 3 metres of car, followed by 15 metres of smoke.

Q: Why is the Trabant's rear window heated?
A: To keep your hands warm while you push it.

Glossary

exhaust (noun) – gases or steam that are produced by an engine as it works

model (noun) – a type of vehicle that a company makes

nostalgic (adjective) – remembering happy times in the past

Grammar

1 Look through the text and try to find examples of the verb forms below.

- regular and irregular past tense verbs
- a continuous tense
- the present perfect
- *going to* future
- a first conditional
- past simple passive

2 Complete the text below with the correct form of the verbs.

The Model T

The American Ford automobile company _____ (*exist*) since 1903, and is one of the biggest car manufacturers in the world.

One of its first cars _____ (*be*) the Model T. It _____ (*build*) by the Ford Motor Company from 1908 to 1927. The president of the company, Henry Ford, _____ (*want*) a car that was practical and not expensive for the American worker. The Model T _____ (*cost*) around $300 and _____ (*go*) up to 70km an hour. It was one of the first cars to be produced on an assembly line. By 1930 Ford _____ (*produce*) more than 10 million Model T cars, making it the most popular car in the world.

As newer cars came out in the 20s and 30s, people _____ (*start*) making jokes about the Model T. But today there _____ (*be*) still fan clubs of the Model T, and people still _____ (*drive*) them at old car shows.

3 Complete the questions with the correct form of the verbs.

1 When _____ (*do*) you get your driving licence?
2 _____ (*do*) you have a car? What kind?
3 What _____ (*be*) your first car?
4 What is the fastest you _____ (*ever travel*) in a car?
5 What is the furthest you _____ (*ever travel*) in a car?
6 _____ (*have*) you ever _____ (*have*) an accident?
7 If you _____ (*can have*) any kind of car, what _____ (*you choose*)?
8 _____ (*be*) the traffic bad where you live?
9 _____ (*be*) it difficult to find parking where you live?
10 Who _____ (*be*) the best driver in your family?

G Grammar focus – explanation & more practice of verb forms on page 150

Speaking

Choose **six** of the questions from exercise 3 above. Work in pairs and ask each other the questions.

Old Unit 10

UNIT 10 New & Old

Part 4

Listening
Two classic board games

Grammar
Both, neither

Vocabulary
Games

Pronunciation
Sentence stress & intonation

Speaking
A board game

Listening

1 Look at the pictures of two classic board games. Do you know these games? Have you ever played them? Tell a partner.

2 2.77 Listen to a talk about the invention of these games. How many things do they have in common?

3 Listen again. What do these words and numbers mean?

Great Depression	architect
by hand	two or more	750 million+
200 million	80+	25+

Extend your vocabulary – words that mean *make*

Make is a very general word. We sometimes use words with more specific meanings that sound more natural in a particular context.

things made in factories	build, manufacture, produce
buildings	build
problems, changes, effects	cause, produce, generate
new things	design, develop, invent, create

Replace the word *make* in the sentences with a more suitable word. More than one answer may be possible.

1 The traffic in the afternoon *makes* lots of problems.
2 They are *making* a new bank in the centre of town.
3 These cars are *made* in a Korean factory.
4 Alfred Butts *made* the game of Scrabble.
5 We've *made* a new computer program.

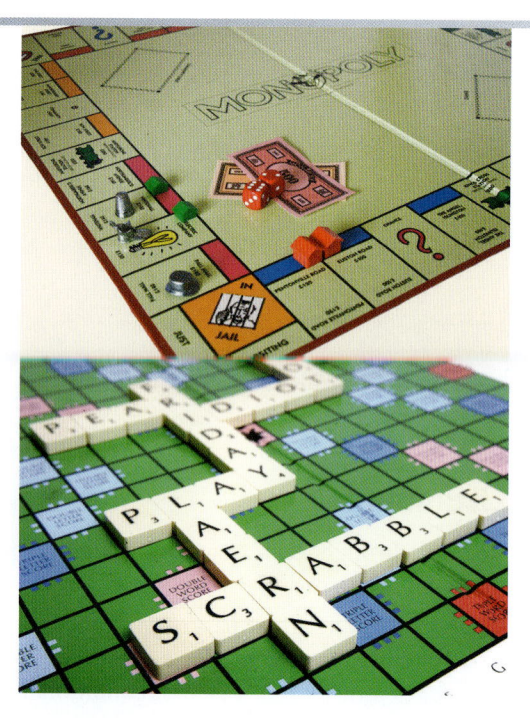

Grammar

Both games are successful today.
Neither game was successful at first.
Both of them are successful worldwide.

- use *both* to talk about two things. *Both* is used with a plural noun and a plural verb
- use *neither* to say something negative about two things. *Neither* is used with a singular noun and verb
- use *both of / neither of* with a plural noun or pronoun

1 Work in pairs. Make sentences about Scrabble and Monopoly using these prompts plus *both* or *neither*.

1 games are American
2 inventors didn't have a job
3 games are played on a board
4 games were not accepted by toy companies at first
5 games are published in over 25 languages

2 Work in pairs. How many sentences can you make with these ideas in three minutes?

Both of us …

Neither of us …

G **Grammar focus** – explanation & more practice of *both & neither* on page 150

120 Unit 10 **Old**

Vocabulary

1 Complete the texts with the words in the box.

| board | dice | miss a turn |
| money | points | square | turn |

Scrabble

Scrabble is played with letters. Different letters are worth different _____.

Each player has seven letters per _____. You put the letters on the _____ and make words.

The object is to get as many points as possible. If you can't make a word with your letters, you _____.

Monopoly

In Monopoly, players roll a _____ and move their counter around the board.

Each _____ on the board represents a property. If you land on someone else's property, you have to pay them. The object is to collect property and make _____.

2 Look at the pictures of other classic board games. Match each sentence to one of the games.

1 The object is to **reach the end** of the board first.
2 You **move around the board** and answer questions.
3 There are sixty-four black and white **squares** on the board.
4 The objective is to **win** different coloured **pieces** when you answer correctly.
5 There are snakes and ladders on the board. You **go down** snakes and **up** ladders.
6 The object is to **capture** your opponent's king.

3 Work in pairs and discuss these questions.
- Have you ever played any of these games? Do you like them?
- What other board games do you know?

Pronunciation

1 Put the words in the correct order to make useful game phrases.

1 the roll dice
2 turn it's your
3 a card pick
4 turn miss a
5 again go
6 highest goes rolls first whoever
7 your is which piece
8 cheating no

2 🔊 **2.78** Listen and check your answers. Then listen and repeat the phrases. Try to copy the intonation.

Speaking

Work in groups of three or four. You are going to play a board game. Turn to page 131 and read the rules. Then play the game.

Snakes and ladders

Trivial Pursuit

Chess

Old Unit 10

UNIT 10 Function globally ending a conversation

Warm up

Work in pairs and choose two of the situations below. Have a one-minute conversation for each situation.

Situations
1. You are strangers. It's very hot outside. A: start talking to B about the weather.
2. You are friends. A: you are learning to drive. Tell B about it.
3. You work together. A: you are going somewhere special on holiday. Tell B about it.
4. A: you are the boss. The company is closing. Tell B the bad news.

Listening

1 🔊 **2.79–2.80** Listen to two conversations. Match each one to a situation above.

2 Listen again and answer the questions.
Conversation 1: How does each man feel?
Why do you think they feel this way?
Conversation 2: Does the woman have good memories of the past? Why?

Language focus: ending a conversation

1 Put the words in the correct order to make useful phrases.
1. going be I'd better
2. now really I go to have
3. off to rush sorry
4. I be going should

2 🔊 **2.81** Listen and check your answers. Then listen and repeat the phrases.

3 🔊 **2.82** Listen to the end of five conversations. Which words do you hear? Complete the words with the correct letters.
1. a _ _ _ _ y
2. r _ _ _ t
3. O _
4. w _ _ l
5. a _ _ r _ _ _ t

Speaking

Work in pairs and choose **one** of the tasks below.

A Repeat the warm up activity using the new expressions you have learnt.

B Create a conversation using **only** the words and phrases in the box. You can use each phrase more than once. Then practise the conversation.

| Anyway. | Bye. | Goodbye. | OK. | OK, then. | Right. |
| See you. | Well. | Well, I'd better … | Yes, of course. |

Unit 10 **Function globally**

Global voices

Warm up

1 Write down three words you have learnt recently.

2 Work in pairs and give definitions for your words. Try to guess what your partner's words are.

Listening

1 **2.83–2.89** Listen to seven people talking about their favourite words and expressions in English. Number them in the order you hear them.

awesome and legendary ___   Oh my god! ___
gorgeous ___   perhaps ___
harmony ___   you know ___
love ___

2 Listen again and choose the correct answers.
1 Arthur, from France, likes the expression because he hears it in *songs / movies*.
2 Diego, from Italy, thinks there *are / aren't* a lot of very interesting words in English.
3 Kristina, from Russia, heard people use her favourite word when they talked about *clothes / the weather*.
4 Elodie, from Switzerland, likes her favourite word because of the *spelling / pronunciation*.
5 Semih, from Turkey, says his favourite words make him feel *happy / funny*.
6 Bea, from England, thinks her favourite words are useful because *they give her time to think / they mean lots of different things*.
7 Guy, from England, likes his word because of the sound, the structure and because *it doesn't exist in any other language / it exists in lots of other languages*.

Language focus: *you know*

1 Bea talks about the expression *you know*. Read about how we use this expression in the box. Which uses did Bea talk about?

> **Language note:** We can use *you know* ...
> a for emphasis.
>   It's a difficult test, **you know**.
> b while we think about what to say next.
>   This is a brand new phone. It's a, **you know**, phone with video and music and everything.
> c when we are giving extra information about something.
>   Have you seen my English book? **You know**, the black one.
> d before we start to talk about a person or thing.
>   **You know** the Japanese restaurant near the school, well, it's closing.

2 Add *you know* to the sentences below.
1 This is an old card game. (add emphasis)
2 I don't feel well. (add *a headache, sore throat*)
3 He won an Olympic medal. (add emphasis)
4 I had never heard that before. (begin with *You know*)
5 It was a big change in her life. (add *she was never the same again*)

Speaking

1 Write down two or three of your favourite words or expressions in English.

2 Work in small groups. Tell each other about your favourite English words or expressions and why you like them.

> **Useful phrases**
> • My favourite expression is ...
> • I like it because ...
> • I don't know why.
> • I agree. It's a good word.
> • I don't know. I don't like it very much.

Arthur, France   Diego, Italy
Kristina, Russia   Elodie, Switzerland   Semih, Turkey   Bea, England   Guy, England

Writing a report on studies

Reading

1 Magdalena's new English teacher has asked her to write a report on her previous language course. Read her report. Did she enjoy the course? Why?

Last summer I studied English for one month in language school in Oxford. We had classes every morning for three hours and in the afternoons we had free time or went on excursions. My class was elementary level and there were twelve students in the class, from all over the world. I stayed with host family.

We studied book called *Move* and sometimes we played games and listened to songs. We did a lot of speaking and listening activities and we did some grammar exercises as well. There was study centre in the school. Sometimes I worked there in the afternoons.

I enjoyed the course very much. I really liked speaking with my classmates and our teacher was very patient and kind. I wasn't so keen on studying grammar. I think I made progress in my speaking, but I should try to speak more. I also need to improve my grammar and writing.

2 Fill in Magdalena's end-of-course report.

Magdalena has completed a _____ - month course at _____ level. She has worked hard, both in class and after class in the _____. She has made good progress, especially in her _____. However, she could still improve this, and also needs to work on her _____ and _____.

Language focus: *a / an* for new information

We use *a* or *an* when we write about a singular noun for the first time. Magdalena wrote:

Last summer I studied English for one month in language school in Oxford.

She should write:

Last summer I studied English for one month in a language school in Oxford.

Find three more places where Magdalena forgot to use *a* or *an*, and correct them.

Writing skills: giving reasons

Make your writing more interesting by giving reasons using *because* or *as*.

I enrolled on a language course as / because I wanted to improve my English.

1 Put these reasons in the correct places in Magdalena's report.

1 … because I wanted to practise speaking outside the class.
2 … as this was a good way to practise on my own.
3 … because the classes were always varied and never boring.
4 … as I am quite shy.
5 … as I still make a lot of mistakes.

2 Complete the sentences with a reason.

1 I want to improve my English as _____.
2 Sometimes studying English is difficult because _____.

Preparing to write

Work in pairs and make notes about your present English course. Use the useful phrases below to help you. Follow this format:

Paragraph 1: information about the course (level, length, number of students)
Paragraph 2: what you did during the course
Paragraph 3: feelings about the course, progress and areas to improve

Describing language activities and skills

- We did a lot of / some listening / speaking activities.
- We did a lot of / some grammar exercises / games / communicative activities.
- I really enjoyed speaking but I wasn't so keen on grammar.
- I need to improve my reading / writing / study skills.
- I need to extend my vocabulary / work on my pronunciation.
- I made progress in my listening / writing / grammar.
- I should try to speak more / be more accurate.

Writing

Write a report like Magdalena's for your next English teacher. Use your notes to help you. Check your report for *a / an* and correct past tense forms.

Global review

Grammar

The writer of this text has forgotten to use *the* eleven times. Put it in the correct places.

China is largest country in East Asia. Population of China is over 1.3 billion, and capital city is Beijing. One of most famous buildings in Beijing is *Forbidden City*. This is where last Emperor of China lived, and today it is visited by millions of tourists every year.

Sport is very popular in China, and 2008 Olympic Games were held in Beijing. Every morning many people practise *qigong* and *tai chi chuan* in city's parks. *Go* is another famous game that was invented in China. It is played with counters on a board, and objective is to control largest part of board.

Vocabulary

Complete the puzzle by reading the clues.

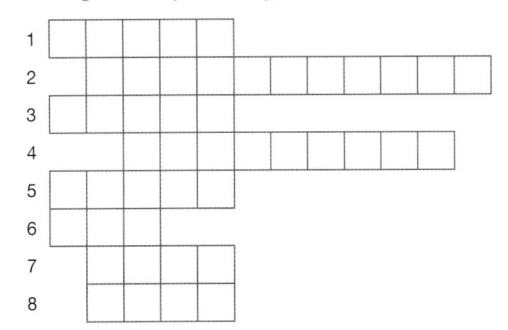

1 I've just bought a _____ new washing machine.
2 A fast form of public transport in a city.
3 Too much traffic can _____ pollution.
4 We should try to reduce our carbon _____.
5 You put your counters on this to play Scrabble.
6 You have to _____ on a bus before you travel.
7 When everyone else has played, it is your _____.
8 How do you get to work? I _____ a motorbike.

Speaking and Writing

1 Work in small groups. Describe a long journey you have made and list what you had to do. Who used the most forms of transport?

2 Work in pairs and find three new words you have learnt in this book. Then complete the definitions.
1 _____ This is a person who _____.
2 _____ This is a place where _____.
3 _____ This is a thing which _____.

3 Work with another pair and read your definitions. Try to guess the words.

Study skills

Evaluating your pronunciation

1 Work in pairs and discuss the questions.
1 How would you describe your pronunciation of English?
  a I speak like a native speaker.
  b My pronunciation is generally clear and comprehensible
  c I have a noticeable accent but my pronunciation is mostly comprehensible.
  d I have a strong accent and am sometimes hard to understand.
2 How would you like your pronunciation to be?
3 Which of these areas of pronunciation have you studied in this class?
  a vowel sounds   f sentence stress
  b consonant sounds   g rhythm
  c consonant clusters   h intonation
  d word stress
  e the relationship between sounds and spellings
4 Which area is the strongest for you?
5 Which area do you need to work on most?

2 Work in pairs. Answer the questions.
1 Which is your favourite English sound?
2 Which is your least favourite?
3 Which sound do you find most difficult to pronounce?

3 Which of these strategies for improving pronunciation have you tried?

* Practise reading a short text aloud. Record it and listen to it, or ask a friend to listen and comment.
* Repeat the lines from a DVD or a song.
* Use a pronunciation book and CD.
* Practise repeating the pronunciation of new words with an electronic dictionary such as the Macmillan English Dictionary.
* Choose an area of pronunciation or a sound you want to improve. Focus on it for a few minutes every day when you are speaking.
* Other ideas.

4 Compare your ideas with a partner and decide how you can improve your pronunciation. What will you try?

Communication activities: Student A

Unit 1, Speaking (page 11)

1 Complete the questions with the correct word – *do* or *are*.

2 Ask your partner the questions.

3 Answer your partner's questions.

Family questions

- _____ you have a big family?
- How many brothers and sisters _____ you have?
- _____ you have family in other countries?
- _____ you in touch with them?
- How often _____ you in touch with your grandparents or grandchildren?
- _____ you have family reunions? How often?

Unit 2, Reading (page 18)

1 Read the text about vegemite. Are there any interesting or surprising facts in the text? Write them down.

2 Read the text again. Write down a few key words to help you tell your partner about the text.

3 Tell your partner about vegemite.

Vegemite

Vegemite is a dark brown food paste from Australia. You can put it on sandwiches, toast or crackers. It tastes salty and bitter and is not very popular in the world except in Australia and New Zealand. Vegemite has strong cultural associations in those countries, and many say it is a comfort food. Vegemite has very high levels of vitamin B, and during the 1940s the Australian army bought large amounts of it for the soldiers. According to the Prime Minister of Australia's website, Vegemite is 'the taste of Australia' and some Australians even take a jar with them when they travel to other countries.

jar of vegemite

crackers

Glossary

bitter (*adjective*) – has a strong sharp taste that is not sweet

jar (*noun*) – a glass container for food, with a lid and a wide opening

paste (*noun*) – a food that is made by crushing meat, fish or vegetables

Unit 6, Grammar (page 69)

1 Write the questions for numbers 1–5 of the quiz. Use the comparative form of the adjective.

Which is faster, the speed of light or the speed of sound?

2 Work with a student from group B. Ask your questions.

3 Listen to questions 6–10 and try to answer them. Write the correct answers in the table.

	Column A		Column B	Answer
1	microscope	modern?	X-ray	microscope
2	speed of light	fast?	speed of sound	speed of light
3	theory that the Earth is round	old?	theory of gravity	theory that Earth is round
4	oil	expensive?	coal	oil, but coal is more polluting
5	hydrogen	heavy?	nitrogen	nitrogen is more than 10 times heavier than hydrogen
6	Jupiter		Saturn	
7	100°F		100°C	
8	one metre		one yard	
9	one megabyte		one gigabyte	
10	-40°F		-40°C	

Unit 9, Vocabulary (page 102)

1 Watch your partner and guess what's wrong.

2 Mime the symptoms below. Your partner must guess what's wrong.
1. You have a headache.
2. Your wrist hurts. / You have a sore wrist.
3. You're sneezing.
4. Your back hurts. / You've got a sore back.

Unit 10, Writing (page 115)

1 Read the definitions of the new words. Copy them down and then write two incorrect definitions for each word.

2 Work with a pair who chose different words. Read out your words and definitions.

3 Listen to the other pair's words and definitions and try to guess which is correct.

A blog is a diary or journal which is on the internet.
Spanglish is a language which is a mixture of Spanish and English.

Communication activities: Student A

Communication activities: Student B

Unit 1, Speaking (page 11)

1 Complete the questions with the correct word – *do* or *are*.

2 Answer your partner's questions.

3 Ask your partner the questions.

Friends questions

- How often _____ you talk to your neighbours?
- _____ you in touch with anybody you went to primary school with?
- _____ you go out with your colleagues from work or school?
- _____ you keep in touch with friends by email, phone, or face to face? How often?
- _____ you have any online friends or acquaintances?

Unit 2, Reading (page 18)

1 Read the text about popular comfort food for men and women. Are there any interesting or surprising facts in the text? Write them down.

2 Read the text again. Write down a few key words to help you tell your partner about the text.

3 Tell your partner about comfort food in North America.

bowl of sweets

Comfort food for men and women

An article published in the American journal, *Physiology and Behavior*, shows differences between men and women and their choice of comfort food.

A survey of over 1,000 North Americans found that women often prefer snack-related comfort food while men prefer more meal-related comfort food. In particular, more women said they liked food like sweets and chocolate while men liked things such as pizza, pasta, steak or casseroles. Women often felt guilty and less healthy than men about their comfort food choices.

The researchers think that the differences between men and women may be because men like hot, prepared meals (that someone else made) while women look for easy comfort food that needs less preparation.

casserole

Glossary

casserole (*noun*) – a deep dish with a lid, used for cooking in the oven, or the mixture of food that is cooked

guilty (*adjective*) – ashamed and sorry because you have done something wrong

prefer (*verb*) – to like or want something more than something else

Unit 6, Grammar (page 69)

1 Write the questions for numbers 6–10 of the quiz. Use the comparative form of the adjective.

Which is further from the sun, Jupiter or Saturn?

2 Work with a student from group A. Listen to questions 1–5 and try to answer them. Write the correct answers in the table.

3 Ask your questions.

	Column A		Column B	Answer
1	microscope		X-ray	
2	speed of light		speed of sound	
3	theory that the Earth is round		theory of gravity	
4	oil		coal	
5	hydrogen		nitrogen	
6	Jupiter	far from the sun?	Saturn	Saturn
7	100°F	hot?	100°C	100°C; 100°F is only 37°C
8	one metre	long?	one yard	a metre is 1.09 yards
9	one megabyte	big?	one gigabyte	a gigabyte
10	-40°F	cold?	-40°C	they are the same temperature

Unit 9, Vocabulary (page 102)

1 Mime the symptoms below. Your partner must guess what's wrong.

1. You have a toothache.
2. You have a sore leg. / Your leg hurts.
3. You're coughing.
4. You've got a fever.

2 Watch your partner and guess what's wrong.

Unit 10, Writing (page 115)

1 Read the definitions of the new words. Copy them down and then write two incorrect definitions for each word.

2 Work with a pair who chose different words. Listen to their words and definitions and try to guess which is correct.

3 Read out your words and definitions.

> *A metrosexual* is a young man who enjoys good clothes, an attractive home and a good personal appearance.
> *Spam* are emails that are sent to many people and are not wanted.

Additional material

Unit 2, Function globally (page 26)

PIZZA PALACE

Pizza (choose your own toppings)
Mushrooms ....
Salami ....
Ham ....
Cheese ....
Tomato ....
Onion ....
Green or Red Pepper ....

Drinks
Cola ....
Water ....
Fruit Juice ....

The Liner Diner

Please wait to be seated.

* *Choose from our large self-service buffet.*
* *Great selection of fish and seafood. Ask your waiter for recommendations.*
* *Order your drinks and coffee from the waiter.*

BARNABY'S CAFÉ

Today's special
Cream of chicken soup
or
Green salad

Vegetarian lasagne
or
Traditional steak and potato pie

Dessert
Ice cream
Fresh fruit

Unit 9, Reading (page 106)

Short cut
He had travelled by car for 11 miles of the marathon!

A helping hand
Olympic officials had helped him cross the line.

The extra distance
Ramzan thought that he hadn't finished the race.

A new Olympic record
He had never swum in a pool of that size before.

Unit 10, Speaking (page 117)

1 Read the full quotes below. Do you think they are positive, negative or neutral about America?

2 Do you know any famous quotes about your country? Tell your partner.

❝ All great change in America begins at the dinner table. ❞
Ronald Reagan, former US President

❝ I think the most un-American thing you can say is 'You can't say that'. ❞
Garrison Keillor, American writer

❝ England and America are two countries separated by a common language. ❞
George Bernard Shaw, Irish writer

❝ America is a mistake, a giant mistake. ❞
Sigmund Freud, Austrian psychologist.

❝ There is not a black America and a white America and Latino America and Asian America – there's the United States of America. ❞
Barack Obama, US President

Unit 10, Speaking (page 121)

Rules

1. Play this game in groups of three or four. You need one coin and one board to play.
2. Each person needs a counter. Put the counters on the square marked Start.
3. Decide who is going first.
4. The first player tosses a coin. If the coin lands heads up, move your counter forward two squares. If the coin lands tails up, move your counter forward one square.
5. If you land on a grey square, follow the instructions. If you land on a red square, speak in English for one minute about the topic on the square.
6. The winner is the person who gets to the end of the board first.

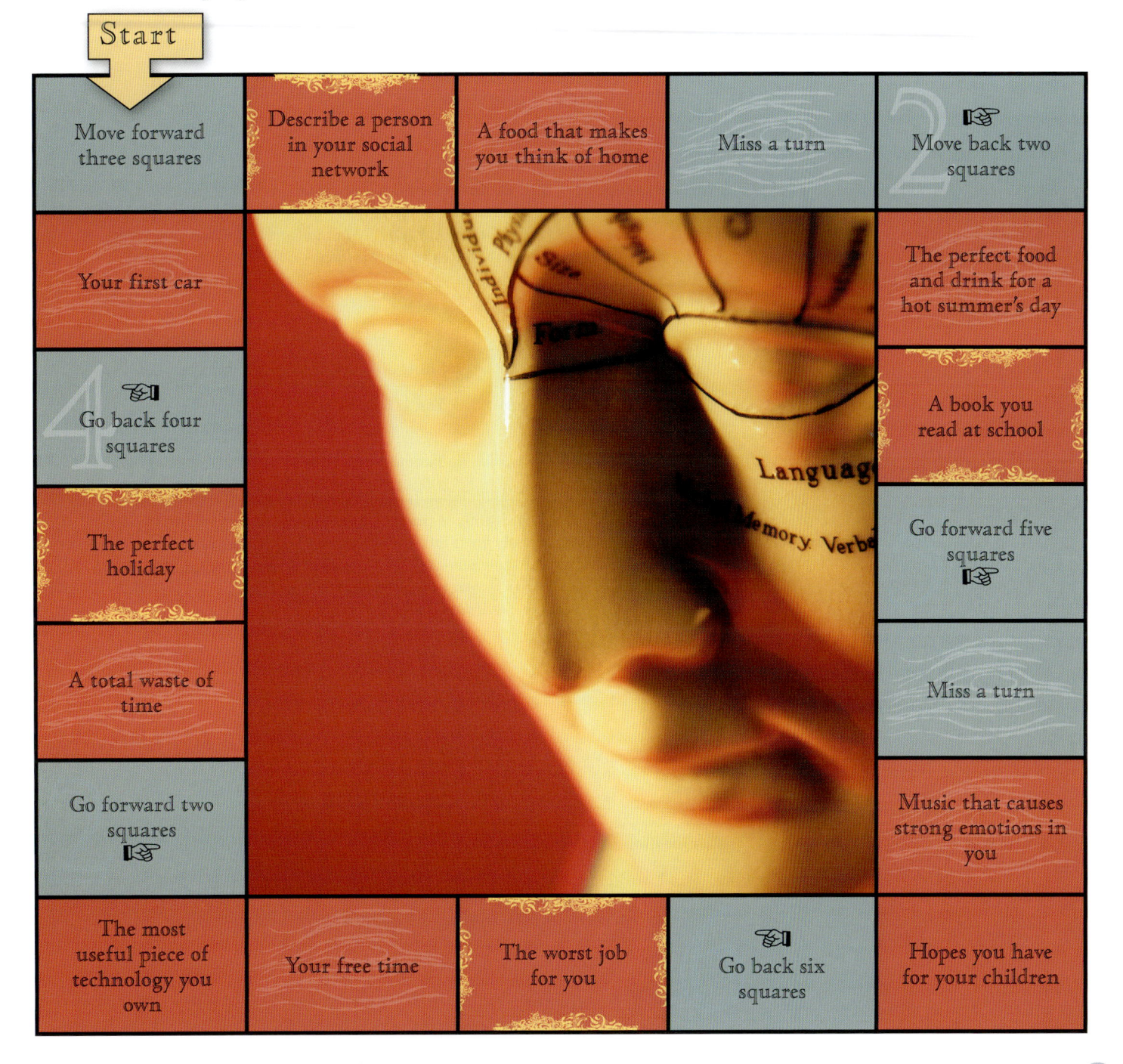

Start

Move forward three squares	Describe a person in your social network	A food that makes you think of home	Miss a turn	Move back two squares
Your first car				The perfect food and drink for a hot summer's day
Go back four squares				A book you read at school
The perfect holiday				Go forward five squares
A total waste of time				Miss a turn
Go forward two squares				Music that causes strong emotions in you
The most useful piece of technology you own	Your free time	The worst job for you	Go back six squares	Hopes you have for your children

Grammar focus

Unit 1

Word order in question forms

Yes / No questions

In *yes / no* questions the verb goes before the subject:
They **are** from Spain. ⟶ **Are** they from Spain?

In present simple or past simple questions, the auxiliary verb *do / did* goes before the subject.
She speaks English. ⟶ **Does** she speak English?
She learnt French. ⟶ **Did** she learn French?

Wh- questions

Question words (*What? Where? Who? When? Why? How?*) go at the start of a question.
Where do you live? **When** were you born?
What is your favourite sport?

What and How questions

Use *how* and *what* with nouns and adjectives or adverbs to start questions.
What pets do you have?   **What** kind of dog is it?
How expensive was it?   **How** often do you feed it?

Use *like* in questions to ask about appearance or personality and characteristics.
What does she look **like**? – She's tall and wears glasses.
What's that new restaurant **like**? – Noisy but the food is good.

Present simple, frequency

Affirmative	Negative	Question	Short answers *Yes*	Short answers *No*
I/You/We/They **work**.	I/You/We/They **don't work**.	**Do** I/you/we/they **work**?	**Yes**, I/you/we/they **do**.	**No**, I/you/we/they **don't**.
He/She/It **works**.	He/She/It **doesn't work**.	**Does** he/she/it **work**?	**Yes**, he/she/it **does**.	**No**, he/she/it **doesn't**.

Use the present simple to talk about:
- habits and routines.
  He **gets up** at seven o'clock.
  They **don't go** to bed late.
- things that are always true.
  The sun **rises** in the east.
  Water **boils** at 100°C.

We use frequency adverbs and expressions of frequency with the present simple. Frequency adverbs (*always, usually, often, sometimes, hardly ever, never*) go between the subject and the verb, except with the verb *to be*.
We **always** have lunch at 1 pm.
He is **always** late for class.

Expressions of frequency (*every day, twice a week, on Mondays*, etc.) usually go at the end of the sentence. They go at the beginning of the sentence when we want to emphasise when or how often.
We go shopping **on Saturdays**.
On Saturdays, we go shopping.

Present continuous

Affirmative	Negative	Question
I am ('m) working.	I am ('m) not working.	Am I working?
You/We/They are ('re) working.	You/We/They are not (aren't) working.	Are you/we/they working?
He/She/It is ('s) working.	He/She/It is not (isn't) working.	Is he/she/it working?

Use the present continuous to talk about:
- things happening now or about now.
  We **are watching** TV.   I'**m learning** English.
- temporary situations.
  He **is living** in London at the moment.

The present continuous is often used with time expressions such as *now, these days, at the moment* and *this week / month / year*.

Some verbs (stative verbs) aren't used in the present continuous: *agree, appear, believe, forget, hate, hear, know, like, love, mean, need, own, prefer, realise, remember, see, seem, want*

Unit 1 Exercises

Word order in question forms

1 Decide if these questions are in the correct (✔) or incorrect (✘) order. Then correct the mistakes.
1 They are from Japan?
2 Where do your parents live?
3 Did learn you a language at school?
4 Who is your favourite actor?
5 Do like you chocolate?
6 How many students there are in the class?

2 Use the words to write the questions.
where born? Where were you born?
1 family from? _____
2 speak any languages? _____
3 job? _____
4 live? _____
5 married? _____
6 children? _____
7 play any sports? _____
8 favourite writers? _____
9 like music? _____

What and How questions

3 Write the questions.

How tall is he? He's nearly two metres tall.
1 What _____? My car's red.
2 How _____? I'm thirty.
3 What _____? My teacher's tall with short, dark hair.
4 How _____? The school is ten kilometres from here.
5 What _____? I have a Visa and an American Express.
6 How _____? It doesn't rain here very often.
7 What _____? She's nice, really friendly.

Present simple, frequency

4 Put the words in the correct order to make sentences.

his parents / on Sundays / my boyfriend / visits
My boyfriend visits his parents on Sundays.
1 check / every day / their email / they
2 TV / in the daytime / watch / hardly ever / we
3 goes / once a week / she / to the cinema
4 meet / at weekends / sometimes / I / colleagues from work
5 all evening / spends / he / on the internet / often
6 usually / my wife / before me / gets up
7 for a meal / go out / we / every Saturday night

Present continuous

5 Complete the dialogue with the correct form of the present simple or present continuous.

A: Where (1) _____ (you / work) at the moment?
B: In a hotel in Italy. My boyfriend (2) _____ (live) in Italy at the moment too.
A: (3) _____ (you / like) it there?
B: It's great. I (4) _____ (prefer) the lifestyle in Italy. In London everybody (5) _____ (work) long hours. People (6) _____ (not enjoy) life as much.
A: (7) _____ (you / speak) Italian?
B: Not very well, but I (8) _____ (take) classes now and I (9) _____ (learn) the language quite quickly. We (10) _____ (not plan) to go back to England for a while.

Unit 2

Countable / uncountable nouns, *some*, *any*

Countable and uncountable nouns

Countable nouns can be singular or plural. Most plural forms end in *s*.
*Put it on your **plate**. Where are the **plates**?*

Some plural countable nouns are irregular:
child – children
woman – women
man – men
Uncountable nouns don't have a plural form.
*Do you take **milk** and **sugar** in tea?*

> **Language note:** Some words can be countable or uncountable.
> *I like coffee. (= the drink)*
> *Can I have a coffee? (= a cup of coffee)*

These are some common uncountable nouns: *accommodation, advice, bread, furniture, information, news, traffic, weather*

some and *any*

Use *some* and *any* with plural nouns or with uncountable nouns. We usually use *some* in affirmative sentences and *any* in negative sentences and questions.
*Do you have **any** plates?*
*We need to buy **some** milk.*

Use *a / an* with singular nouns.
*I don't have **a** plate. You need **an** egg for that recipe.*

a lot of, a little, a few, (not) enough, much, many

Use quantifiers before a noun to show the quantity or amount of something.
- *a little* and *much* are used with uncountable nouns:
  ***a little** coffee*, *too **much** sugar*
- *a few* and *many* are used with plural countable nouns:
  ***a few** apples*, *too **many** bananas*
- *a lot of* and *(not) enough* are used with uncountable nouns and plural nouns: ***a lot of** pasta*, ***not enough** vegetables*

> **Language note:** *much / many* are usually used in negative sentences and questions or with *too*.
> *A lot of / lots of* is usually used instead of *much / many* in affirmative sentences. *There's **a lot of** salt in this dish.*
> We use *a lot* to answer the question *How much / many ...?*

The infinitive with *to*

Use the infinitive with *to* after some verbs: *agree, arrange, decide, forget, hope, learn, manage, mean, need, offer, prefer, promise, refuse, remember, try, want, would like*
You need to eat slowly. Remember to add sugar.

> **Language note:** we don't use *to* after modal verbs such as *can / can't* and *must*. (See Grammar focus 5 page 140 for more on modals.)
> *I **can drink** one glass of wine, but no more.*

> Use the infinitive with *to* after adjectives.
> *It's **healthy to eat** salad. It's **good to try** different foods.*

Infinitive of purpose

We use the infinitive with *to* when we talk about the purpose of something or why we do something.
I eat lots of vegetables to get important vitamins. (= because I want to get)
You use a corkscrew to open wine. (= so that you can open)

> **Language note:** We can use *in order to* instead of *to* in these sentences. *For* isn't used in these sentences.
> *I eat lots of vegetables **in order to get** important vitamins.*
> Not: ~~I eat lots of vegetables for to get important vitamins.~~

Unit 2 Exercises

Countable / uncountable nouns, *some*, *any*

1 Complete the sentences with *a / an*, *some* or *any*.

1 I'm going shopping. Do we need _____ eggs?
2 Can I have _____ large cola and two coffees please?
3 I'd like _____ information about restaurants in the area.
4 There's _____ bread left, but there isn't _____ butter.
5 I'm making _____ big cake for my son's birthday.
6 I need _____ advice about vegetarian food.
7 Let's buy _____ new furniture for the dining room.
8 I need _____ onion for this dish.

a lot of, a little, a few, (not) enough, much, many

2 Underline the correct quantifier in each sentence.

1 **A:** I'm afraid there's too *much / many* milk in this.
   B: Sorry, I forgot you only like a *few / little* in coffee.
2 **A:** How *much / many* biscuits would you like?
   B: *A lot / A lot of*!
3 **A:** We have *lots of / much* space. Why don't you come and visit?
   B: Thanks but I *don't have enough / have too little* days off.
4 **A:** My wallet was here *a little / a few* minutes ago!
   B: I'm afraid there are *lots of / many* pickpockets here, sir.

3 Choose one of the dialogues in Exercise 1. Think about what is happening and who is speaking. Write the next two lines.

The infinitive with *to*

4 Read the text about a Japanese drink. Complete the text with *to* or nothing (–).

Sake is rice wine. The Chinese first learnt __to__ make sake, but now it is the traditional drink of Japan. To make sake you need (1) _____ cook rice in water. It is important (2) _____ use a special kind of rice. You can (3) _____ serve sake warm or cold. In Japan people prefer (4) _____ drink warm sake in winter and cold sake in summer. You are meant (5) _____ drink sake with friends. Tradition says you mustn't (6) _____ pour sake for yourself. So if you drink sake in Japan, remember (7) _____ pour it only for other people.

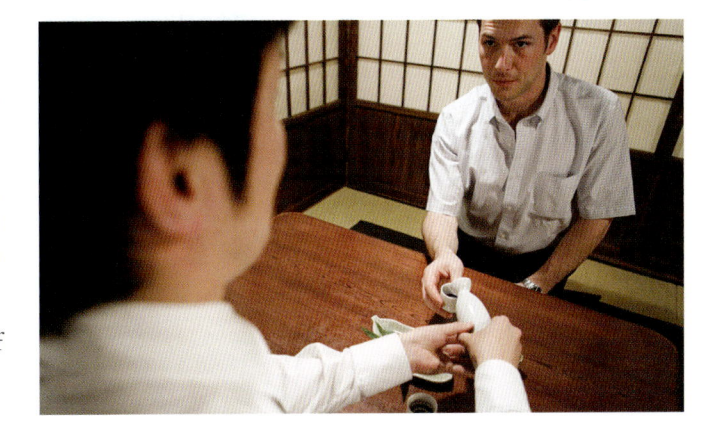

Infinitive of purpose

5 Make six sentences.

1	I went to the baker's	a	meet our friends.
2	He looked round the café	b	celebrate her birthday.
3	She smiled at me	to c	show she wasn't angry.
4	He went into the garden	d	buy some bread.
5	We cycled into town	e	find a good table.
6	They organised a party	f	pick some tomatoes.

Grammar focus Unit 2   135

Unit 3

Past simple and past continuous

Past simple

Affirmative	Negative	Question
I/You/He/She/It/We/They worked.	I/You/He/She/It/We/They did not (didn't) work.	Did I/you/he/she/it/we/they work?

-ed spelling

- for most verbs add ed: *look – looked*
- for verbs ending in *e*, add *d*: *smile – smiled*
- for verbs ending in *y*, change the *y* to *ied*: *study – studied*. (But verbs ending in vowel + *y* are regular: *play – played*).
- for verbs ending in consonant-vowel-consonant, double the consonant and add *ed*, eg *stop – stopped*

Use the same form for all persons (*I, you, he, she, it, we, they*) except for the verb *to be*.
Some verbs have an irregular affirmative form:
have – had, go – went, see – saw, think – thought.
Use the past simple to talk about completed actions in the past.
I **watched** a good film at the weekend.
I **bought** a book about history of art last week.

Past continuous

Affirmative	Negative	Question
I was working.	I was not (wasn't) working.	Was I working?
You/We/They were working.	You/We/They were not (weren't) working.	Were you/we/they working?
He/She/It was working.	He/She/It was not (wasn't) working.	Was he/she/it working?

Use the past continuous to describe an activity or situation in progress in the past.
He **was watching** a film on TV.
We often use the past continuous for activities that are interrupted by a completed action. It is used in contrast with the past simple.
He **was watching** a film on TV when the phone **rang**.

―――――――――――――X―――――――
watching a film   *phone rang*

While is often used with the past continuous. *When* is often used with the past continuous and the past simple.
I fell asleep **while** I was reading a book.
I was reading a book **when** I fell asleep.

Used to

Affirmative	Negative	Question
I/You/He/She/It/We/They used to work.	I/You/He/She/It/We/They didn't use to work.	Did I/you/he/she/it/we/they use to work?

We use *used to* to talk about regular actions in the past which don't happen now.
I **used to play** the guitar. (= but I don't play it now)

We also use *used to* to talk about situations in the past which aren't true now.
There **used to** be an art gallery in our town. (= but there isn't one there now)

Language note: There is no present form of *used to*. We only use *used to* to talk about regular actions in the past.
Not: I use to download music.

Unit 3 Exercises

Past simple and past continuous

1 Use the prompts below to write what was happening yesterday lunchtime in the park.

1 What / people / do / in the park / at midday yesterday?
2 two workers / dig / a hole
3 a man / read / a newspaper / on a bench
4 a woman / eat / a sandwich – but she / not enjoy / it
5 two children / play / hide and seek
6 an old woman / walk / her dog
7 two tourists / take / photos

2 Underline the correct form of the verb in each sentence.

1 We *were cleaning / cleaned* the windows when it *was starting / started* to rain.
2 While she *was looking / looked* in the mirror, she *was noticing / noticed* her first grey hairs.
3 It *was getting / got* dark when I *was switching on / switched on* the lights.
4 They *were dropping / dropped* the sculpture while they *were carrying / carried* it inside.
5 While she *was closing / closed* the curtains, she *was seeing / saw* somebody outside.
6 I *was painting / painted* the bedroom wall when I *was falling off / fell off* the ladder.

Used to

3 Complete the sentences with *used to* or *didn't use to* and an appropriate verb.

1 He _____ to cassettes, he didn't use to listen to CDs.
2 He _____ the violin, but now he plays the guitar.
3 He _____ an MP3 player but he has one now.
4 He _____ to classical concerts, he used to go to music festivals.
5 He _____ miserable, now he feels relaxed and happy.
6 He _____ opera but he likes it now.

Grammar focus Unit 3

Unit 4

Future hopes and plans

Use verbs such as *hope, plan, want, would like* (+ infinitive with *to*) to talk about future hopes that aren't definite.
I **want** to work in a developing country.
I'**d like** to be an aid worker.

Use *look forward to* (+ verb with *-ing*) to talk about definite future plans.
I'm **looking forward to** working in Africa next year.

Future plans and intentions (*going to*, present continuous)

Going to

Affirmative	Negative	Question
I **am** ('**m**) **going to** work.	I **am not** ('**m**) **not going to** work.	**Am** I **going to** work?
You/We/They **are** ('**re**) **going to** work.	You/We/They **are not** (**aren't**) **going to** work.	**Are** you/we/they **going to** work?
He/She/It **is** ('**s**) **going to** work.	He/She/It **is not** (**isn't**) **going to** work.	**Is** he/she/it **going to** work?

We use *going to* to talk about what we have already decided or intend to do in the future.
He's **going to** train to be a doctor. (= It is already decided)
They're **going to** work for an NGO.

Language note: *going to go* is often replaced by *going*.
I'm **going to go** to France next year = I'm **going** to France next year.

Present continuous

See Grammar focus 1 on page 132 for an explanation on how to form the present continuous.

Use the present continuous to talk about future plans, in particular for arrangements with a date and time, eg plans with friends or travel arrangements.
I'm **meeting** friends this evening. (= I've made an arrangement with them)
We're **going to** Egypt on holiday this year. (= We've already arranged the holiday)

Prediction and ability (*will*, *be able to*)

Will

Affirmative	Negative	Question
I/You/He/She/It/We/They **will** ('**ll**) work.	I/You/He/She/It/We/They **will not** (**won't**) work.	**Will** I/you/he/she/it/we/they work?

Use *will* to talk about predictions or beliefs about the future. It is often used with the verbs *think, hope* and *to be sure*.
I think there'**ll be** a nuclear accident.
I'm sure there **will be** more homeless people in the future.

Be able to

Use *will be able to* to talk about ability or possibility in the future. We don't use *will can*.
We **won't be able to** stop pollution.

Language note: compare *will* and *going to*.
We're **going to** reduce carbon emissions.
(= definite plan / intention)
I think we'**ll** reduce carbon emissions.
(= prediction, may or may not happen)

Future time clauses

Future time clause		Main clause
If When Before After As soon as	+ present tense (usually present simple)	future form (usually *will*)

Use future time clauses with a present tense to talk about future predictions.
If we **reduce** carbon emissions, we'**ll reduce** global warming.
It is possible to change the order of the future time clause and main clause.
When you **see** the film, you'**ll be** really frightened.
Will we have dinner **before** we **go** to the cinema?

Language note: we use *if* for things that might happen but aren't certain. We use *when* for things that are certain.

Unit 4 Exercises

Future hopes and plans

1 Match the sentences.

1. She's a doctor. She wants
2. He's five years old. He hopes
3. I'm a teacher. I'm looking forward
4. I'm a student. I'm planning
5. They worry about pollution. They'd like
6. We're aid workers. We're looking forward

a   to working on a new project in Latin America.
b   to work for an environmental organisation.
c   to fight disease in developing countries.
d   to starting the new school year.
e   to get a good job when I leave college.
f   to get a bike for his birthday.

Future plans and intentions (*going to*, present continuous)

2 Complete the sentences. Use the correct form of *going to*.
1. We _____ (*give*) our children a future!
2. This government _____ (*not help*) our country!
3. When _____ (*you / stop*) this war?
4. How _____ (*we / feed*) our children?
5. We _____ (*not give up*)!
6. Who _____ (*help*) the poor?
7. I _____ (*fight*) for what I believe!
8. Cars _____ (*destroy*) our environment.

3 Complete the dialogues with the correct form of the present continuous.

1. A: They're holding a big climate change conference at the end of the year.
   B: Where _____?
2. A: When are you meeting Lisa again?
   B: _____ after work tomorrow actually.
3. A: I'm going on holiday in June.
   B: Where _____?
4. A: What time is David coming round?
   B: _____ today, I'm afraid.
5. A: Are you working on Saturday?
   B: No, _____ at all this weekend.

Prediction and ability (*will, be able to*)

4 Complete the text with *will* or *won't*.

What do we know about global warming? Well, global temperatures (1) _____ increase. Sea levels (2) _____ rise and in some areas there (3) _____ be floods. But in other areas there (4) _____ be enough rain. That means farmers in some areas (5) _____ be able to grow food any more. And some animals and plants (6) _____ be able to exist in changing environments, so there (7) _____ be fewer types of animals.

5 Underline the correct verb.
1. We *are having / will have* lunch with friends tomorrow.
2. I hope you *are going to enjoy / will enjoy* your visit.
3. What *are you going to do / will you do* this evening?
4. I'm sure we *will find / are finding* a solution.
5. She's *going to be / will be* an engineer when she leaves school.
6. What time *will you meet / are you meeting* them?
7. What do you think *is happening / will happen* tomorrow?
8. I'*m going to check / 'm checking* my email in a minute.

Future time clauses

6 Complete the sentences with the correct form of the verb in brackets.

1. I think the baby _____ (*start*) to cry as soon as we _____ (*get*) on the bus.
2. If you _____ (*do*) the shopping, I _____ (*cook*) dinner.
3. You _____ (*be*) shocked when you _____ (*read*) that book.
4. After he _____ (*finish*) work, he _____ (*go*) to the airport.
5. She _____ (*be*) upset if he _____ (*forget*) her birthday.
6. I _____ (*send*) you a text when we _____ (*arrive*).

Unit 5

Have

Affirmative	Negative	Question
I/You/We/They **have** a car.	I/You/We/They **don't have** a car.	**Do** I/you/we/they have a car?
He/She/It **has** a car.	He/She/It **doesn't have** a car.	**Does** he/she/it have a car?

Use *have* as a main verb to talk about possessions, relationships or characteristics.
I **have** two brothers.
She **has** dark hair.

Language note: We can't use short forms when we use *have* as a main verb. Not: ~~I've a cat.~~

Instead of *have* we can also use *have got* for possession. *Have got* is often used in spoken and informal English.
I'**ve got** two brothers.
She **hasn't got** dark hair.
Have you **got** any money?

Use *have* as a main verb with certain nouns to talk about actions or experiences. For example:
- have breakfast / lunch / dinner / a drink / a coffee
- have a party / a holiday / a swim / an accident / a good time
- have a chat / a conversation / a meeting
- have an illness / a headache / a problem

Modal verbs

Use *must* and *have to* to talk about things that are necessary. We often use *must* and *have to* for rules. *Have to* is often used for something which is necessary because of a law or because someone else says it.
I **must** finish this report.
He **has to** give a presentation tomorrow. (= His boss said so)

Use *must not (mustn't)* to express prohibition.
You **mustn't** wear jeans and trainers in the office.

Use *don't have to* to say that something isn't necessary, but it is possible or allowed.
Men **don't have to** wear a tie at work. (= but they can if they want to)
Use *can* to say that something is possible or allowed.
You **can** buy food in the staff canteen. Or you **can** eat your own sandwiches there.
Use *can't* to say that something is not possible or allowed.
You **can't** eat lunch at your desk.

-ing forms

The *-ing* form of the verb can be:
- the subject of a sentence
Working long hours is very stressful.
Playing chess is very relaxing.
- the object of some verbs, for example: *love, like, dislike, enjoy, mind, can't stand*
I like **playing** basketball.
I can't stand **jogging**.

- used after prepositions: *good / bad at, interested in, tired of, excited about, bored with, instead of, in spite of*
He's very good at **skiing**.
I'm excited about **going** on holiday.

Present perfect

Affirmative	Negative	Question
I/You/We/They **have ('ve) worked**.	I/You/We/They **have not (haven't) worked**.	**Have** I/You/We/They **worked**?
He/She/It **has ('s) worked**.	He/She/It **has not (hasn't) worked**.	**Has** he/she/it **worked**?

The present perfect is formed with the verb *have* + past participle. The past participle of regular verbs is the same as the past simple. (see Grammar focus 3 page 136). Irregular verbs often have different forms, eg go – went – gone.

Use the present perfect to talk about an unspecific time in the past. Compare the present perfect and the past simple.
I **have been** to Disneyland. (= no specific time, present perfect)
I **went** to Disneyland last summer. (= specific time, past simple)

We often use the present perfect with *ever* and *never* to talk about experiences up to the present.
Have you **ever been** to an amusement park? (= at any time in your life)
I'**ve never been** on a roller coaster. (= up to now)

Language note: *have been to* = have visited a place.

Compare: She'**s been** to Germany. (= and now she has come back home).
She'**s gone** to Germany. (= and she's still there).

Unit 5 Grammar focus

Unit 5 Exercises

Have

1 Complete the sentences with the correct form of *have*.

1 She _____ a baby yesterday – a little girl.
2 They _____ got a car, they cycle everywhere.
3 We _____ a party on Sunday evening. Would you like to come?
4 Do you know him? He _____ glasses and he _____ much hair.
5 I _____ breakfast most days because I'm never hungry in the morning.
6 I'm afraid he _____ got time right now.
7 We _____ a printer at home so I bought one yesterday.
8 _____ a minute, please Madam?

Modal verbs

2 Read the rules and choose the correct meaning.

1 Employees mustn't make private phone calls.
  a Private phone calls aren't allowed.
  b You can make private phone calls if you want.
2 Employees don't have to work fixed hours.
  a You need to work at the same time every day.
  b You choose when you work.
3 Employees have to follow the dress code.
  a You can wear what you want.
  b There are some clothes that you can't wear.
4 Employees can take breaks when they need them.
  a You take a break when you want to.
  b You need to tell the manager when you take a break.
5 Employees must clock in and out when they start and finish.
  a It's necessary to clock in and out.
  b It isn't necessary to clock in and out.
6 Employees can't call in sick without a doctor's note.
  a It's possible to call in sick without a doctor's note.
  b You need a doctor's note to call in sick.

-ing forms

3 Put the words in the correct order to make sentences.

1 type / he / without / looking / can
2 training / two / had / weeks / we / of
3 new / starting / she's / job / about / her / excited
4 part / looking / is / an / good / job / the / important / of
5 at / tea / work / hate / coffee / making / I / and
6 magazines / she's / working / instead of / always / reading

Present perfect

4 Write the dialogues with the correct form of the present perfect.

1 A: you / ever / try / skiing?
  B: Yes / we / go / skiing / in France / twice / so far.
2 A: what / you / done / with the remote control?
  B: I / not see / it / but / your mum / just / watch / a programme.
3 A: my son / stop / collecting / stamps.
  B: he / ever / think / about collecting / coins?
4 A: you / be / on holiday / this year?
  B: I / have / a busy year at work / so / I / not have / any time to relax.
5 A: She still / not finish / talking / on the phone.
  B: I hope / she / not call / that friend in Brazil.

2 Choose one of the dialogues. Think about what is happening and who is speaking. Write the next two lines.

5 Choose the correct ending.

1 They've built two amusement parks outside the city …
  a and they are going to build another.
  b two years ago.
2 They went on a roller coaster last summer and …
  a they love it.
  b they loved it.
3 She's been to the water park …
  a yesterday.
  b lots of times.
4 I've never been in a haunted house because …
  a I'm scared of the dark.
  b I was scared of the dark.
5 He bought a burger in the food area but …
  a it didn't taste very good.
  b it hasn't tasted very good.
6 We've visited a great theme park in South Korea …
  a when we were on holiday.
  b and one in Hong Kong too.

Unit 6

Comparative and superlative adjectives and adverbs

	Adjective	Comparative	Superlative
One syllable adjectives and adverbs: add -er/-est	fast slow big	fast**er** slow**er** big**ger**	the fast**est** the slow**est** the big**gest**
Adjectives ending in e: add -r/-st	nice	nic**er**	the nic**est**
Adjectives ending in y: change the y to ie and add –r/-st	dry	dr**ier**	the dr**iest**
Two or more syllable adjectives and adverbs that end in -ly: more/most + adjective or adverb	important quickly	**more** important **more** quickly	the **most** important the **most** quickly
Irregular adjectives and adverbs	good well bad	**better** **worse** **badly**	the **best** the **worst**

Language note: For one-syllable adjectives ending with one consonant, double the final consonant and add -er / -est. Some two syllable adjectives, especially adjectives ending in y can be used in either form (*more* + adjective or with -er / -est) angry – angrier / *more angry*

Use comparative adjectives to compare two things or people. Comparative adverbs compare two actions. *Than* is used after comparatives.
*People in warm countries are **happier** than people in cold countries.*
*I can run **faster** than you.*

Comparative adjectives and adverbs (*a bit, much, as … as*)

We can modify comparative adjectives and adverbs with *a bit* or *much*.
*That DVD player is **a bit** cheaper. This one is **much** cheaper.*

Use *(not) as … as* to make comparisons.
*My job is **as** exciting **as** yours.* (= both our jobs are equally exciting)
*My job isn't **as** exciting **as** yours.* (= your job is more exciting than mine)

Use *less* with longer adjectives to mean *not as much*.
*She's **less** intelligent than her sister.* (= her sister is more intelligent)

Superlatives

Use superlatives to compare someone or something in a group with all the other things in that group.
*This computer is **the cheapest** in the shop.*
*Shopping online is **the most convenient** method.*

Use superlatives with the present perfect.
*My girlfriend is **the most interesting** person **I've ever met**.*

Use superlatives with *in the …*
*The internet is **the best** invention **in the** world.*
*I'm **the tallest** person **in the** class.*

Phrasal verbs and objects

A phrasal verb is a two-word verb consisting of a verb + a particle. Some phrasal verbs take an object and some phrasal verbs don't.
• verb + particle
*Can you **log on**?*
• verb + particle + object
***Turn on** the computer.*

When phrasal verbs take an object, the object can usually go in two places:
• after the verb and particle
***Turn on** the computer.*
• between the verb and particle
***Turn** the computer **on**.*
If the object is a pronoun, it can only go between the verb and particle:
***Turn** it **on**.*
Not: ~~Turn on it.~~

Unit 6 Exercises

Comparative and superlative adjectives

1 Write the comparative and superlative forms of the adjectives in the table.

Adjective	Comparative	Superlative
tall		
hot		
content		
safe		
good		
expensive		
enjoyable		
cheap		
beautiful		
heavy		

Comparative adjectives (a bit, much, as … as)

2 Write comparisons using the prompts below.

1 he / be / patient / with the children / her
2 she / be / happy / now / last year
3 most people / get / a bit / fat / when / they / get / old
4 I / sleep / good / in my own bed / in a hotel
5 money / not be / as / important / health
6 this chair / be / much / comfortable / that one
7 some new robots / be / as / intelligent / humans
8 my home computer / starts / slowly / my work computer

Superlatives

3 Complete the sentences with the superlative form of the words in the box.

| expensive | fast | good | high | popular | strange |

1 The blog of a Chinese film actress has the _____ number of readers on the internet.
2 The _____ name for @ is *elephant's trunk* in Danish.
3 The _____ domain name cost $7.5 million.
4 Social networking is the _____ growing sector of the internet.
5 'How to kiss' and 'Who is God' were the _____ search questions in 2007.
6 Books are the things that sell the _____ on the internet.

Phrasal verbs and objects

4 Complete the sentences with the correct phrasal verb.

1 The music is too loud.
   Well, turn _____!
2 The TV isn't working.
   You need to plug _____.
3 These web pages are really interesting.
   Can you print _____?
4 How do I put the word into the search engine?
   Just type _____.
5 The phone's ringing.
   Well pick _____!
6 The computer is frozen.
   You have to shut _____.
7 We need to find out train times.
   Can you look _____?
8 I've found his email address.
   I'll write _____.

Grammar focus Unit 6   143

Unit 7

Present perfect with *for* and *since*

for ...	*since* ...
years	1999
ages	the 1960s
six months	this morning
a long time	2pm
	he was a child

Language note: don't use the present perfect with time expressions like *in the 90s, in 2005*. Use the past simple with these expressions.

Use the time expressions *for* and *since* with the present perfect to talk about unfinished time. *For* states the length of time and *since* is used with the beginning of the time.
How long have you worked here?
I've worked here **for** ten years.
I've worked here **for** ages.
I've worked here **since** 2000.
I've worked here **since** I was 25.

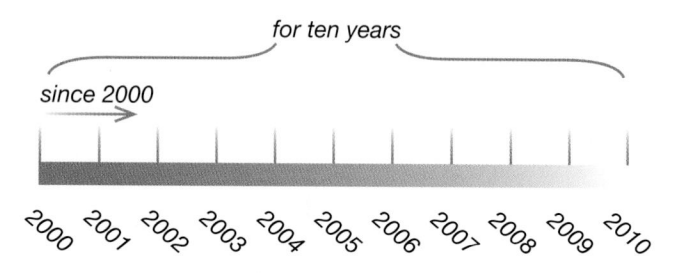

Present perfect with *yet* and *already*

Affirmative	Negative	Question
I/You/We/They have **already** eaten.	I/You/We/They haven't eaten **yet**.	Have I/you/we /they eaten **yet**?
He/She/It has **already** eaten.	He/She/It hasn't eaten **yet**.	Has he/she/it eaten **yet**?

Use *already* with the present perfect to emphasise that something has happened before now.

The structure is auxiliary + *already* + past participle. It is usually used in affirmative sentences.
I've **already** been to the bank.
I've **already** checked our account.

Use *yet* with the present perfect to talk about something that has not happened, but will probably happen soon.

Use *yet* in negatives and questions. *Yet* goes at the end of the sentence.
The money hasn't gone into my account **yet**.
Have you paid the bills **yet**?

Unit 7 Grammar focus

Unit 7 Exercises

Present perfect with *for* and *since*

1 Complete the sentences with *for* or *since*.
1. I've had this job _____ 2002.
2. She's known him _____ 20 years.
3. We've wanted children _____ ages.
4. I've liked travelling _____ I went on my first school trip.
5. I've been working here _____ a long time.
6. They haven't had anything to eat _____ 6am.
7. We've had the same TV _____ the 1990s.
8. I haven't seen her _____ days.

2 Complete the text with the present perfect or the past simple form of the verb in brackets.

Microwaves (1) _____ (*be*) a popular time saver for years. An American company (2) _____ (*produce*) the first microwave in 1947 – it was almost 1.8 metres tall! Families (3) _____ (*use*) smaller modern microwaves since the 1970s. But many people don't think it is safe. So, is microwaved food safe? The answer is 'yes' if you (4) _____ (*cook*) the food for the right length of time. Microwaves (5) _____ (*be*) particularly popular since companies (6) _____ (*start*) producing freezer to microwave 'ready-meals' in the late 1980s. The UK (7) _____ (*be*) the largest European consumer of microwave ready meals for years. But a report in 2008 (8) _____ (*say*) British people are now starting to eat more healthily.

Present perfect with *yet* and *already*

3 Write the dialogues. Use *already* and *yet*.
1. A: you / pay / the electricity bill?
   B: no but I / pay / the water bill.
2. A: we / not hear / about that loan.
   B: I / call / the bank / twice about it.
3. A: we / spend / all our money for this month.
   B: oh dear, / you / check / the lottery ticket?
4. A: our / railway shares / make / a profit.
   B: good / but the water shares / not improve.
5. A: you / have / the letter about your inheritance?
   B: no, the solicitor / not send / anything.

4 Correct the mistakes in these sentences.
1. Tom has lived in Germany for he was a child.
2. Has Emma got already married?
3. He hasn't done his homework already.
4. They have finished the book yesterday.
5. She's worked here since three months.
6. We haven't done this already.

Unit 8

The passive voice

Present passive		Past passive	
I **am**	shocked.	I **was**	shocked.
You/We/They **are**		You/We/They **were**	
He/She/It **is**		He/She/It **was**	

Form the passive with the verb *to be* + past participle.

Use the active voice to focus on the agent. (the person or thing who does the action)

    agent   *active verb*   *object*
Zaha Hadid designed the building.

Use the passive voice to focus on the action.
*The building **was designed** in 2005.*

If we want to say who did the action we can use *by* + agent.
*The building **was designed** in 2005 by a famous architect.*

We use the passive when we do not know who did the action (the agent), or it is not important.
*My bag **was stolen**.* (= I don't know who stole it)
*A bomb **was left** in the station.* (= we don't know who left the bomb)

Language note: the passive is more frequent in formal speech and writing.

First conditional

if clause		Main clause
If	+ present simple	I/you, etc. *will/can/might* (not) + verb

Use the first conditional to talk about a possible future situation.
*If it **is** bad weather, I'll watch TV. But if it's sunny, I'll go to the beach.*

Use *will*, *might* or *can* in the main clause:
- *will*: the speaker thinks it's likely that the situation will happen
- *might*: the speaker is not sure that the situation will happen
- *can*: the speaker is not sure if it will happen or not

The *if* clause can be the first or second clause in the sentence.
If we take the train, we'll enjoy the journey more.
We'll enjoy the journey more if we take the train.

Second conditional

if clause		Main clause
If	+ past simple	I / you, etc. *would / could* (not) + verb

Use the second conditional to talk about an unreal future situation. It is unlikely or almost impossible that the situation will happen.

*If I **didn't have** to work, I'd **go** to the beach today.*
(But I have to work so I won't go to the beach)
*If I **had** lots of money, I **could travel** round the world.*
(I don't have lots of money and it's unlikely that I will have lots of money in the future)

Language note: we sometimes say *If I were* instead of *If I was*. Both verbs are correct. *Were* is especially common in the expression *If I were you ...* when giving somebody advice.

Unit 8 Exercises

The passive voice

1 Write about eight modern buildings. Use the present or past passive. Sometimes you need *by*.
1. The Empire State Building in New York / use / in the *King Kong* film.
2. The two Emirates Towers in Dubai / connect to / a huge shopping centre.
3. 30 St Mary Axe in London / call / 'the Gherkin' / Londoners.
4. Sydney Opera House / build / to look like a ship.
5. The Guggenheim Museum in Bilbao / often / compare / to a fish or water.
6. The Petronas Towers in Kuala Lumpur / occupy / international companies.
7. The new Jewish Museum in Berlin / design / the architect Daniel Libeskind.
8. The Pompidou Centre in Paris / name / after a French president.

2 Rewrite these sentences with the passive so they mean the same.
We sold our flat last week.
Our flat was sold last week.
1. Somebody built the flats in the 1980s.
2. They call the building *Huntingdon House*.
3. Restaurants and cafés surround the building.
4. They painted the walls in our flat white.
5. We put in a new kitchen last year.

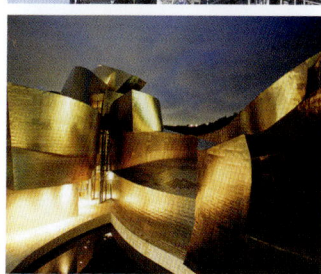

First conditional

3 Complete the sentences with the correct form of the first conditional.
1. If I _____ (*give*) you my email address, _____ (*you / send*) me the details?
2. I _____ (*call*) the police if I _____ (*see*) him again.
3. If you _____ (*not have*) a ticket you _____ (*not / can / get*) on the bus.
4. He _____ (*might / take*) you to the airport if he _____ (*have*) time.
5. If the weather _____ (*be*) nice, we _____ (*can / go*) to the top of the tower.
6. If we _____ (*go out*) for a meal, we _____ (*not have to*) go food shopping.
7. She _____ (*not listen*) to him if he _____ (*not tell*) her the truth.
8. If the internet _____ (*not work*) again, I _____ (*complain*) to the company.

Second conditional

4 Complete the conversation with the correct form of the second conditional.
A: What would you do (1) _____ (*if / you / be*) me?
B: Well, if I were in your shoes, (2) _____ (*I / go*) on a long trip.
C: Yes, I'd take a month's holiday tomorrow (3) _____ (*if / my boss / give / me*) time off.
B: If I had the choice, I think (4) _____ (*I / go / walking*) in New Zealand or Peru.
C: Yes, I'm sure I'd forget all my problems (5) _____ (*if / I / do*) something like that.
B: Perhaps your boss would help (6) _____ (*if / you / explain*) everything to her.

5 Match the conditional sentences.
1. If I went to America,
2. If we went on the bus,
3. If we take the credit card,
4. If I don't wear sandals,
5. If we go camping,
6. If I had a problem,

a. we won't have to look for accommodation.
b. I'd go to San Francisco.
c. we won't have to take lots of cash.
d. my feet will be too hot.
e. we'd save lots of money.
f. would you help me?

Grammar focus Unit 8 147

Unit 9

Modal verbs of advice

Use *should / shouldn't* (+ infinitive without *to*) to give advice and make suggestions.
You **should** go to bed if you don't feel well.
You **shouldn't** read in poor light – it's bad for your eyes.

We often use the structure *I (don't) think* with *should*.
I **don't think you should** drink any more.
Not: *I think you shouldn't drink any more.*

Ought to can be used instead of *should* but it is more formal. *Should* is more common.
You **ought to** take an aspirin.
You **ought not to** watch TV without your glasses.

Must is similar to *should* but it is stronger and more definite (see Grammar focus 5 page 140 for more on *must*).
You **must** take an aspirin.

Could / couldn't, had to / didn't have to

(For modals of obligation and possibility in the present, see Grammar focus 5 page 140)

Use *had to / didn't have to* to talk about past obligation.
I **had to** take tablets for a long time.
I **didn't have to** stay in hospital long.

Use *could / couldn't* to talk about things that were possible or not possible in the past.
When I was in hospital, I **couldn't** get out of bed.
We **could** have visitors in the afternoon.

Past perfect

Affirmative	Negative	Question
I/You/He/She/It/We/They had ('d) worked.	I/You/He/She/It/We/They had not (hadn't) worked.	Had I/you/he/she/it/we/they worked?

Use the past perfect to talk about an event in the past that happened before another event or a specific time in the past.
He cried because they **had lost** the match.
I **hadn't been** to a football match before last Saturday.

With *before* and *after*, we can use the past simple instead of the past perfect as the order of events is clear.
Before I started doing regular sport, I was overweight.
Before I started doing regular sport, I had been overweight.
The players celebrated **after** the match finished.
The players celebrated **after** the match had finished.

Use the past participles *been* and *gone* in the same way as in the present perfect (see Grammar focus 5 page 140).

they had lost the match   he cried

Past |————————↓————————↓————————| Present

Reported statements

Use reported statements to say what another person said.
I'm not feeling well. ⟶ He said that he wasn't feeling well.
I'm going to the doctor's. ⟶ He told me that he was going to go to the doctor's.

In reported statements, the verb goes one tense *back*.

Direct statements	Reported statements
present simple 'I *like* your new hairstyle.'	**past simple** She said (that) she *liked* my new hairstyle.
present continuous 'I'm *getting* married.'	**past continuous** He said (that) he *was getting* married.
present perfect 'We've *bought* the tickets.'	**past perfect** She said (that) they *had bought* the tickets.
past simple 'I *missed* the bus.'	**past perfect** He said (that) he *had missed* the bus.
will 'I'*ll see* you later.'	**would** She said (that) she *would* see me later.
am/is/are going to 'I'*m going to* join a gym.'	**was/were going to** She said she *was going to* join a gym.

In reported statements other words can also change:
- pronouns: 'We're meeting at **my** flat.' ⟶ He said that **they** were meeting at **his** flat.
- places: 'I got **here** by train.' ⟶ He said he had got **there** by train.
- this / that: 'I've just bought **this** book.' ⟶ He said he had just bought **that** book.
- times: 'I met her **last week**.' ⟶ He said he had met her **the week before**.

Be careful with *say and tell*:
- we say something (to somebody)
- we tell somebody (about something)
The doctor **told** me I was stressed. I **said** I knew that.

Unit 9 Exercises

Modal verbs of advice

1 Complete the second sentence so that it has a similar meaning to the first. Use *should* or *shouldn't*.

I think you need to stop smoking.
I think you should stop smoking.
1 Don't worry about it.
   You _____.
2 Go and see your doctor.
   You _____.
3 You don't drink enough water.
   I think you _____.
4 You drink too much coffee.
   I don't think _____.
5 Don't go to bed so late.
   You _____.

Could / couldn't, had to / didn't have to

2 Complete the text with *could*, *couldn't*, *had to* or *didn't have to*.

Yesterday, I broke my ankle while I was running. I (1) _____ walk so I (2) _____ phone my girlfriend and she (3) _____ take me to the hospital. Luckily I (4) _____ wait long for an X-ray. The doctor put a bandage on my foot and said I (5) _____ go home. Unfortunately I (6) _____ move for days and my girlfriend (7) _____ do everything for me. The only good thing was that I (8) _____ go to work.

Past perfect

3 Join the sentences. Use the past perfect.
1 She ran 20 km. She was tired.
   She was tired because _____.
2 I finished playing tennis. I took a shower.
   When _____.
3 The swimmer failed a drugs test. He lost his medal.
   The swimmer lost his medal because _____.
4 She was optimistic. She won the race.
   Before she won the race, _____.
5 The referee sent a player off. The team played with ten men.
   After _____.
6 She hurt another player. She paid a fine.
   _____ because _____.

Reported statements

4 Read the dialogue and report back the conversation between a doctor and a patient.

D: Good morning. You're obviously having trouble with your back.
P: Yes, I woke up this morning and I had problems getting out of bed.
D: Have you had this problem before?
P: No, I've never experienced that before.
D: OK, I'm just going to take a look. You'll feel a pain …
P: Ow! That hurt! … But my back feels much better.

She said that I was obviously having trouble with my back.
I told her that (1) _____ and _____.
She asked me if (2) _____.
I said that (3) _____.
She said that (4) _____.
Then she told me that I (5) _____.
I said that it (6) _____ but that my back _____.

Grammar focus Unit 9   149

Unit 10

Defining relative clauses

Defining relative clauses give more information about a person or a thing. Relative clauses are formed with *that / which* to describe things, *who* with people and *where* with places.

> **Language note:** we can use *that* instead of *who* and *which* but not instead of *where*.

He's the doctor **who / that** saved my life.
It's something **which / that** I don't like talking about.
I know a good Italian restaurant **where** we often go for lunch.
Not: ~~I know a good Italian restaurant that we often go for lunch.~~

Definite article (*the*)

Use *the* when a person or thing has been referred to before.
*We've found a new flat so we were painting **the** flat all last night.*

Use *the* when there is only one of this person or thing or it is clear which one it is.
*My parents met **the** Queen once.*

> **Language note:** we use *a / an* (for singular nouns) or zero article (for plural nouns) when we talk about things in general.
> *New Zealand is **a** country with many mountains, rivers and lakes.*

The can also be used:
- when it's part of a superlative phrase
*You're **the best thing** that has happened to me.*
- when it is part of a name (such as a river)
the *Mekong,* **the** *Black Sea,* **the** *Titanic,* **the** *Golden Gate Bridge*
- for nationalities and groups in society
the *British,* **the** *unemployed*

Verb form review

Present simple	I **work**.	See Grammar focus 1 page 132
Present continuous	I'm work**ing**.	See Grammar focus 1 page 132
Past simple	I work**ed**.	See Grammar focus 3 page 136
Past continuous	I **was** work**ing**.	See Grammar focus 3 page 136
Present perfect	I **have worked**.	See Grammar focus 5 page 140
Past perfect	I **had worked**.	See Grammar focus 9 page 148
will	I **will work**.	See Grammar focus 4 page 138
going to	I am **going to work**.	See Grammar focus 4 page 138

active	The company **makes** cars.	See Grammar focus 8 page 146
passive	The cars **are made** in Germany.	See Grammar focus 8 page 146
first conditional	If the bank **gives** me a loan, **I'll buy** a small second-hand car.	See Grammar focus 8 page 146
second conditional	If **I had** the money, **I'd buy** a fast sports car.	See Grammar focus 8 page 146
modals: obligation & possibility (present)	**can / can't** **must** **have to / didn't have to**	See Grammar focus 5 page 140
modals: advice	**should / shouldn't, ought to / ought not to**	See Grammar focus 9 page 148
modals: obligation & possibility (past)	**could / couldn't** **had to / didn't have to**	See Grammar focus 9 page 148

Both, neither

Use *both* to talk about two things. *Both* is used with a plural noun and a plural verb.
Both *cars are quite old.*

Use *neither* to say something negative about each of two things. *Neither* is used with a singular noun and verb.
Neither *car is very reliable.*

Use *both of* and *neither of* with a plural noun or pronoun.
Neither of *the cars is economical. Let's sell* **both of** *them.*

Unit 10 Exercises

Defining relative clauses

1 Complete the dialogues with *who, which, that* or *where*.

1. A: Who's that?
   B: He's a chef _____ has written lots of best-selling cookery books.
2. A: Can you recommend a hotel in New York?
   B: Yes, there's a good hotel _____ we stayed last year.
3. A: Hi, what's new?
   B: Well, I got the job _____ I told you about last time.
4. A: Where's the dictionary?
   B: Over there. It's the big blue book _____ is on that shelf.
5. A: Who were the first Europeans there?
   B: I think it was the Vikings _____ sailed there first.
6. A: What's that big building there?
   B: Oh, that's the new supermarket _____ you can shop 24 hours.

Definite article (*the*)

2 Complete the sentences with *a / an*, *the* or nothing (-).

New South Wales is (1) _____ state in (2) _____ south-east of Australia. It is (3) _____ oldest and most populated state in Australia and its capital Sydney is home to famous sights such as (4) _____ Sydney Opera House. It has (5) _____ very diverse climate with hot summers and cold winters. (6) _____ state has great locations for visitors: (7) _____ beautiful beaches, national parks and snowy mountains.

Verb form review

3 Underline the correct verb.

1. The first plane that *had to / could* be controlled in the air *was invented / invented* in 1903.
2. The plane *flew / has flown* for 12 seconds.
3. The Wright brothers *were making / had made* bicycles when they *became / were becoming* interested in planes.
4. They *built / were building* the plane after they *have watched / had watched* how birds fly.
5. The biggest passenger plane, the Airbus A380 *made / is making* its first flight in 2005.
6. Since then, several airlines *have ordered / had ordered* A380s.
7. Airbus *is planning / is going to plan* to produce an even bigger plane in the near future.
8. If everything *went / goes* according to plan, the new plane *will be / is being* nearly 80 metres long.

Both, neither

4 Rewrite the sentences about two friends using *both / neither* or *both of / neither of*. Sometimes more than one answer is possible.

1. The two friends live in a big city.
2. They aren't married.
3. The friends don't have a car.
4. Each friend owns property.
5. The two friends enjoy playing chess.
6. They've written books but their books haven't been published.

Grammar focus Unit 10   151

Audioscript

Unit 1

1.02
1 Sorry, yes. My last name is Torrance. That's T–O–R–R–A–N–C–E.
2 I live on Janssen Street. I'll spell that for you: J–A–N double S–E–N
3 Write this down. The name of the state is K–E–N–T–U–C–K–Y. That's Kentucky.

1.03
1 A: Oh, when was this photo taken?
   B: That one? Five years ago, I think.
   A: Mmmm. It's quite a good photo of you.
   B: I don't know. I don't think I looked good with that beard.
   A: I think you look nice and, mmm, intelligent.

1.04
2 A: How's the baby?
   B: Oh *great*. Great.
   A: It's a 'she', right?
   B: Yes, yes. I'll show you a photo. She looks like her father.
   A: Oh, yeah, bald just like her dad! How old is she?
   B: Six months now.
   A: She looks really happy. She's got a great smile.

1.05
3 A: Who's this a photo of?
   B: Don't you know? It's Bella!
   A: Bella? Oh yes! She looks so different here. How long ago was this?
   B: At the end of university.
   A: Wow. Her hair was much *longer* then, and so *curly*.

1.06
4 A: What does the suspect look like?
   A: I can't hear you. What does the suspect look like?
   B: The suspect is a white, older man.
   A: Anything else?
   B: Just a second ... yes. He's got grey hair and a moustache.
   A: What kind of car does he drive?
   B: An old white Volvo.
   A: Thanks.

1.07
1 Pilar is my Spanish neighbour. She's on vacation in Mexico, and I've got her cat and her plants.
2 OK, Hans. Hans and I aren't really friends. He's more of an acquaintance. He's director of the German department.
3 Ken is a colleague of mine at the university. He teaches French, and I teach German.
4 I take a computer class in the evening. Sofia is my classmate.

1.09
The theory of Six Degrees of Separation works like this. Imagine you and John are colleagues. John is married to Mary, but you don't know her personally. So you and Mary have one degree of separation. Mary has a sister, Jane. Jane and you have two degrees of separation. Jane's neighbour, let's call him Robert, works for a big hotel in the city centre. You and Robert, Jane's neighbour, have three degrees of separation. Robert doesn't own the hotel. He works for Mr. Smith, the president. You and Mr Smith ... four degrees of separation. Mr Smith, because he's an owner of a big expensive hotel, he's often in touch with important people. He's friends with the Ambassador for example. So you and the Ambassador have five degrees of separation. And well, the Ambassador goes to New York three times a year, and he knows the Secretary General of the United Nations. So, if you make all the right connections it means that you and the Secretary General of the United Nations have six degrees of separation.

1.10
A: What are you doing?
B: So, what do you do?
C: Excuse me, we're trying to work.
D: You're not listening!
E: How's it going?

1.11
1 A: Hello.
   B: Hello.
   A: First time here?
   B: Sorry?
   A: I said, is this your first time here? At the conference.
   B: Yes. Yes.
   A: Well, hello. My name's George.
   B: Hi George. Nice to meet you.

1.12
2 A: Oh, look at the time. It's getting late.
   B: What time is it?
   A: Eleven o'clock. And I have a class tomorrow.
   B: Oh. Well, OK then.
   A: Yes. Thanks for everything.
   B: No problem.
   A: Goodnight.
   B: Bye.

1.13
3 A: And this is from me.
   B: Aww.
   B: Oh my ...
   A: It's a dog! Isn't that great?
   B: Er, yes. A dog. Thank you very much.
   A: You're welcome. Happy birthday.

1.14
4 A: Hello? Oh hi, listen I'm on the train. It's not a good time right now...
   B: Hey!
   A: Wait a minute ... Oh, I'm sorry. I didn't see you and ...
   B: That's all right.
   A: Here, let me help you with your bag.
   B: No, it's fine.

Unit 2

1.18
Zao Shen is the god of the kitchen. He is a figure in Chinese mythology. He watches families and tells the other gods if a family is good or bad. He has the power to make families rich or poor. Zao Shen also protects the home from evil spirits. Many homes in China, Taiwan and Southeast Asia have a picture of Zao Shen in the kitchen.

1.20
Human beings need water to live. A human being can live for weeks without food, but only a few days without water. We often hear that our body is two thirds water, but what exactly does water do to help the human body?

Water helps to protect important parts of the body, such as the eyes. The brain is 75% water. We also need water to breathe, and to keep our body temperature normal. Water carries nutrients and oxygen to all parts of the body. Blood is, in fact, 92% water. In addition, water helps to convert food into energy and removes waste from the body. It is also very good for a person's skin. Even the bones in our body are made up of 22% water.

The human body gets water not only from water itself but also from other drinks and food. Water is a major part of many foods, particularly fruit and vegetables, which may contain from 85 to 95% water. Because the amount of water we need may change with climate, level of activity, diet and other factors, there is no one recommendation for how much daily water you need to drink. However, adults typically need at least two litres (eight cups) of water a day, from all sources.

1.23
1 A: Good evening.
   B: Hello. It's a table for two, please. We've got a reservation.
   A: Name?
   B: Moore, that's M – double O-R-E.
   A: Ah, yes. Just this way.
   A: Now, what would you like to order?
   C: I'll have the fish.
   B: Just a minute. I haven't seen everything on the menu yet.
   C: Sorry, then can we have another minute to decide?
   A: Of course.

1.24
2 A: Here you go. Anything to drink?
   B: Sorry, I think there's a mistake here. I wanted a hamburger, not a hot dog.
   A: OK, sorry. Just a minute. One hamburger, please.
   B: Thanks.
   A: Anything to drink?
   B: Uh… A diet Coke, please.
   A: Small, medium or large?
   B: Small, please.

1.25
3 A: More coffee?
B: No thanks, I'm fine.
A: Did you enjoy your breakfast?
B: It was lovely, thanks.
A: Good.
B: Could I have the bill?
A: You have to pay over there for the buffet service.
B: Sorry, where?
A: Over there, next to the plants and the exit sign.
B: Oh, I see it. Thanks again.
A: You're welcome.

1.27
1 Mo, Iran
Typical traditional Persian food. It consists of rice and minced lamb, kebabs and chickens and dried fruit.

1.28
2 Gianfranco, Italy
Pizza. Of course not Pizza Hut but Napoli pizza. Yes, pizza, lasagne and pasta.

1.29
3 Elena, Russia
Borsch – it's very interesting – it's like a salad. But it's boiled in water, I don't know, with beetroot, with onion, potato, with meat, or maybe with chicken, or maybe with turkey. Yeah and it's very tasty really.

1.30
4 Marlies, Germany
A schnitzel dish. It's kind of a meat, it's fried and you most often have it with French fries and salad or potato salad which is rather typical of German food again.

1.31
5 Matt, US
Candy makes me think of home. There are certain candy brands that whenever I see them they remind me of my childhood and they remind me of growing up in the United States.

1.32
6 Sonia, Spain
Spanish tortilla makes me think of home and that's a very typical answer but I think it is a very simple dish which is made from eggs and potatoes and it's made like any other tortilla.

Unit 3

1.38
In 1877, Thomas Edison made one of the first ever sound recordings. Edison predicted that sound recordings would be used for office dictation, speaking books, education, talking clocks and music.
In 1903, the first records were released with recordings on both sides. People used to listen to these on record players called gramophones.
In the nineteen-twenties sound recording met film. The first films with sound were called 'talking pictures'.
In 1962 the company Philips introduced the audio cassette tape player. One year later the first discotheque in America opened in Los Angeles.
The seventies and eighties saw the introduction of VHS video, cassette Walkman and CD. The CD revolutionised the music industry.
It was in the early nineties that digital music and video appeared. In 1996 the first digital music player was sold in Japan. One year later the first MP3 player came out. But it wasn't until the beginning of the 21st century that digital music and MP3 players really began to become popular. In 2001 Apple released the first iPod, a portable MP3 player.
The history of sound recording has always been to make devices that are smaller, but contain more sound. The first record played for only six minutes and needed a large machine to play it on. The current generation of music players go in your pocket and can hold more than 15,000 songs, video and photographs.

1.42
Music has always been a very important part of film and television. A film can be completely transformed depending on the kind of music you use.
For example, if you want the audience to feel scared you want to use some kind of tension music. Here is an example of music that makes people feel tense or scared. It uses violins played on a very high note and very quickly.
Gentle music is good for making an audience feel calm and safe. I use guitar, violin or even piano. This kind of music is good with love scenes.
I sometimes use choral music for certain special scenes, or to make people feel sad. I use this for when a character dies in a film.
Finally, sometimes individual characters or ideas in a film have their own kind of music. I did the music for the British television programme *Robin Hood*, and every time the character of Robin appears you hear this kind of music. It uses trumpets, which are always good instruments for heroes.
In the past, to record the music for a film, the orchestra used to play in front of a large screen showing the movie, so the composer could get the timing just right. Now with computers, it isn't so necessary. Everything is much easier, and we do a lot of the work in the studio.

1.44
1 A: So, what did you think?
B: I don't know. Horror films, well, they should be thrilling, you know, be a bit scary.
A: I think so too.
B: And that film wasn't.
A: Oh come on, it was.
B: No, I don't agree. It was not scary.

1.45
2 A: Now, you believe that there are too many big budget action films in the cinema.
B: That's right.
A: And that there should be more space for films from around the world. More 'world cinema'.
B: Exactly. There are lots of great films from other countries, but we only see our own American films here. And I don't think that's right.
A: I agree with you there, John. So what films do you think we should see?
B: Well …

1.46
3 A: What about this one?
B: What, a musical?
A: I know you think that musicals are terrible.
B: Absolutely, you're absolutely right. They are awful!
A: Well, maybe but … I read this one was different. We always see the same films anyway.
B: Oh please. We see lots of different films. Last week we saw a French film.
A: Fine, you choose the DVD then.

Unit 4

1.48
A: …?
B: OK, well. My name's Josh Gross and this is Helle Hansen.
C: Hi.
B: And … well, we're aid workers with the Danish organisation Milene Nielsen Foundation. Helle, do you want to… say something about it?
C: It's starting a new project in Guatemala next month. We're going to be in a small village …
B: In the mountains.
C: In the mountains. It's a very poor place.
A: …?
C: We're going to work with the children there.
B: Basically, we're going to be responsible for the children during the day. Playing, cooking…
C: Cleaning …
A: …?
B: I'm a teacher originally, and Helle has a background in child psychology. We both wanted to help people.
C: I fell in love with Guatemala when I was there on a holiday two years ago. The people are friendly and the country is beautiful. I remember thinking: 'I'm coming back here one day.'
B: It's going to be my first time in Guatemala. I'm looking forward to going on this trip very much.
C: Yeah, me too.
A: …?
B: Good question. I guess I would say that hope is the most important thing. If you don't have hope, you don't have anything.
C: Yes, this is especially true when you're working with people who have, really, *lost* hope. If you have hope, well that helps you keep going.

Audioscript 153

Audioscript

A: …?
B: Thanks. We'll let you know how it goes.
C: Thank you.

1.52

A: *An Inconvenient Truth?* Isn't that a documentary from a few years ago about global warming? No, I haven't seen it, no. I heard it was interesting.
B: Well, of course I knew about global warming a bit before I saw the film… but, well …. wow. I mean, it really makes me think about what I'm going to do. If we don't do something now, we'll have serious problems in the future.
C: All I want to say is that I saw this film. It was a great documentary, and it's very, very important.
D: Oh, yes I remember this film. I saw it after Al Gore won the Nobel Peace Prize. I learnt a lot. It was different from a usual Hollywood film.
E: I didn't like it. These kinds of documentary films are always frightening. And anyway, when this climate change happens, I'll be dead. So I don't want to worry about it now.
F: I haven't but my son saw this film at school, in his geography class. He was talking about it all evening. He said: "You'll think differently after you see it." I think it's good that he learns about this kind of thing at school.

1.53

1 A: Oh. Look at the time. My train's leaving soon.
   B: Shall I pay for these?
   A: That would be great.
   B: OK. Wait. I don't have enough for both of them.
   A: Hold on. How much is it?
   B: £2.75.
   A: I'll pay for it. Here's five. I really have to go now though.
   B: Thanks again. Have a good trip, and see you next Monday!
   A: Bye! See you Monday.

1.54

2 A: Hey! What time do you need to get to the airport?
   B: I'm planning to be there two hours before the flight. Why?
   A: Well, look at the time. The airport train leaves in five minutes.
   B: Oh no.
   A: I'm sorry, we were talking and I didn't see the time…
   B: No, don't worry. I … I won't take the train. I'll take a taxi.
   A: A taxi? They're quite expensive. Let me drive you to the airport.
   B: Really? That would be great. Thanks.
   A: No problem. We can continue our conversation in the car.

1.55

3 A: Can I help you?
   B: Yes, thanks. Erm, I … I've missed my train. Can I use this ticket for the next train?
   A: Yes, you can. The next train is the six o'clock fast train. You'll need to pay an extra ten euros for that. Or you can take the six fifty train and you don't have to pay anything extra.
   B: OK, I'll take the six fifty train then. Thank you.
   A: You're welcome.

1.56

1 A: Are you ready to order?
   B: Yes. I'll have a salad.
2 A: I don't understand this.
   B: That's all right. I'll help you.
3 A: The next train is in twenty minutes.
   B: Shall we take it or wait?
4 A: Here, let me take those bags.
   B: Thanks, but it's OK. I'll carry them.

1.57

1 Abdul, Libya
   Actually I'm learning English because it will be helpful for my career.

1.58

2 Olga, Russia
   I'm learning English because first of all I want to be a teacher of English in my country.

1.59

3 Mert, Turkey
   I would like to work for some companies who work in Canada and USA and they need really good English skills and I have to speak English very well and to work for them.

1.60

4 Naif, Saudi Arabia
   Well I believe that English is very important nowadays as you cannot continue studying without using English because it's the international language nowadays.

1.61

5 Arthur, France
   I am learning English because I love it. I love the English culture, the American culture, its movie, its music.

1.62

6 Dain, South Korea
   English is a world language so we need to study English. It's essential. And personally I want to be a politician or I want to be a diplomat, which my father wants. So I think English is the most important thing for a politician or a diplomat so that's why I am studying English in Britain now.

Unit 5

1.63

1 Oh, hello, good to see you. Listen, somebody has to work this Saturday morning. Susan has called in sick. Now, I know that you've worked every Saturday this month, but there isn't anyone else. That all right? You can take next Saturday off.

1.64

2 Excuse me? Yes, come here, please. Now, I don't know if anybody told you, but we have a dress code here. Employees mustn't wear jeans to work. It's not allowed. You don't have to wear a jacket and tie, but try to be a little bit more formal.

1.65

3 No, no, NO. How many times do I have to say this? You *can't* use the computer to send private emails and you *can't* send personal messages to each other on the computer. You are on company time, and you *must respect* that time. That means *working* everybody, and *not talking*.

1.66

4 It's *OK*, you know. Of course you can go on your lunch break now. You don't have to come in to my office and ask me every time. I like to keep things informal around here, and as long as everyone does their work then I don't see a problem. All right? By the way, I recommend the Italian restaurant on the corner if you don't know where to go. *Very* good pasta.

1.69

Good afternoon. My name is Robert Macarthur, and I'm here to talk to you about the serious leisure perspective.
The serious leisure perspective comes from the expert on leisure, Robert Stebbins, at the University of Calgary in Canada. He has been working on this theory since 1974. According to Stebbins, there are two main forms of leisure: casual leisure and serious leisure.
Casual leisure is just that, casual. Sitting about at home is casual leisure. Doing nothing is casual leisure. Watching television, reading a book. Maybe just going for a walk or chatting with friends over dinner. People enjoy doing these activities because they feel good, because they're relaxing, because they're fun.
For many of us here in America, leisure has a bad reputation because it's not work. We live in a society that says work is more important than leisure because leisure is lazy.
But there is another form of leisure, called serious leisure. Serious leisure activities are activities which lead to personal development. Doing a sport regularly, like cycling, running, skiing, or swimming are examples of serious leisure.
Serious leisure activities can also include making things, or collecting things. Here, for example, is an image of a website for collectors of rubber ducks. This is funny, yes, but an example of serious leisure too.
Finally, serious leisure can mean volunteer work. By volunteer work, I mean unpaid work helping

people other than your family. For example, volunteering in a local hospital. Or in a school. Or in a home for old people.

I believe serious leisure is important because it's fun, yes, but it also satisfies a need in us, it can change our lives.

And now, moving on to my own research …

1.73

1 A: Right. Hello and thanks again for coming. The purpose of today's meeting is to give you all the information about …
   B: Excuse me. Could I just ask a question?
   A: Yes, Mrs Davies.
   B: My son doesn't have all the books yet. Is this a problem?
   A: Not at all. We can talk about the books in just a moment.
   C: Can I add that my daughter doesn't have the books either? They haven't arrived.
   A: Thank you, Mr Brown. Please don't worry about it now …

1.74

2 A: And I think you will find that the starting salary is *very* good.
   B: Yes. Thank you. May I ask about working hours again? I'm not sure that I understood. What time do you expect me to arrive in the morning?
   A: Seven o'clock.
   B: Fine. Seven o'clock. That's early.
   A: We need people early in the morning to talk to our European offices.
   B: Of course.
   A: Is there a problem?
   B: No, not at all. Not at all.

1.75

3 A: OK, so the next item on the agenda is …
   B: Can I say something here?
   A: Is it about wages?
   B: No, it isn't.
   A: All right then. Because we aren't talking about wages in this meeting.
   B: Can I just say that the dress code we have now is terrible. Terrible.
   A: Thank you, David.
   B: I *hate* these ties.
   A: I know … which is why we're talking about a change in the dress code.
   B: Can I also mention that the trousers are so *uncomfortable*.

Unit 6

2.02

1 I did this last summer. It was an interesting part-time job – much more interesting than the other jobs I've had. There were 15 of us in total. The study was in Texas and the scientists were looking at the effects of no gravity on the human body. For the study we had to stay in bed for 15 days. Every day the scientists put us in a special machine that turned us around and around upside down for an hour really quickly. I felt like my brain was in my stomach after the first day. But … at the end of the project I got $6,000

– enough to get me to Los Angeles and to look for work as an actor.

2.03

2 Many people think my work is just disgusting, but I think it's interesting. I spend all day working in people's rubbish. It's not as bad as you think. Not always, anyway. I often work at a city landfill, you know, the place where they put all the rubbish. Sometimes I study specific kinds of rubbish. I'm finishing a project at the moment on office rubbish: paper, plastic, that kind of thing. Office rubbish is much less disgusting than restaurant rubbish. That was last year's project.

2.07

1 www.ebay.it, that's I-T for Italy.
2 j324@hotmail.com
3 www.facebook.com
4 www.itt.com/english
5 Jason_17@gmail.com
6 www.myspace.com
7 www.amazon.de, not com, D-E…
8 sean@yahoo.co.uk, that's S-E-A-N at Y-A-H-O-O dot C-O dot U-K

2.08

1 A: OK. Try now.
   B: No. It's still not working.
   A: Nothing? Can you see anything on the screen?
   B: Yes. But when I click on the internet button nothing happens.
   A: And now?
   B: Yes! It's working now. Oh *thank you thank you*. What did you do?
   A: The cable was old. I took a new cable and connected it up to the internet again.

2.09

2 A: So, tell me the problem again?
   B: OK, when I try to print out a document the computer prints out a *different* document.
   A: You mean, not the one you want to print?
   B: That's right.
   A: Have you tried …
   B: I've tried everything!

2.10

3 A: No, no, it's OK, the computer person is here now. You're here.
   B: Yes? What's the problem?
   A: Well, I try to open my email … and … I get this.
   B: Urg … yuk.
   A: Yeah. Disgusting, huh?
   B: Yeah. OK. Shut down the computer and leave it.
   A: Is it a virus or something?
   B: I'm afraid so.

2.11

4 A: Oh no. No!
   B: What's wrong?

A: The laptop's gone down again!
B: Did you save your work?
A: No.
B: You should really back up all your work. I always do.
A: Great …Thanks for the advice.

2.12

5 A: OK, ready to do this?
   B: Yep. Definitely.
   A: First, click on this button here.
   B: OK … done.
   A: Now log on to the system.
   B: What?
   A: Log on. Type in your username and password.
   B: Oh.
   A: What?
   B: I can't remember my password!

2.15

A: Hi, excuse me. I noticed your bag. Are you going to the Technology conference?
B: That's right.
A: Me too! Could we share a taxi?
B: Sure.
A: The conference centre, please.
C: OK.
A: Have you been to San Francisco before?
B: Er, no. No I haven't.
A: Neither have I. Nice weather.
B: Mm.
A: My name's Frank, by the way.
B: Nice to meet you. Claudia.
A: Hi Claudia. Where are you from, Claudia?
B: Frankfurt.
A: Wow. Frankfurt. You don't have a German accent at all.
B: I went to school in England.
A: So did I. Well, I'm English so … I guess that's normal.
B: Yes, I guess.
A: So … do you work for ABT Technology?
B: Yes. I work in the Frankfurt office. This is my first conference.
A: Oh, I've been to lots of conferences. They're very boring you know.
B: Really?
A: Oh yes. The worst part is listening to our president, Lance Thomas.
B: Really?
A: Gosh yes. His talks are so boring. But the evening party is quite good. Do you like parties?
B: No, not really.
A: Ah. Me neither. Not really.
B: Thanks, Frank.
A: You're welcome. Are you staying in the conference hotel?
B: No, I'm not.
A: Ha. Neither am I. It's horrible. Where's your hotel?
B: I er… I don't know. Oh look, here's my husband.

Audioscript

A: Oh. Oh.
B: Lance, this is Frank. Frank, this is my husband Lance.
A: Oh ...Er ...
D: Nice to meet you, Frank. Glad you could be here.
A: Hi.

2.16
1 Honor, England
I think that the most useful technical advance for me has been the internet, yes, because I can do things like booking tickets and so forth.

2.17
2 Arthur, France
Television is very important for the information and for entertainment.

2.18
3 Sara, Italy
The most important useful technological advance is, we could say now is a computer. It's very important. I think that nobody could really live or work without a computer.

2.19
4 Antonis, Greece
I think the plane. The aeroplanes, yeah.

2.20
5 Maxim, Russia
I think that most important technological advance for me it is SMS services, of course so mobile phone, but especially SMS services.

2.21
6 Starla, England
For me the most technological advance I'd say is the internet because it's convenient and quick and saves you a lot of time.

2.22
7 William, Ghana
Well, I think the internet is the most important, especially when you are looking for information.

Unit 7

2.25
The concept of time in the English language, and in western culture in general, is very much linked to money. Time can be seen as a form of currency. You can spend time and money, or save it. Time can be wasted. You can give someone your time, just like you can give them money. We have free time, extra time, spare time and overtime. We can convert time into money, and money into time. Time, money and work are intimately connected.

2.35
1 A: Do you speak English?
B: A little.
A: How much is the shirt?
B: This one?
A: No. The checked one.
B: Hundred and fifty.
A: A hundred and fifty? That's expensive.
B: You can have it for a hundred and twenty-five.
A: A hundred and ten?
B: Sorry, no. A hundred and twenty-five.
A: No thanks. I'll leave it.
B: OK! OK! A hundred and ten.

2.36
2 A: Hello. Can I help you?
B: Can I have some of these, please?
A: Which ones, love?
B: The red and white ones. They'll look nice in the living room.
A: Right. Here you are. Three pounds.
B: Thank you.
A: Would you like one of these small plants? They're lovely at this time of year.
B: Oh. All right. How much is it?
A: Only 75p.
B: I'll take it. Here you are.
A: Here's your change.
B: Goodbye now.
A: Bye.

2.37
3 A: ¿Puedo ayudarte?
B: Sorry, I don't speak Spanish.
A: Can I help you?
B: No, I'm just looking, thanks.
A: OK.
B: Sorry, yes. How much is this book?
A: Two euros.
B: Only two euros. That's cheap.
A: Yes. I put the price at ten euros. Nobody wants to buy it. At five euros. Nobody wants to buy it. So I made it cheap. Two euros. Do you want to buy it?
B: Oh.
A: What's wrong?
B: I'm the author.
A: The author?
B: Yes. I wrote it. I'll take it. For two euros.

Unit 8

2.41
1 The Tower of London was originally built in 1078. It was used as a home for the kings and queens of England for almost six hundred years, but also served as a prison. Two of the most famous prisoners in the Tower were the young princes Edward and Richard. In 1483, Richard the Third, their uncle and king of England, put them in the tower. They were never seen again. The princes were ten and thirteen years old. Today, people say the tower is haunted by their ghosts.

2.42
2 A: Look, look!
B: Oh, I recognise this place. It's from a film.
A: Yes, it's the house from some scary movie.
B: Right! It was used in the film *Psycho*.
A: Hold on, the guide says … this is probably one of the most well-known film set houses in Hollywood history. The old house and motel next to it were built originally for the Hitchcock film *Psycho* in the 1960s.
B: Mmm.
A: Sometimes, at Halloween, the house and motel are opened for the public to come and stay.
B: Brrr. Staying at this place on Halloween? No thank you.

2.43
3 Well, welcome to Bran Castle, one of the most famous castles in Romania. The castle was occupied by the government in communist times, but was returned to its owners in 2006.
Of course, as many of you know, the castle is known as Dracula's castle. People believe that Vlad Tepes – the original Dracula – lived here. This isn't exactly true, however, but he *was* kept as a prisoner here for some time. The castle is now a famous tourist attraction, and it is visited every year by thousands of people.

2.46
1 A: Well, now is really the time to visit the United States.
B: Really?
A: Oh *yes*. The dollar is not very strong, so things are really cheap.
B: Oh. I wanted to go to France. But, cheap is good.
A: Listen, if you travel this month you'll get an extra twenty per cent discount.
B: This month isn't possible.
A: Next month?
B: Yes. I have a week's holiday next month. Are there any specials then?
A: I'll ask if you like.
B: Yes, please.

2.47
2 A: And here is the main square and the tower. The tower is more than five hundred years old, and is the tallest building in the city. The view from the top of the tower is truly amazing. Today, with this beautiful sunshine, if you go up the tower, you won't regret it.
B: Excuse me, does it cost anything to go up the tower?
A: I'm afraid so. It costs eight euros.

2.48
3 A: These are the carpets. I thought you were going to show me the food part. And have some lunch.
B: Yes, yes. The food is on the other end of the market. Do not worry, my friend. We'll go there later if you want. As your guide, though, I have to show you everything. Look, isn't this amazing?
A: Mmm.

B: Some of these carpets take more than two months to make. They are all made by hand.
A: I'm just hungry, that's all.
B: Are you sure? If you buy one of these carpets now, I can get a good price for you.
A: Oh. Well …
B: She says if you buy two she will give you a *big* discount.
A: OK, then. How much …?

2.51
1 A: Hello, Greenway Holidays.
B: Hi, my name's Pablo Alonso. I'm calling about the English learning holiday.
A: You need to speak to Mrs Knight. I'll put you through.
B: Thank you.
A: Just a moment, please.

2.52
2 B: Hello?
A: I'm sorry, but the line's busy. Do you want to hold?
B: OK, I'll hold.

2.53
3 A: Hello?
B: Hello, is that Mrs Knight?
A: No, I'm afraid she isn't here.
B: Can't you give me information about the English learning holiday?
A: I'm sorry, I can't. Can I take a message?
B: No, that's all right. I'll call back.

2.54
4 A: Hello, Greenway Holidays.
B: Hello, this is Pablo Alonso again. Can I speak to Mrs Knight?
A: I'll put you through.
C: Sandra Knight speaking. Sorry to keep you waiting.
B: Oh, hello. My name's Pablo Alonso. I'm calling about the English learning holiday.
C: What would you like to know?
B: Well, I've looked on your website and I have a few questions about the cost.
C: Right, of course, Mr Alonso. Our prices, I think you'll find, are very competitive …

2.56
1 David, Georgia
So homes in Georgia are very big – some big ones and so we have two kind of homes. There are block of flats – there are many of them and we also have houses. Houses usually are in the outside of the country – in the villages.

2.57
2 Elena, Russia
In my country we have different homes like in England, because in England many people live in cottages, yes, but in my country we have very big houses. Many flats, but not so big, but good, and mostly Russian families have a cottage – it's not a cottage, it's maybe a little house in the countryside where we can grow fruit and vegetables but we don't live in these cottages, but what I can say more. Maybe prices – if you buy – if you sell your flat in Moscow – little flat – you can buy three houses in Great Britain.

2.58
3 Valería, Bolivia
I would say homes in Bolivia are much more coloured. Here, above all in Oxford, all the homes looks very similar I would say but in Bolivia you can find a red house just besides a yellow house and it is a pretty nice combination of colours.

2.59
4 Katie, Northern Ireland
Where I live in Belfast homes are … they're quite varied. In inner city Belfast you have very small red brick terraced houses. Two up two down houses and they're – I think they date from the 1800s – they sort of typify whenever you think of the city you think of red brick terraced houses.

2.60
5 Bea, England
Homes where I live are quite large. In my street in particular the houses have four or five bedrooms. They are usually shared between lots of different house mates. I personally live with two people I didn't know before and now one of them is a very good friend. The houses have kitchens and separate living rooms and dining rooms and the best thing about my house is that it has a large garden.

Unit 9

2.61
The common cold can be caused by more than 200 different viruses.
An adult gets between two and five colds a year, while for children or babies the number is higher; between 6 and 10 colds a year.
From the moment you get a cold to the moment you feel the symptoms is between 24 and 48 hours.
The total time in your life that you will have a cold is two to three years.
The common cold is not a deadly disease, but it is expensive. In the US alone, experts estimate that it costs the economy 3.5 billion dollars in lost time at work and school.

2.65
1 You should eat hot chicken soup as soon as you feel ill.
2 Just drink water. Lots of water.
3 Drink orange juice and lots of vitamin C.
4 I think you should eat foods with vitamin A, like carrots.
5 Drink hot water with lemon and honey in it.
6 I think you should drink water with a spoonful of salt.
7 Breathing hot steam works. Go for a sauna.
8 You should eat garlic. It works, I promise!
9 Just take two aspirin and stay in bed.
10 Cold medicine. Take cold medicine.
11 You shouldn't do any exercise. You should stay in bed. Don't go out.
12 I don't think you should stay in bed. Be active. Go out.
13 What you should do, what you really *ought to* do, is to wash your hands regularly.
14 You should stay dry. Don't wash your hair or go out in the rain.

2.70
A: Harry, is that you?
B: Yes, yes… I'm home.
A: Well, what did the doctor say?
B: Er. Nothing much. She said I was healthy. No serious problems.
A: Oh, that's wonderful. Did she say anything about a diet?
B: A what?
A: A diet.
B: Oh, oh yes. She said, she said… I could eat *some* red meat. Just once a week.
A: That's good. You do eat a lot of meat. What about salt and sugar? Shouldn't you cut down on those?
B: Um. No, no she didn't say anything about salt or sugar.
A: Oh. That's strange. What about coffee?
B: Er, coffee, yes, coffee.
A: You drink five cups of coffee a day. Isn't that too much?
B: Oh yes. She told me that I could only drink … two cups a day.
A: OK. And can you go back to work?
B: Yes. I start tomorrow.

2.72
A: Hello, can I help?
B: Yes, I erm, need something for a sore throat. It really hurts.
A: Well, we have this syrup or these tablets.
B: Which is better?
A: They're both good. The syrup is more expensive.
B: Oh, well … I'll take the tablets then. How many do I take?
A: Just one …
B: Sorry. I'm sorry. And how often should I take it?
A: Just one every four to six hours. Take it before mealtimes. Are you allergic to any medicine?
B: No.
A: Then you'll be fine with this.
B: Can I get some antibiotics too?
A: I'm afraid you need a prescription for that.
B: Oh.
A: You know, you should really see a doctor if that cough continues.
B: I know. I know.
A: Anything else?
B: No thanks.
A: That'll be £4.50 then, please.

Audioscript 157

Audioscript

Unit 10

2.73
A: So, your book *Brave New Words* is all about new words in English. How do new words appear?
B: One of the most common ways of making new words is simply to combine two words which already exist. So for example in the past we had texts, and we had messages, now with mobile phones we have …
A: Text messages.
B: Yes. That's right. Another common way of making a new word is to combine parts of words. Consider brunch. Brunch is a meal that people can have at 11 o'clock in the morning, a combination of breakfast and lunch.
A: So combinations are how new words are made.
B: There are other ways too. Abbreviations, for example, are a common way of making new words. Do you know what a digital versatile disc is?
A: Er …
B: A DVD …?
A: Of course.
B: Yes, the abbreviation becomes the new word. Another way is to give a word a new meaning. We have new meanings for all kinds of words connected to computers – for example mouse and virus.
A: Or windows.
B: Yes. Finally, we can borrow words from other languages. An example of this would be a tsunami – a Japanese word which became very frequent in English after the natural disaster in Asia in 2004.
A: Will all these new words continue to exist?
B: Maybe not. Some will continue, others won't. But the way we create these new words … combination, abbreviation, giving old words new meanings or borrowing words … well these are going to be with us for a long time.

2.77
In 1929 many people in the United States suddenly lost their jobs. This was the beginning of what Americans call the Great Depression, and it lasted for about four years. During the Great Depression, two of the most famous board games in the world were invented: Monopoly and Scrabble. While the games are very different, the story behind each one is similar …
Alfred Butts, the inventor of Scrabble, and Charles Durrow, the inventor of Monopoly, were both American. Neither inventor had a job. Butts had lost his job as an architect in 1929, and Durrow was an unemployed sales representative in 1933.
At the beginning, the inventors made every edition of their game by hand. Neither game was accepted by toy companies at first.
They said that Monopoly was too complicated, and that nobody would be interested in Scrabble.
Both games are played on a board, and can be played by two or more people.
Both games have been extremely popular: according to its makers, more than 750 million people have played Monopoly, and two hundred million copies of Scrabble are sold every year.
Both of them are successful worldwide. They are published in over 25 languages today, and are available in more than 80 countries.

2.79
1
A: Oh, hello, there you are.
B: Hello.
A: Listen, I'm afraid there's some bad news.
B: Oh?
A: Yes. The thing is, the company is closing.
B: Really? When?
A: Tomorrow. The whole thing. It's been sold.
B: Sold?
A: Yep.
B: So… so, what's going to happen to everyone?
A: There'll be an official announcement. Oh, here's my floor.
B: Er … I'm still …
A: Anyway. Sorry to rush off. Talk later, OK?
B: OK. Bye.
A: Goodbye.

2.80
2
A: Phew. Isn't it hot?
B: Hmm. Sorry?
A: I said, isn't it hot?
B: Yes. Yes. Very hot.
A: I can't remember a summer like this since … since the nineteen seventies.
B: Yes. It is very hot.
A: Nineteen seventy-six it was.
B: I don't really remember, I was quite … young then.
A: I guess you were. Well, it was so hot that…
B: Really.
A: Yes. I was in love then …
B: Oh look. Here's my floor.
A: Oh.
B: Well, I have to go. Nice to talk to you.
A: Yes, yes.
B: Goodbye.

2.82
1 I know, I know. It *was* funny. Anyway … talk to you tomorrow OK? Yep.
2 …and so that's what we'll do. Right, that's it. We'll continue after the break, OK?
3
A: What time does the film start?
B: Nine o'clock.
A: Nine o'clock. OK, see you then.
B: OK, bye.
4 Well, I think that's it. Yes, I'll send the email. Bye.
5
A: Was there anything else?
B: No … I don't think so.
A: All right. You can pay over there.
B: Thanks. Bye.
A: Bye.

2.83
1 Arthur, France
My favourite expression in English is 'Oh my god'! That's it! Because we heard this expression very often in movie, in television and I think it's a cliché of the English people or American people. Oh my god.

2.84
2 Diego, Italy
There are a lot of very interesting words in English. My favourite word is for example love.

2.85
3 Kristina, Russia
My favourite words in English. I think when I came to England last year everybody said, oh he looks gorgeous and it's gorgeous, the weather is gorgeous and so it became my favourite word.

2.86
4 Elodie, Switzerland
My favourite words in English are – I really like the word perhaps. I don't know why – because of the sound, because of the pronunciation, I don't know. Perhaps. What else? Well I don't know.

2.87
5 Semih, Turkey
For me, my favourite words in English are awesome and legendary. I don't know why because when I say awesome or legendary it makes me feel happy.

2.88
6 Bea, England
OK my favourite words in English are 'you know' because they're very useful words. When you are not sure what to say you can use them to fill in a sentence and they're very good words to give you time so that you can think about, you can concentrate on what you are thinking and maybe think of different ideas, you know.

2.89
7 Guy, England
One of my favourite words in English is harmony. I think it's a nice word, it's got a nice sound to it. I like the structure of the word. I think the ideas that it represents are very positive, whether you are talking about musical harmony, or artistic harmony, or harmony when people work together well or understand each other well. And I think probably there's a similar word in many other languages, so it's a word that a lot of people understand quite easily.

Macmillan Education
Between Towns Road, Oxford OX4 3PP
A division of Macmillan Publishers Limited
Companies and representatives throughout the world

ISBN 978-0-230-03309-2

Text © Lindsay Clandfield & Amanda Jeffries 2010
Design and illustration © Macmillan Publishers Limited 2010
Grammar Focus section by Rebecca Robb Benne

First published 2010

All rights reserved; no part of this publication may be reproduced, stored in a retrieval system, transmitted in any form, or by any means, electronic, mechanical, photocopying, recording, or otherwise, without the prior written permission of the publishers.

Original design by Barbara Mercer and Katie Stephens
Page layout by eMC Design Limited
Illustrated by Jonathan Burton, Peter Harper, Celia Hart, Robin Lawrie and eMC Design
Picture research by Sally Cole, Perseverance Works Limited
Cover design by Barbara Mercer
Cover photograph used by permission of the Museum of the History of Science, University of Oxford/Keiko Ikeuchi

Author's acknowledgements

First and foremost, I would like to thank Rafael Alarcon-Gaeta for his support and nurturing of this project from the very beginning. The team working on Global have all done an incredible job. My gratitude to Nick Sheard, Stephanie Parker, Stig Vatland and Barbara Mercer for constantly rising to the challenges this book presented and coming out on top every single time. Many thanks also to Selina Hansen for her comments and help on the manuscript.

A lot of the inspiration for this book came from the hundreds of teachers I've had the chance to meet around the world. This would not have been possible without the help of the tireless people at Macmillan who organised my trips and gave me insight into the countries I was visiting.

This book is dedicated to my children Lucas and Marcos, whose curiosity about life and everything has been very motivating to me as an author.

The author and publishers would like to thank all the teachers and consultants who have piloted and reviewed the material. Particular thanks go to the following people: Andrea Córdova, Susana Flores (Anglo Multimedia School of English, Haedo, Buenos Aires, Argentina); Ma. Cristina Maggi, Ma. Cristina Buero de Chinton (Friends' School of English, Adrogué, Buenos Aires, Argentina); Mirta Zampini, Aldana Anchorena, Elizabeth Rainieri, Ma. Soledad D. Mangiarotti, Pamela Sabrina Pecorelli (IECI, Haedo, Buenos Aires, Argentina); Alejandro Jorge Listrani (Cultural Inglesa de Palermo, Ciudad Autónoma de Buenos Aires, Argentina); Lilian Itzicovitch Leventhal (Potential/ Colegio I.L.Peretz, São Paulo, Brazil); Ana Maria Miranda (Cultura Inglesa Ribeirão Preto, Ribeirão Preto, Brazil); Magali de Moraes Menti (FACCAT - Escola Municipal Lauro Rodrigues, Porto Alegre, Brazil); Simone Sarmento (PUCRS, Porto Alegre, Brazil); Laura Lee Lehto (Cultura Inglesa, Fortaleza, Brazil); Viviane Cristine Silva Grossklauss, Analice Sandovetti (Cultura Inglesa Jundiaí, Jundiaí, Brazil); Celia Aguiar de Almeida Costa (Cultura Inglesa de Juiz de Fora, Brazil); Corina Celia Machado Correa (Associação Alumni - São Paulo, Brazil); Jane Godwin (The Four, São Carlos, Brazil); Caroline Toubia (The Holy Family School, Jesuite, Egypt); Amany Shawkey, Heidi Omara (Macmillan Publishers Ltd, Egypt) Caroline Franz , Dana Jelinkova (MVHS Muenchner Volkshochschule, Munich, Germany); Irene Rodriguez, Haydee Gutierrez Palafox, Antonio Morales de la Barrera, Javier Ramos de Hoyos (The Anglo Mexican Foundation, Mexico City, Mexico); Viviana Caruso de Curtius (freelance author and consultant, Mexico City, Mexico); Emma Dominguez (Academic Studies Manager, The Anglo Mexican Foundation, Mexico City, Mexico); Katarzyna Rogalińska-Gajewska (Archibald, Warsaw, Poland); Małgorzata Woźniak, Dorota Pachwicewicz, Agnieszka Kilanowska (Centrum Językowe 'Euroclub', Gdańsk, Poland); Fabiola Georgiana Hosu (Little London School and Nursery School, Dimitrie Cantemir University, Bucharest, Romania); Lydia B. Korzheva (Diplomatic Academy, Moscow, Russia); Ludmila A. Pokrovskaya (Russian Academy of Foreign Trade, Moscow, Russia); Olga S. Petrischeva (Moscow State University of International Relations, Moscow, Russia); Albina Valieva (The International Language School 'Denis School', Moscow, Russia); Karen Dyer, Cathy Harris, Frank Hodgkins (International House, Madrid, Spain); Carlos Trueba (E.O.I Villaverde, Madrid, Spain); Patricia Plaza Arregui (E.O.I. Malaga, Spain); Maria Esther Álvarez Rico (E.O.I. Sagunto, Valencia, Spain); Burcu Tezcan Ünal (Bilgi University, Istanbul, Turkey); Dr. F. Ilke Buyukduman (Ozyegin University, Istanbul, Turkey); Sarah Shaw (The British Council, Chiang Mai, Thailand); Aomboon Burutphakdee (Payap University, Chiang Mai, Thailand); thanks to: Nattinee Khueansri, (Payap University, Chiang Mai, Thailand); Claudia Edwards (London School of English, London, UK); Sally Jones (Regent Oxford, Oxford, UK); Katherine Griggs (Community English School Oxfordshire Adult Learning, Oxford, UK).

A special thank you to Jackie Halsall, Sarah Paterson and all the staff and students at Eckersley, Oxford and Regent, Oxford for all their help with Global voices.

The authors and publishers would like to thank the following for permission to reproduce their photographs:

Cover Credit: By permission of the Museum of the History of Science, University of Oxford/Keiko Ikeuchi.

Alamy/John Arnold Images pp14(r), 48(tmr), Alamy/N.Boyd p99(tr), Alamy/P.Dazeley p85(b), Alamy/Mary Evans p81(t), Alamy/P.Gibbs p121(t), Alamy/S&R Greenhill p124, Alamy/P.Horree p30(bl), Alamy/Imagebroker pp24(d), 50(l), Alamy/Imagestate pp82, 122(bl), Alamy/isifa Image Service s.r.o p100, Alamy/Lordprice Collection p21(br), Alamy/Iain Mas p11, Alamy/J.Marshall/Tribaleye Images p94(b), Alamy/Nagelstock p96(bm), Alamy/North Wind Picture Archive p45, Alamy/C.Pearsall p98(mr), Alamy/C.Pefley p21(tr), Alamy/C.Richardson p24(e), Alamy/Vario Images GmbH & Co K.G pp26(ml), 37(l), Alamy/N.Vereker p50(ml), Alamy/C&M Werner p79(mr), Alamy/J.West p62(r), Alamy/H.Westheim Photography p106(t); Bananastock pp17(b), 59(tl), 59(tm), 59(bm), 137; Brand X pp103(7), 110(bl), 133, 143; Comstock p110(bm); Corbis/K.C.Armstrong p46(br), Corbis/Atlantide Phototravel p96(ml), Corbis/C.Barria/Reuters p48(t), Corbis/BBC p56, Corbis/J.Beeden p95(m), Corbis/ Bettmann Archive pp6(br), 23(bl), 38(ml), 46(bl), 145, Corbis/T.Bognar p147(bl), Corbis/W.Bossen/Stock this Way p73, Corbis/Bursein Collection p30(br), Corbis/F.Cevallos p91(b), Corbis/J.Cooke p72, Corbis/R.Eshel p106(bmr), Corbis/Envision p126(b), Corbis/R.Faris p74(ml), Corbis/R.Galbraith p84(b), Corbis/G.Hall p71(b), Corbis/P.Hardy p131, Corbis/D.Houser p86(br), Corbis/Hulton Deutsch pp31(b), 81(br), 91(t), Corbis/Jagadeesh/Reuters p55(l), Corbis/L.Lefkowitz p96(br), Corbis/T.Levine/Zefa p83(t), Corbis/P.Lissac/Godong p84(t), Corbis/T.McGuire p67(t), Corbis/M.Nicholson p23(br), Corbis/S.Oskar/Zefar p86(tl), Corbis/A.Peisi/Zefa p74(mr), Corbis/O'Brien Productions p14(ml), Corbis/L.Psihoyos p68(m), Corbis/A.Redpath p122(tr), Corbis/N.Sarony p33(b), Corbis/D.Scott p24(f), Corbis/J.Sohm,Visions of America p31(t), Corbis/P.Souders pp30(tl), 48(b), Corbis/Stock Photos p20; Corbis RF pp16,24(c), 103(9), 106(tm), 106(bl), 106(bml), 106(lm), 149, 151(t); Digital Stock p92(tl); Digital Vision p112; Fotolibra/D.Breed p35(h), Fotolibra/G.Headley p94(m), Fotolibra/F.Kay p135(m), Fotolibra/J.Rich p120(t); Guardian News & Media Ltd 2006/C.Johnston p55(r); Getty Images/AFP p96(t), Getty/Aurora p10(l), Getty/Car Culture p119(t), Getty/DK Images p28, Getty Images Entertainment p47(l), Getty/Gallo Images pp42(tl), 99(tm), Getty/T.Gipstein p78(t), Getty/Hola Images p6(tr), Getty/Hulton Archive pp18, 94(l), 108(t), 118(d),

Getty/N.Emmerson p86(bl), Getty/Iconica pp6(m), 26(r), 108(b), 122(tl), Getty/M.Lannen p128(t), Getty/S.McAllister p58, Getty Images News p13, Getty/Photographers Choice pp50(mr), 60(l),78(b), Getty/Photonica pp7, 12,34(l), 48(tml), Getty/Reportage p50(r), Getty/Retrofile/FPG p35(b), Getty/W.Smith p21(tl), Getty/Stone pp6(tl), 34(m), 68(t), 71(t), 81(bl), 88, 102, Getty/Taxi pp6(bl), 59(ml), 74(r), 74(r), 79(l), 86(tr), 121(bl), Getty/The Image Bank pp22(b), 36(t), 70, 98(ml), 109, 122(br), Getty/Time & Life Pictures p106(tml); Image Source pp17(t), 25, 52, 64, 83(mr), 85(t), 98(r), 103(3), 103(8), 135(b), 151(b); Joshua Tree Photography pp 9, 10(r), 19(portraits), 42(b,r), 43, 44, 60(b), 83(tl); Kobal Collection/Anglo Enterprise/Vineyard p47(r); Lonely Planet Images/R.L'Anson p90(t), Lonely Planet/C.Polich p48(bmr); Macmillan Publishers Ltd/P. Bricknell p103(6); Mary Evans pp23(ml), 118(b), 118(h), Mary Evans/Imagno p23(tr); Masterfile/N.Hendricksen p62(l), Masterfile/Jerzyworks p62(mr), Masterfile/M.Roman p62(ml), Moodboard p106(br); Motoring Picture Library pp 118(a), 118(g), 118(f), 119(b); Naturepl/A.Sands p92(ml), Naturepl/J.Freund p95(b); Panos Pictures/G.Akash p59(r), Panos Pictures/T.Derven p120(l), Panos/G.Pirozzi p22(l); Reproduced by permission of Penguin Books Ltd cover of The Beach by Alex Garland (First published by Viking 1996, Penguin Books 1997) copyright © Alex Garland, 1996, p95; cover of High Fidelity by Nick Hornby (Penguin Books Ltd, 2000) copyright © Nick Hornby, 2000, p37; Photoalto pp 59(m), 103(4), 103(5); Photodisc pp83(m), 92(tm), 92(tml), 92(br), 92(tr), 92(tmr), 92(bm), 92(bl); Photolibrary Group/age fotostock pp48-49(b), 84(m), 92(bl), 105(l), 147(r), Photolibrary/Arcangel Images pp35(f), 147(tl), Photolibrary/M.Bail p33(l), Photolibrary/IFA-Bilderteam p25, Photolibrary/Productions Burke/Triolo p24(b), Photolibrary/Digital Vision p98(l), Photolibrary/F1 Online p107(l), Photolibrary/Flirt Collection p60(t), Photolibrary/B.Foubert p21(m), Photolibrary/Fresh Food Images pp103(2), 128(b), Photolibrary/D.Hurst p35(b), Photolibrary/Imagestate p57, Photolibrary/JTB photo pp19(m), 35(e), Photolibrary/G.Kirk p19(t), Photolibrary/R.Llewellyn p34(tm), Photolibrary/T.de Ling/Time Out p26(mr), Photolibrary/Nonstock Jupiter Images p83(b), Photolibrary/Oxford Scientific pp99(tl),105(m), Photolibrary/Photocuisine p103(1), Photolibrary/Phototake Science pp127, 129, Photolibrary/A & G Reporter p48(bml), Photolibrary/H. Rice p24(a), Photolibrary/B.Robert p32(m), Photolibrary/SGM p35(c); Photoshot p26(l), Photoshot/bilderlounge p135(t), Photoshot/J.Blackler p61, Photoshot/P.Seheult p35(d), Photoshot/Tetra Images p32(t), Photshot/WpN p14(mr), Photoshot/World Pictures p96(bl); Plainpicture/Briljans p59(br), Plainpicture/Johner p93(tr), Plainpicture/G.Lenz p54, Plainpicture/O.Boe p14(l); Press Association/AP Photo/K.Kasahara p106(mbl); Prestwick House Literary Touchstone Classics: The Picture of Dorian Gray by Oscar Wilde, Cover Design by Larry Knox, copyright © 2005 by Prestwick House, Inc. revised 2007. Reprinted by permission. All rights reserved.p33(tr), Rex Features pp120(m), 126(t), Rex/M.L.Antonelli p40, Rex/M.Bjorkman p35(g), Rex/C.S.U Archive/Everett p46(t), 69(t), Rex/Everett Collection pp36(bl), 38(l), 90(bl), Rex/S.Meddle p35(a), Rex/Miramax/Everett p38(mr), Rex/Paramount/Everett p49(t), Rex/J.Pepler p121(m), Rex/Sony Pictures/Everett p38(r); Robert Harding/Occidor p90(br); Rubberball p83(mb); Sally Mais Photography p36(br); Science Photo Library p116, Science Photo Library/J.Daugherty p105(t), Science Photo Library/Gusto Images p110(t), Science Photo Library/G.Kidd p110(br), Science Photo Library/M.Kulyk p24(l), Science Photo Library/P.Psaila p68(t); The Art Archive/Musée du Louvre Paris/Gianni Dagli Orti p93(tl), Art Archive/Musée d'Orsay Paris/Alfredo Dagli Orti p31(tm), The Art Archive/Egyptian Museum Cairo/Gianni Dagli Orti p32(b), The Art Archive/Museo del Templo Mayor Mexico/Gianni Dagli Orti p30(bm), The Art Archive/National Gallery London/Eileen Tweedy p31(bm); Dr L. J. Reed, The Centre for Neuroimaging Sciences, Institute of Psychiatry, London p67(b); Topfoto/The Granger Collection pp118(e), 118(c), Topfoto/R.Voillet p107(r); Wellcome Library London p104; www.eggling.com, made in Japan by Seishin Togei Inc,distributed by Noted p114(t), Macmillan Reader, Frankenstein Corbis/Bettmann p69(b). Commissioned photography by Joshua Tree Photography pp 27, 51, 75, 99 (portraits),123; Roger Scruton p115 (portrait)

The author and publishers are grateful for permission to reprint the following copyright material: Extract from 'Six Degrees of Separation' by John Guare, copyright © John Guare 1999, reprinted by permission of Methuen Drama, an imprint of A&C Black Publishers Ltd. Extract from 'The Beach' by Alex Garland, copyright © Alex Garland 1997, reprinted by permission of Riverhead Books, an imprint of Penguin Group (USA) Inc. for website and printed World rights, excluding EEC & UK territories. Audio and printed rights for territories EEC & UK acquired from Andrew Nurnberg Agency. Adapted material from 'The Book Of Lists' by Amy Wallace and David Wallechinsky, copyright © Amy Wallace and David Wallechinsky, first published in Great Britain by Canongate Books Ltd., 14 High Street, Edinburgh, EH1 1TE, reprinted by permission of the publisher. Poem – 'Routine' by Stuart Doggett, reprinted by permission of the author. Extracted material from 'Exploring Comfort Food Preferences Across Age and Gender' copyright © Elsevier Science 2003, reprinted by permission of the publisher. Extract from 'This much I know: Rajeshwari Singh: Call-centre operator, 20, Delhi' by Amelia Gentleman, copyright © Amelia Gentleman 2006, first published in The Guardian 26.11.06, reprinted by permission of the publisher. Extract from 'Six Degrees of Separation' by John Guare, copyright © John Guare 1990, reprinted by permission of International Creative Management, Inc. USA. Extract from retold version of 'Frankenstein' by Margaret Tarner for Macmillan Readers, copyright © Margaret Tarner 2005, reprinted by permission of the publisher. Extract from retold version of 'The Picture of Dorian Gray' by F.H.Cornish for Macmillan Readers, copyright © F.H.Cornish 2005, reprinted by permission of the publisher. Material from 'Brave New Words' by Kerry Maxwell, copyright © Kerry Maxwell 2007, reprinted by permission of the author. Adapted material from 'Trade Secrets: Food & Drink' by Alexandra Fraser, copyright © Alexandra Fraser 1999, reprinted by permission of Orion Non-fiction, an imprint of Orion Publishing Group, London. Extract from 'High Fidelity' by Nick Hornby, copyright © Nick Hornby 1995, reprinted by permission of Penguin Group UK. Material from article 'The Worst Jobs in Science 2007' by Jason Daley. Screenplay Excerpt from 'Bram Stoker's Dracula' copyright © 1992 Columbia Pictures Industries, Inc. All Rights Reserved, courtesy of Columbia Pictures. Material from article 'Concerned Citizens' published in Education Citizenship and Social Justice by Associate Professor Cathie Holden at University of Exeter, copyright © Cathie Holden 2006, reprinted by permission of the author. Fitter Happier – Words and Music by Thomas Edward Yorke, Jonathan Richard, Guy Greenwood and Dan Rickwood. Warner/Chappell Music Limited (PRS). All Rights Reserved.
We are very grateful to Andy Price for generously allowing us to interview him and include extracts of his music.

These materials may contain links for third party websites. We have no control over, and are not responsible for, the contents of such third party websites. Please use care when accessing them.

Although we have tried to trace and contact copyright holders before publication, in some cases this has not been possible. If contacted we will be pleased to rectify any errors or omissions at the earliest opportunity.

Printed in Thailand

2016 2015 2014 2013
16 15 14 13 12

PRE-INTERMEDIATE

global business class eWorkbook

Contents

Global Business Class eWorkbook at a glance	2–3
Language Practice	4–5
Print and Work	6–7
Listen	8–9
Watch	10–11
On the Move	12
Reference Tools	13
Tests and Portfolio	14
Technical information	15

Global Business Class eWorkbook at a glance

The Global Business Class eWorkbook combines the best of both worlds: everything you would find in a printed Workbook for home study and multimedia resources to enhance revision and ongoing learning.

The Global Business Class eWorkbooks are mainly intended for self study or home study. They contain a set of resources to support and enhance the material in the Coursebook. The eWorkbook can be used with your computer or you can save some of the material and use it with other devices (for example, mp3 players).

If you prefer to work on paper you can print your work.

When you launch a level of the Global Business Class eWorkbooks you will see the following options:

Where to start?

You can start by going to help [?] or by reading this booklet.

If you want to have a clear overview of the whole content you should select the Contents Map icon.

You can see the result of the last self-check test you have done.

You can see all the resources linked to each of the units, and you can view them either by type or by the recommended order in which you should use them.

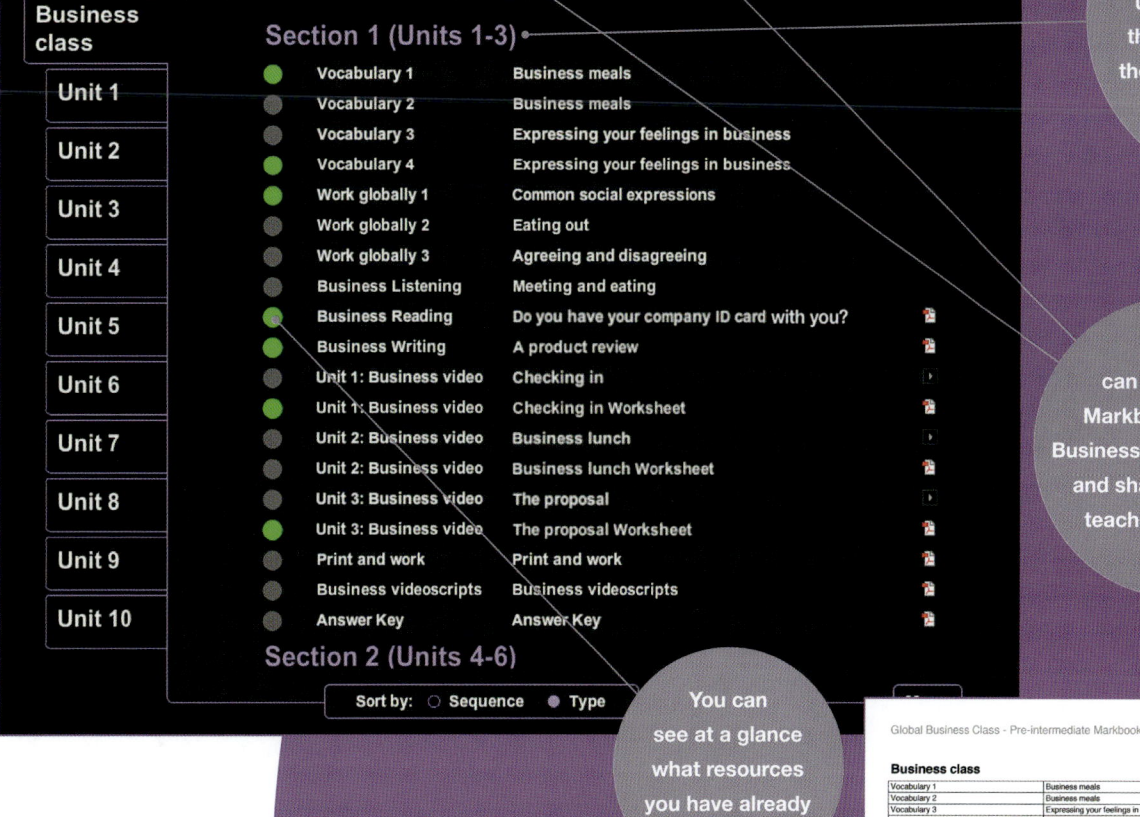

You can export your Markbook and your Business Class Markbook and share it with your teacher if you want to.

You can see at a glance what resources you have already accessed.

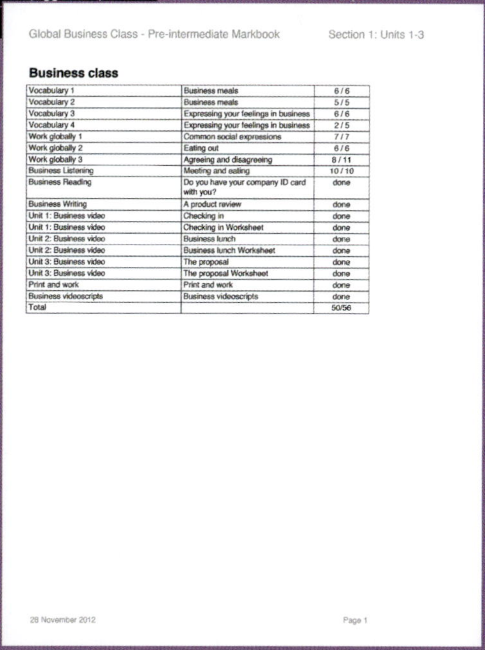

'Business Class' contains additional resources and practice activities to help you learn the key language and skills to communicate and succeed in the global business environment

Language Practice

The Language Practice section includes activities that provide consolidation of the language presented in the Coursebook. It includes practice of all language skills: grammar, vocabulary, pronunciation, reading, listening and writing.

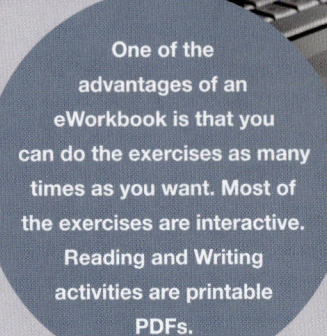

One of the advantages of an eWorkbook is that you can do the exercises as many times as you want. Most of the exercises are interactive. Reading and Writing activities are printable PDFs.

You can navigate the material by unit or by language skill. If you choose to work by unit, you will be taken to a list of all the activities related to that particular unit.

If you choose to work by skill, you will be taken to a list of all the different activities related to that particular skill.

When you choose an activity practising grammar, vocabulary, listening or pronunciation you will be taken to a screen like this one.

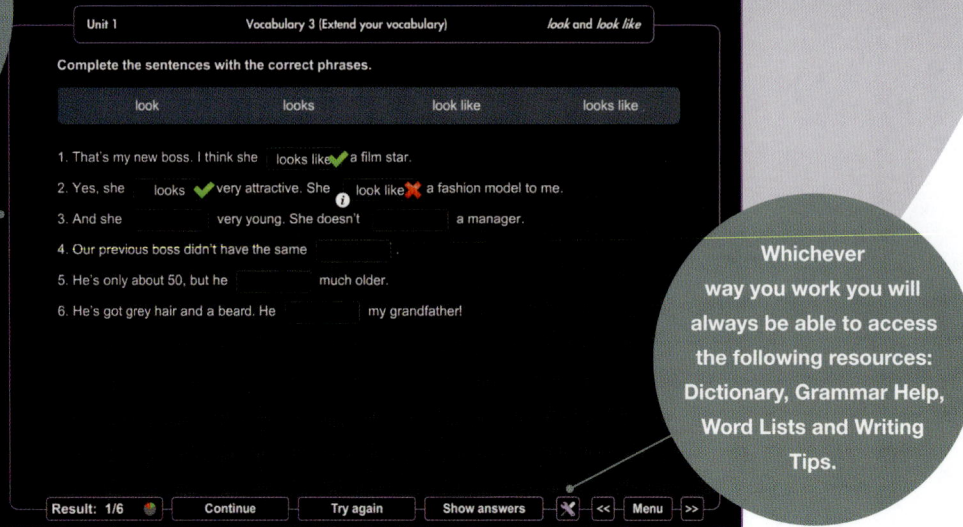

Whichever way you work you will always be able to access the following resources: Dictionary, Grammar Help, Word Lists and Writing Tips.

Global Business Class eWorkbook

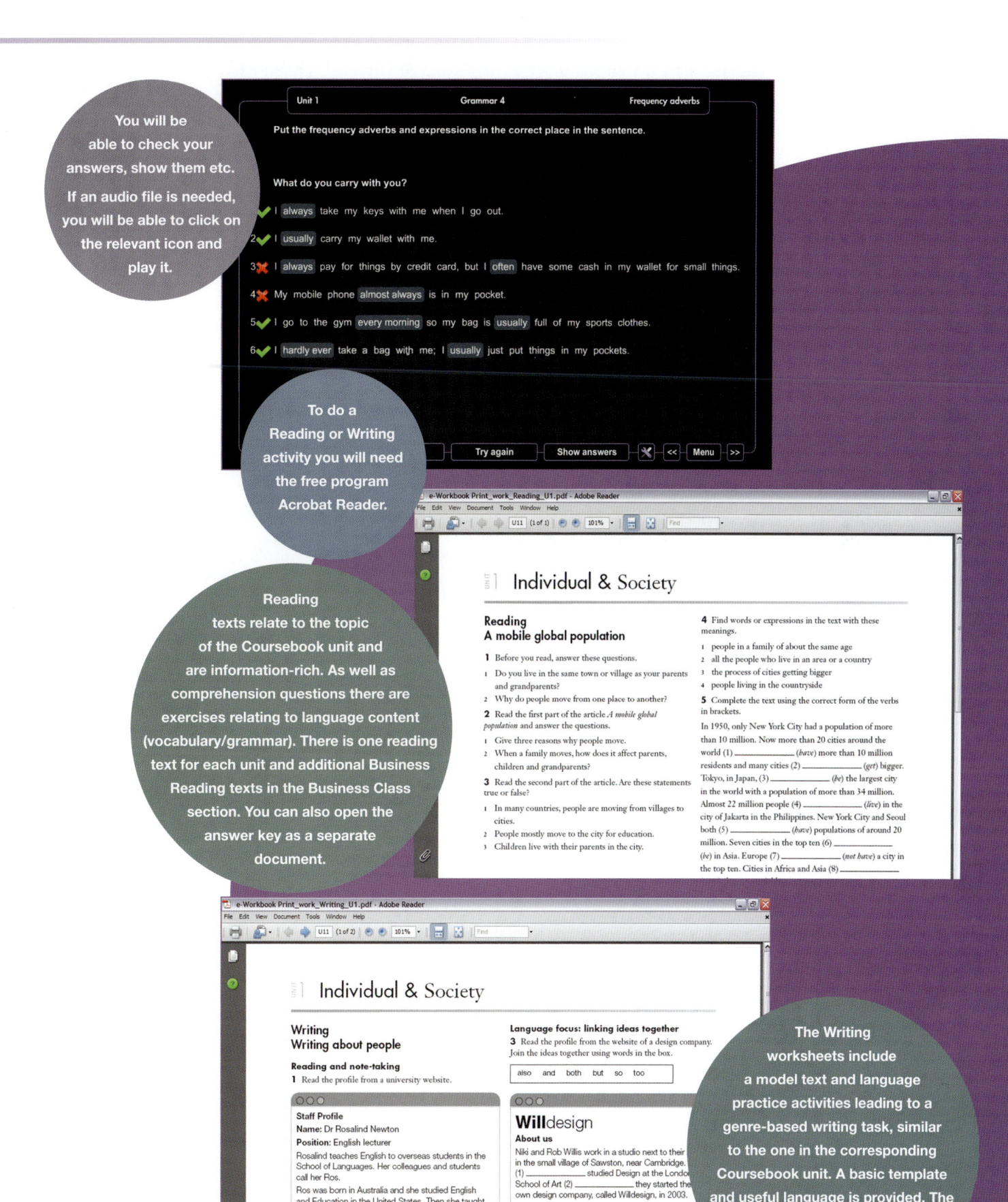

You will be able to check your answers, show them etc. If an audio file is needed, you will be able to click on the relevant icon and play it.

To do a Reading or Writing activity you will need the free program Acrobat Reader.

Reading texts relate to the topic of the Coursebook unit and are information-rich. As well as comprehension questions there are exercises relating to language content (vocabulary/grammar). There is one reading text for each unit and additional Business Reading texts in the Business Class section. You can also open the answer key as a separate document.

The Writing worksheets include a model text and language practice activities leading to a genre-based writing task, similar to the one in the corresponding Coursebook unit. A basic template and useful language is provided. The Business Class section contains additional Business Writing worksheets.

Global Business Class eWorkbook

Print and Work

This section offers a pen-and-paper version of the activities in the Language Practice section, plus downloadable audio tracks when needed. It is designed to suit a different learning style. If you prefer to work away from the computer, this gives you exactly the same as what you would expect in a printed workbook with the added advantage that you only print the pages that you need.

Within the Business Class menu there is also an option to select a pen-and-paper version of the Business Class activities, and the answer key for each section.

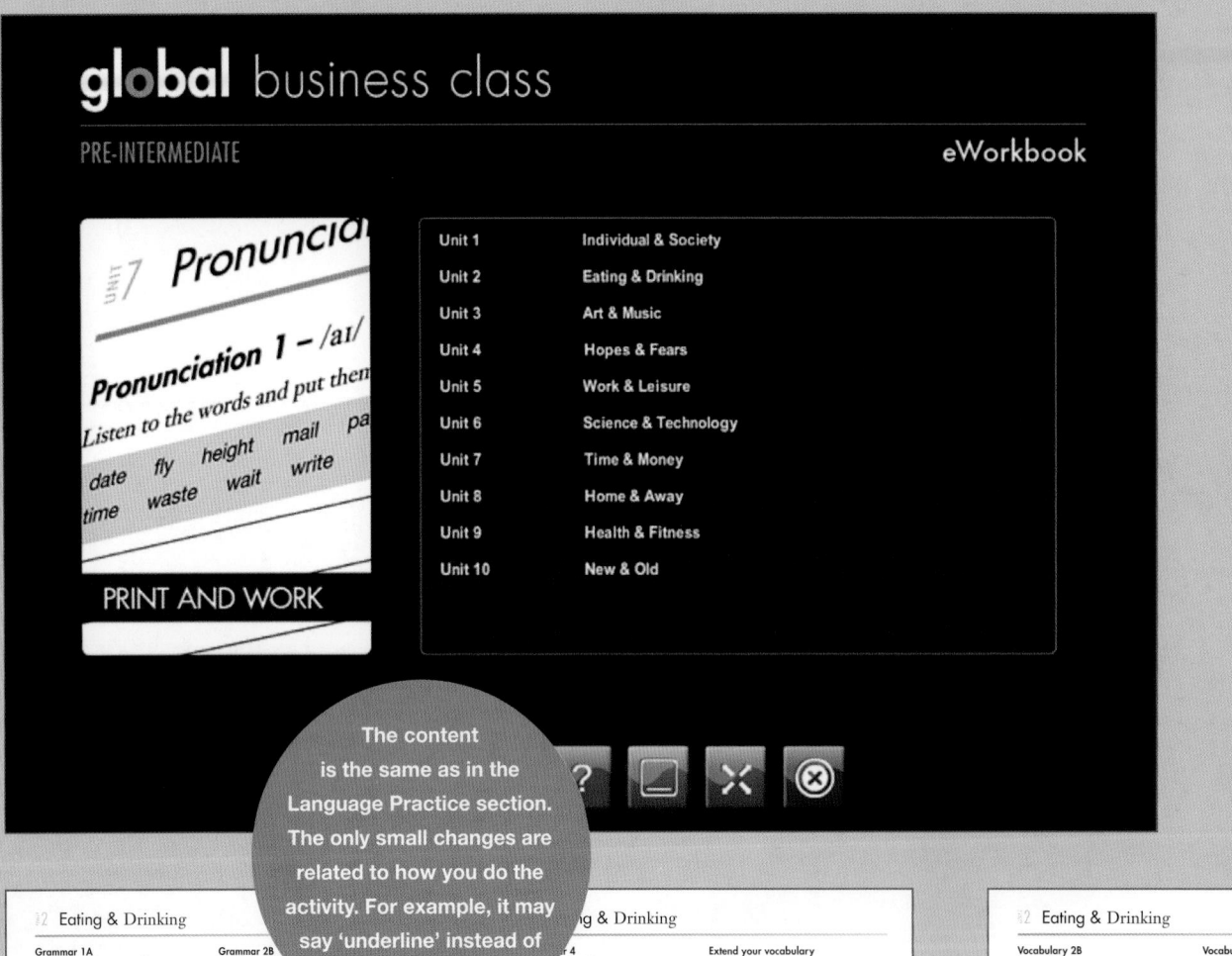

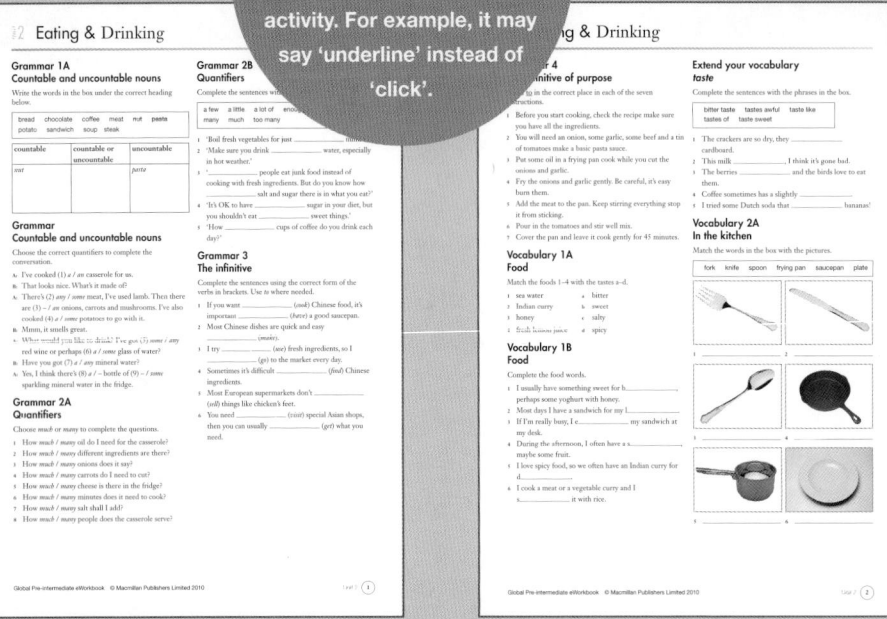

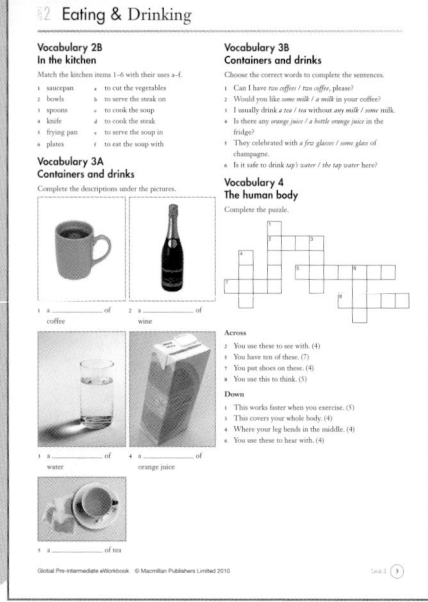

The content is the same as in the Language Practice section. The only small changes are related to how you do the activity. For example, it may say 'underline' instead of 'click'.

Global Business Class eWorkbook

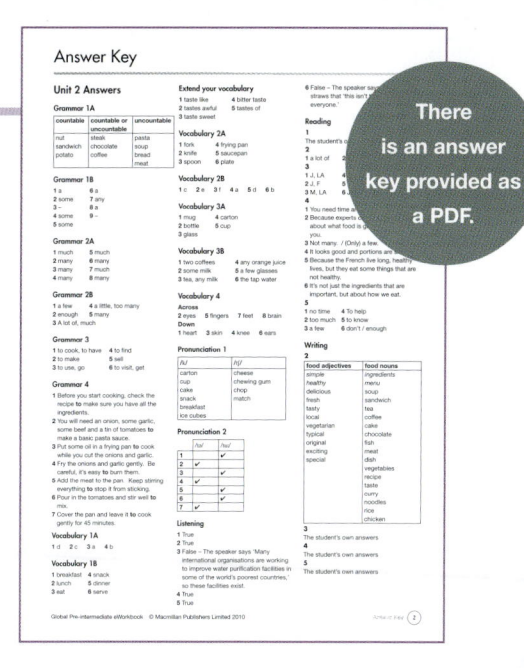

- There is an answer key provided as a PDF.
- If audio files are needed to complete an activity, you will have the option of playing them or downloading them.

Global Business Class eWorkbook

Listen

This section offers access to all the Listening material in the eWorkbook. It includes the following:

- Access to the listening activities in the Language Practice section
- Audio material designed to be used 'on the move'
- Access to the listening tracks from the Class Audio CDs
- Access to the listening activities in the Business Class section

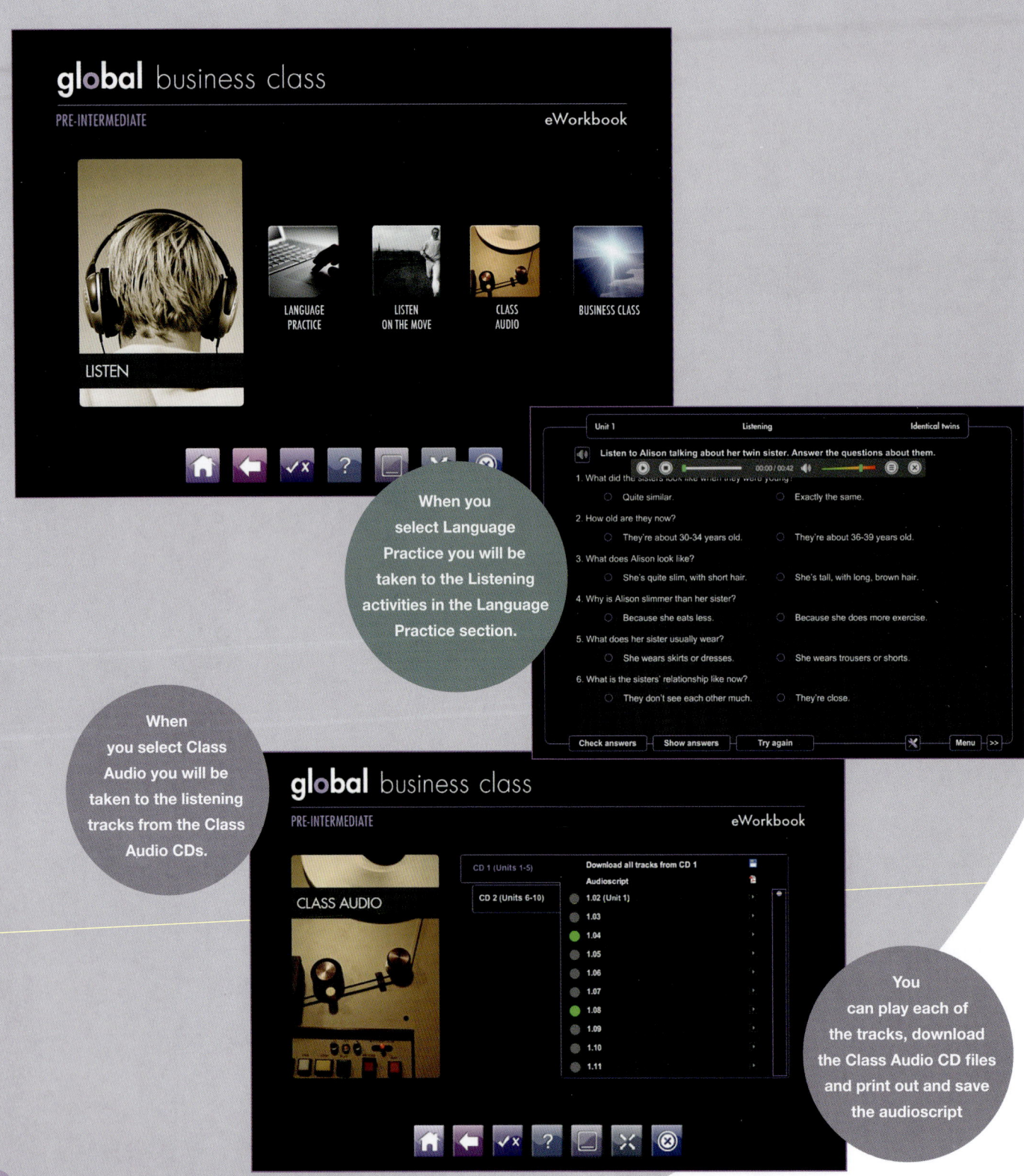

When you select Language Practice you will be taken to the Listening activities in the Language Practice section.

When you select Class Audio you will be taken to the listening tracks from the Class Audio CDs.

You can play each of the tracks, download the Class Audio CD files and print out and save the audioscript

Global Business Class eWorkbook

Listen on the Move includes audio material not linked to specific activities, i.e. different from the listening material in the Language Practice section. There are three types of audio material.

In Conversation contains situational dialogues (e.g. at a restaurant, taking a taxi). The situations relate to the situations in the 'Function Globally' pages in the Coursebook.

Vocabulary Builder contains lists of vocabulary items introduced in the Coursebook which are organised by topic.

Useful Phrases features mini-dialogues that contain the 'Useful phrases' in the Coursebook (e.g. 'agreeing and disagreeing').

You can play this material by clicking on play or you can download the files and copy them onto an mp3 player or other devices.

You can also print or download a PDF with the audioscript for all this material.

As its name indicates, this is ideal for learning on the move.

Global Business Class eWorkbook 9

Watch

When you select Watch in the main menu you are taken to a screen where all the video clips in the eWorkbook are listed.

You can either watch the videos on your computer or download the files. When you watch the videos on your computer you can select to watch them with or without subtitles.

When you click on 'download' you can copy the files to a selected location. You can download the files in a number of formats, for example for iPod, iTouch, iPhone or other common mobile phones.

You can also download the scripts as a PDF.

10 Global Business Class eWorkbook

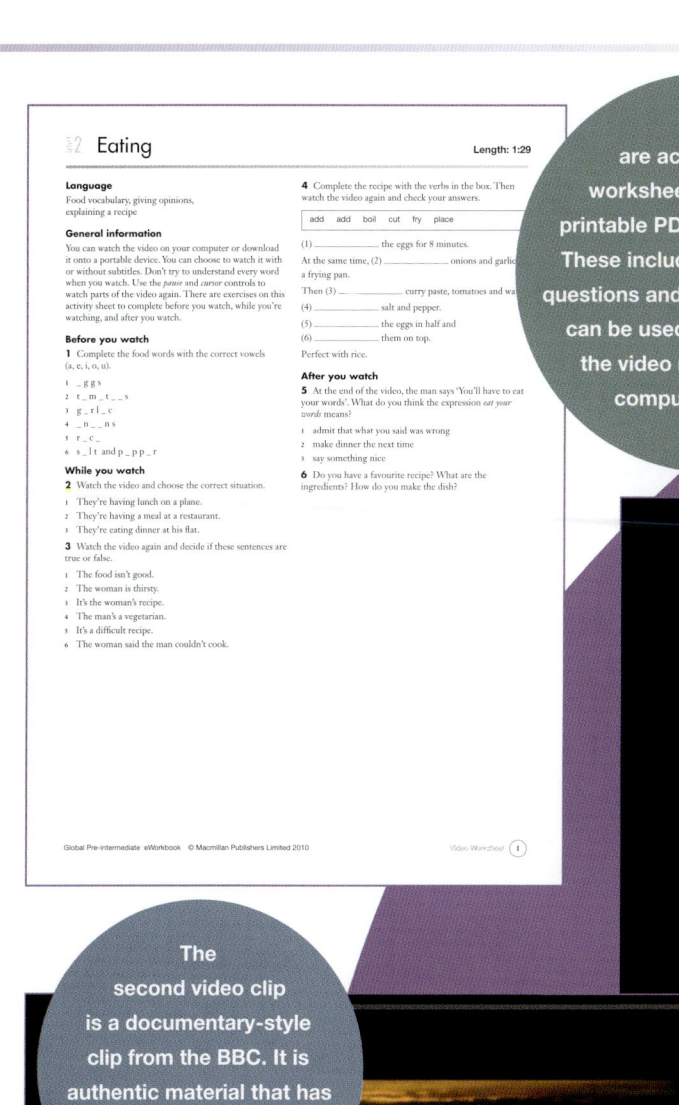

There are accompanying worksheets, available as printable PDFs, one per video. These include comprehension questions and language work and can be used when you watch the video material on your computer or on the move.

There are three video clips per unit. One of them follows a similar style to the user generated content available on popular video websites.

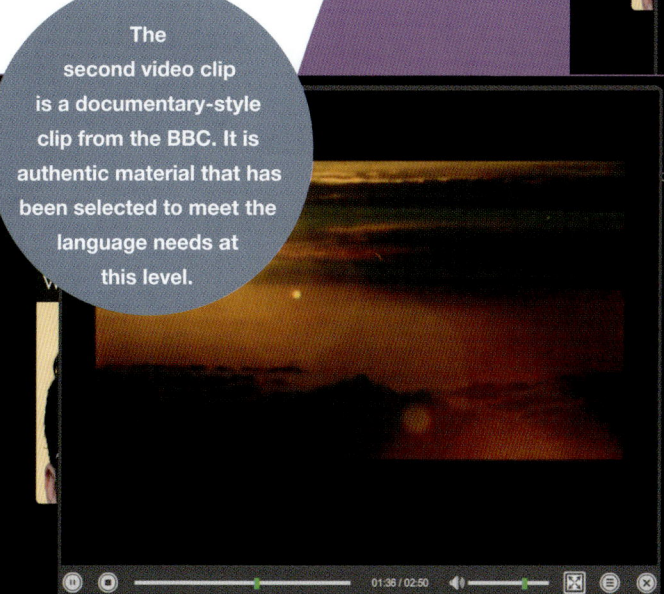

The second video clip is a documentary-style clip from the BBC. It is authentic material that has been selected to meet the language needs at this level.

The third video clip is in a similar style to the first clip and focuses on key communication skills and language for business. You can access the Business Class videos from within the Business Class or Watch menus.

Global Business Class eWorkbook

On the Move

This section includes content also accessible through the Listen and Watch sections offered in one place for ease of access.

When you select this option you are taken to a screen that offers you the option of downloading audio material or video material.

ON THE MOVE

> If you want to access video material, select Watch.

> If you want to access audio material, select Listen on the Move or Class Audio.

> Audio files are offered as mp3 files.

> Video files are offered in a variety of formats.

> In addition, there are PDFs with other assets associated with the audio or video material (eg worksheets to use alongside video clips).

Global Business Class eWorkbook

Reference Tools

The Global Business Class eWorkbook contains powerful Reference Tools to help you with your work.

These tools can be accessed directly from the main menu on the home page or when you are doing an activity.

WORD LISTS & DICTIONARY

GRAMMAR HELP

WRITING TIPS

The Dictionary Tool is a link to the Macmillan English Dictionary Online (you need to be online to access this feature).

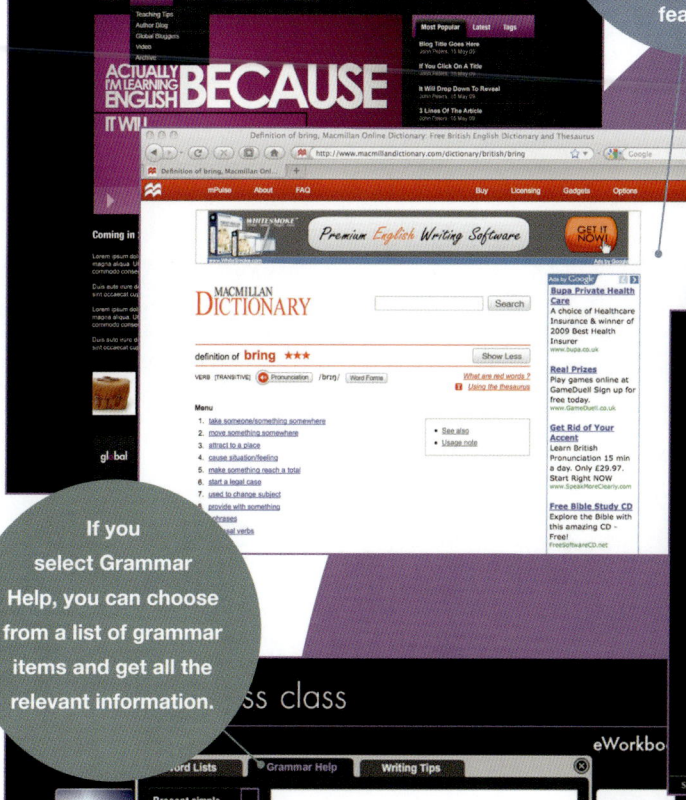

Word Lists include the key words that you need to learn in each of the units.

If you select Grammar Help, you can choose from a list of grammar items and get all the relevant information.

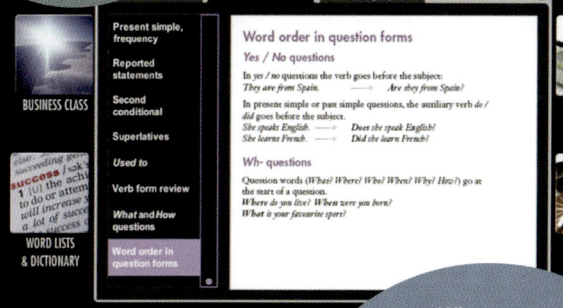

When you select Writing Tips you are given a list of topics. Each of them includes a brief explanation on a particular aspect of writing, such as the use of capital letters, spelling, punctuation, paragraphing, etc., followed by a series of multiple-choice questions to ensure that the main points have been understood.

Global Business Class eWorkbook 13

Tests and Portfolio

You can test yourself at any point using the Global Business Class eWorkbook. You can set yourself tests either by a set time or a set number of questions.

When you finish the test you will be given a score. Your last three scores will be recorded.

When you select Portfolio in the main menu you are taken to a screen offering information about the Common European Framework, User needs, Language passport and Self-assessment Checklists.

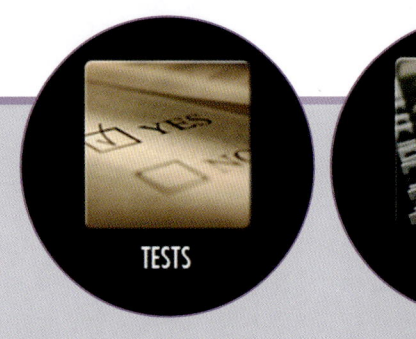

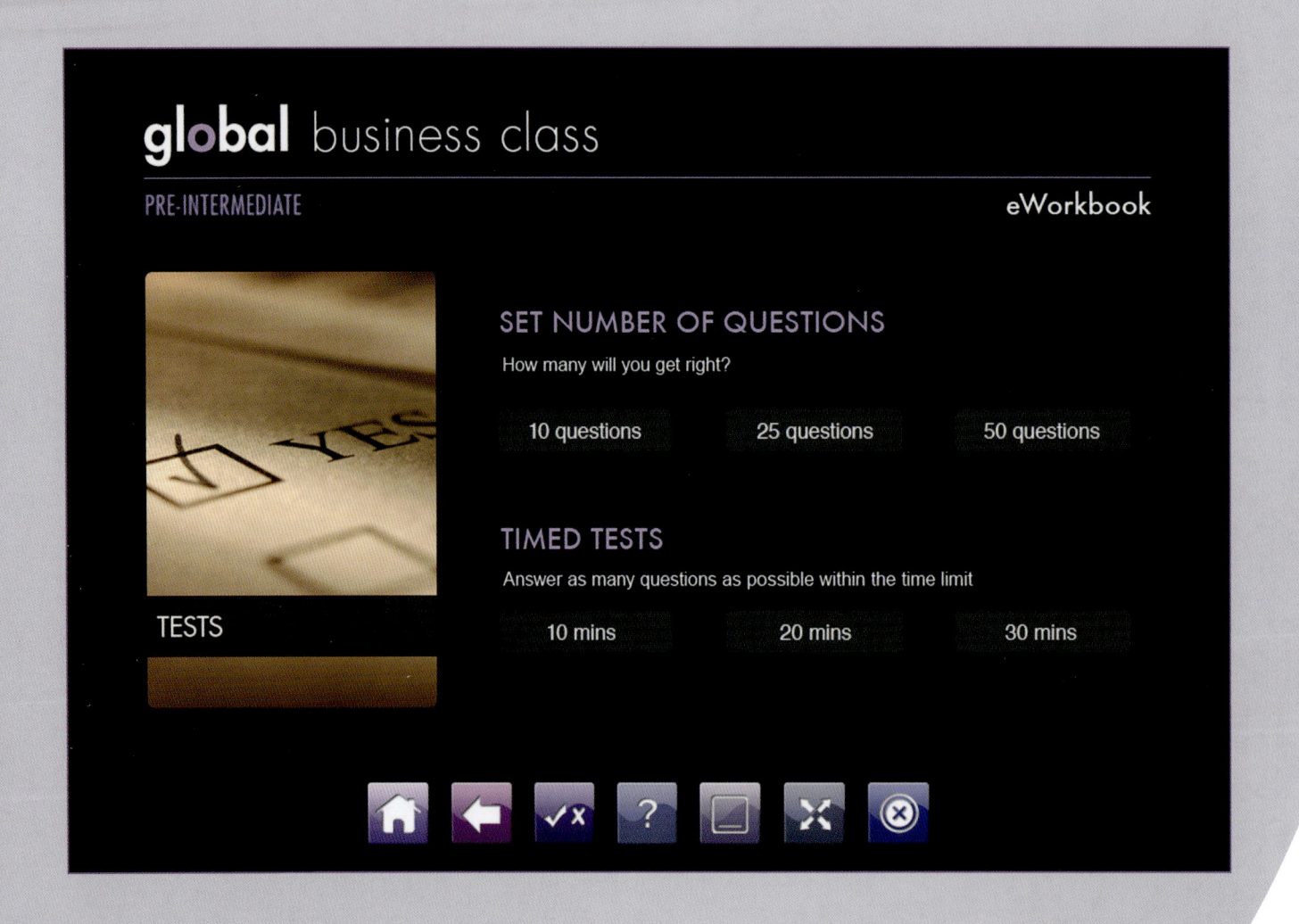

TESTS

PORTFOLIO

global business class

PRE-INTERMEDIATE

eWorkbook

TESTS

SET NUMBER OF QUESTIONS
How many will you get right?

10 questions   25 questions   50 questions

TIMED TESTS
Answer as many questions as possible within the time limit

10 mins   20 mins   30 mins

Global Business Class eWorkbook

Installation instructions

Before you install the *Global Business Class eWorkbook*, please make sure that your computer meets the minimum system requirements mentioned below.

To install and run *Global Business Class eWorkbook*

Windows
Insert the DVD-ROM and choose 'Run' from the auto play menu.

Macintosh
Please select the DVD-ROM drive and double click Install from the Install_Mac folder. Follow the on-screen instructions.

Once installed, you may wish to drag the application icon from the applications folder to your dock for easy access.

Alternatively, double click the application from the applications folder to launch.

Trouble installing your eWorkbook?
Go to the *Macmillan Product Support* website at help.macmillan.com/

You'll find a section that deals with problems that a small number of users have reported.

Minimum System Requirements

Windows
Processor: Pentium 4, 2ghz or faster
Hard disk: Minimum 2 GB free, 3 GB free on the system drive
Operating systems: Vista, XP SP2, Windows 7
32 MB Video RAM
1 GB RAM Audio sound card
DVD drive
Internet Connection (For Registration/live updates)
System administration rights for installation

Macintosh
Intel Core™ Duo 1.33 GHz or faster processor
1 GB RAM
32 MB video RAM
Operating systems: Mac OS X v.10.4, 10.5, 10.6, 10.7
Hard disk: Minimum 2 GB free, 3 GB free on the system drive
DVD drive
Internet connection (For registration/live updates)
System administration rights for installation

Important Information

Appropriate rights are required to install software on your computer and to write end-user data to your computer's hard disk. If end-user rights are restricted, it might not be possible to save the results score in the activities. Please seek expert advice if you do not have the necessary rights

If you have obtained your Macmillan CD-ROM from an authorised supplier, then our software is guaranteed to contain no viruses or similar threats. If you have any doubts about the authenticity of your CD-ROM, please consult your supplier.

A security program can occasionally report a false alarm, also known as a false positive. When this occurs, the program mistakenly thinks there is a threat, although no threat exists.

If a false alarm is reported, please send details to help@macmillan.com and include the name and version of your security program. A screenshot or image of the problem is helpful too. Please also send the title, ISBN, and version number that are printed on the label of your CD-ROM, and the name and version of your operating system. We will then attempt to have the virus definition database that is used by the security program updated as quickly as possible.

All Macmillan CD-ROMs are copyright. Copying is prohibited. Any attempt to copy this CD-ROM will violate the license agreement, invalidate the warranty, and cancel your entitlement to customer service and technical support.

END USER LICENCE AGREEMENT FOR *Global Pre-Intermediate Business Class eWorkbook* **(ISBN: 978-0-230-44375-4)**
This is an agreement between you (the "**User**") and Macmillan Publishers Limited (the "**Supplier**").

1. Licence
The Supplier grants the User a personal, non-exclusive, non-transferable licence to use the Supplier's software product, *Global Pre-Intermediate Business Class eWorkbook* as acquired with this licence (the "**Program**"). The Supplier grants the User the licence to use one copy of the Program (i) on a single stand-alone computer for use by the User and one or more people provided that only one person uses it at any one time, **and** (ii) on a second computer for the purpose of preparing lessons (provided the Program is only used on one stand-alone computer at a time). The User shall not: (i) loan, rent, lease or license the Program; (ii) copy or authorise copying of the Program, reverse-engineer, disassemble or decompile the Program (other than to the extent permitted under applicable law), (iii) operate the Program from a network or mainframe system unless with prior consent.

2. Copyright and other intellectual property rights
The intellectual property rights in the Program and any documentation or materials supplied with the Program are owned by and remain with the Supplier or its third party licensors.

3. Statutory rights
If the User is a consumer and has in that capacity purchased the Program, the exclusions and limitations contained in this agreement do not affect any statutory rights to which the User is entitled as a consumer and which may not under applicable law be excluded or limited.

4. Warranty
Subject to clause 3, the Supplier warrants that the Program and any disc or other medium on which the Program is supplied will be free from defects which have a materially adverse effect on its use in accordance with this agreement. The Supplier does not warrant that the Program will be entirely free from errors or that the information accessible via use of the Program is entirely accurate or error free. The User's sole remedy for breach of this warranty is to return the Program and all documentation to the Supplier, together with proof of purchase, and the Supplier will, at the User's option, either replace the Program or provide the User with a full refund.

5. No other warranties
SUBJECT TO CLAUSE 3, EXCEPT AS EXPRESSLY PROVIDED OTHERWISE BY THIS AGREEMENT, NO CONDITIONS, WARRANTIES, REPRESENTATIONS OR OTHER TERMS APPLY WITH RESPECT TO THE PROGRAM OR USER DOCUMENTATION (INCLUDING ANY SUCH TERMS AS TO QUALITY, PERFORMANCE, SUITABILITY OR FITNESS FOR A PARTICULAR PURPOSE).

6. Limitation of liability
SUBJECT TO CLAUSE 3 AND SAVE AS EXPRESSLY PROVIDED OTHERWISE BY THIS AGREEMENT:
(A) THE SUPPLIER SHALL NOT BE LIABLE TO THE USER OR TO ANY THIRD PARTY FOR: LOSS OF PROFITS; LOSS OF SALES OR BUSINESS; LOSS OF USE OF COMPUTER EQUIPMENT, SOFTWARE OF DATA OR ANY INDIRECT OR CONSEQUENTIAL LOSS HOWSOEVER SUCH LOSS ARISES; AND (B) THE SUPPLIER'S TOTAL AGGREGATE LIABILITY UNDER THIS AGREEMENT SHALL BE LIMITED IN ALL CASES TO THE PRICE OF THE PROGRAM; PROVIDED THAT NOTHING IN THIS AGREEMENT LIMITS THE SUPPLIER'S LIABILITY TO THE USER IN THE EVENT OF DEATH OR PERSONAL INJURY RESULTING FROM THE SUPPLIER'S NEGLIGENCE OR FOR ANY OTHER LIABILITY THAT MAY NOT BE EXCLUDED OR LIMITED UNDER APPLICABLE LAW.

7. Termination
The User's licence to use the Program automatically terminates if the User fails to comply with any provisions of this agreement.

8. Title
The Supplier shall at all times retain ownership of the Program but the User shall retain title in the media on which the Program is supplied.

9. Entire agreement, applicable law and jurisdiction
This agreement is the complete and exclusive statement of the agreement between the User and the Supplier with respect to the Program. This agreement is governed by English law and both parties submit to the exclusive jurisdiction of the English Court.

END-USER SOFTWARE LICENCE AGREEMENT (SLA) between the company which is granting this licence ("Macmillan Publishers Limited") and end-user ("Licensee"). By installing this Software product you agree to this licence.

1. DEFINITIONS
"**Software**" means the computer programs provided to Licensee by Macmillan and/or computer programs in which Macmillan has proprietary rights and/or sublicence rights granted by a third party licensor, and any related materials or documents, and any subsequent revisions provided to Licensee. "**Configuration**" means central processing unit ("CPU") or any group of CPUs, connected by a local area network, that operate together for the purpose of performing the functions of the Software and/or restricting the use of the Software to the maximum number of licensed users.

2. SCOPE OF AUTHORISED USE
2.1 You may install this software in up to two computers. The Software is furnished under a personal, non-transferable, non-exclusive licence in executable/object code solely for Licensee's own use. Further installations than those defined above may become chargeable. Please contact Macmillan if you require additional licensed copies of this application
2.2 Licensee shall not copy nor permit any party to copy Software, except to make a single copy solely for backup or archival purposes as necessary for use on the Configuration, but only with the inclusion of copyright and proprietary notices. If Licensee is unable to operate Software on the Configuration due to an equipment malfunction, the Software may be used temporarily on another Configuration during the period of equipment malfunction. Licensee shall not sublicense or transfer or otherwise make Software available to any third party. Licensee shall not modify, decompile, disassemble or otherwise reverse engineer Software or create derivative works based on the Software. The Licensee may only exercise rights under s50 of the Copyright Designs and Patents Act 1988 or similar legislation if it has first asked Macmillan to disclose the required information and Macmillan has declined to do so.
2.3 Licensee shall allow Macmillan and its nominated representatives reasonable access to its premises to audit Licensee's compliance with this Agreement.

3. TITLE AND OWNERSHIP; CONFIDENTIALITY
Title to, ownership of the Software and any patent, copyright, underlying trade secret and other intellectual property rights in it or any of its parts shall not transfer to Licensee but shall remain in Macmillan or its third party licensors. Software is confidential and proprietary to Macmillan and/or its third party licensors and Licensee shall observe the proprietary nature thereof. Licensee shall not disclose, provide or otherwise make available Software or any part (which includes without limitation, database structures and message formats) or copies thereof to any third party. Licensee shall take action by instruction or agreement with its employees who are permitted access to Software, to protect the confidentiality of Software. Licensee shall keep Software and such materials secure, and prevent unauthorised access, copying or use thereof. Licensee agrees to notify Macmillan immediately it becomes aware of any unauthorised knowledge, possession, or use of Software or any such materials by any person or entity. Additional terms may apply where the Software is owned by a third party and provided by Macmillan under licence; in such cases, those terms will be provided separately.

4. LIMITED WARRANTY
A. Macmillan warrants that all unmodified Software, when used under the conditions described in the applicable Macmillan published specifications furnished to Licensee, if any, will conform to said Macmillan published specifications at time of shipment and for a period of ninety (90) days. If Licensee determines that a non-conformity exists which is a substantial deviation from the Macmillan published specification, Licensee shall provide proper written notification to Macmillan, within the warranty period, explaining the alleged nonconformity. Upon receipt of such written notification Macmillan's or its third party Licensors' sole liability and Licensee's sole and exclusive remedy shall be for Macmillan to use reasonable efforts to provide, at no cost to Licensee, programming corrections by telephone and/or mail to correct such documented nonconformity. Provided Macmillan determines that the alleged nonconformity is a

defect in the unaltered version of the Software and is not the result of (i) Licensee's use of the Software other than in accordance with the Macmillan published specification; or (ii) modifications to the Software made by parties other than Macmillan; or (iii) damage due to improper use or neglect, Macmillan shall use reasonable efforts to remedy such nonconformity by issuing corrected information to Licensee, including corrected documentation or code or a work-around if available. Macmillan does not warrant that the operation of Software will be uninterrupted or error free or that all errors will be remedied. Macmillan does not warrant that Software will meet Licensee's specific requirements or operate with any hardware or software other than as specified in the Macmillan published specification, if any shall have been provided.
B. Macmillan does not warrant the performance of Macmillan products if used with third party products not approved by Macmillan.
C. NEITHER MACMILLAN NOR ANY OF ITS THIRD PARTY LICENSORS MAKES ANY OTHER REPRESENTATION OR WARRANTY REGARDING THE SOFTWARE, INCLUDING EXPRESS OR IMPLIED WARRANTIES OF SATISFACTORY QUALITY, MERCHANTABILITY AND FITNESS FOR A PARTICULAR PURPOSE AND NONINFRINGEMENT OF THIRD PARTY RIGHTS AND ALL OTHER WARRANTIES ARE HEREBY EXPRESSLY DISCLAIMED. SOME JURISDICTIONS DO NOT ALLOW THE EXCLUSION OF IMPLIED WARRANTIES, SO THE ABOVE LIMITATIONS MAY NOT APPLY TO YOU. LICENSEE RETAINS FULL CONTROL OVER AND RESPONSIBILITY FOR THE USE OF SOFTWARE. MACMILLAN DOES NOT WARRANT THE MERCHANTABILITY OF ANY OF LICENSEE'S PRODUCTS THROUGH THE USE OF THE SOFTWARE. THIS WARRANTY GIVES YOU SPECIFIC LEGAL RIGHTS. YOU MAY HAVE OTHER RIGHTS, WHICH VARY FROM JURISDICTION TO JURISDICTION.

5. LIMITATION OF LIABILITY
IN NO EVENT IS MACMILLAN OR ITS THIRD PARTY LICENSORS LIABLE FOR DAMAGES INCLUDING, BUT NOT LIMITED TO LOSS OF PROFITS, OPPORTUNITY, DATA OR FOR INDIRECT, INCIDENTAL, SPECIAL OR CONSEQUENTIAL DAMAGES ARISING OUT OF OR IN CONNECTION WITH THE USE OR PERFORMANCE OF SOFTWARE, EVEN IF NOTICE HAS BEEN GIVEN OF THE POSSIBILITY OF SUCH DAMAGES. THIS LIMITATION OF LIABILITY SHALL NOT APPLY TO LIABILITY FOR FRAUD AND DEATH OR PERSONAL INJURY RESULTING FROM MACMILLAN'S NEGLIGENCE TO THE EXTENT APPLICABLE LAW PROHIBITS SUCH LIMITATION. SOME JURISDICTIONS DO NOT ALLOW EXCLUSIONS OR LIMITATIONS LIABILITY, SO THIS EXCLUSION AND LIMITATION MAY NOT APPLY TO YOU. IN NO EVENT WILL MACMILLAN OR ITS THIRD PARTY LICENSORS BE LIABLE FOR ANY AMOUNT GREATER THAN THE INITIAL LICENCE FEE PAID FOR THE SOFTWARE WHICH ALLEGEDLY CAUSED THE DAMAGE, EVEN IF MACMILLAN SHALL HAVE BEEN INFORMED OF SUCH DAMAGES OR OF ANY CLAIM BY ANY THIRD PARTY.

6. INFRINGEMENT INDEMNITY
Macmillan shall defend any action, suit or proceeding brought against Licensee which alleges that any Macmillan proprietary Software infringes a U.S. or U.K. patent or copyright that Macmillan is aware of, on the condition that Licensee promptly notifies Macmillan of the action and gives Macmillan the opportunity, full authority, information and assistance for the defense of the action. Macmillan shall pay all resulting damages and costs awarded against Licensee but shall not be responsible for any settlement made without its consent. Macmillan may, at its option and expense: (i) replace or modify Software so that infringement will not exist; (ii) remove Software involved and refund Licensee a portion of the price paid therefore as depreciated or amortised by an equal annual amount over the lifetime of the Software as established by Macmillan; or (iii) obtain for Licensee the right to continue using the Software. Macmillan and its third party licensors disclaim all other liability for copyright, patent or other infringement, including any incidental or consequential damages. Macmillan shall have no liability for any infringements or claims thereof based upon: (i) the combination of Software with products not supplied by Macmillan, (ii) modification or alteration of Software by Macmillan in accordance with Licensee's instructions or by parties other than Macmillan, or (iii) failure to install updates provided by Macmillan.

7. TERM AND TERMINATION
7.1 This Licence shall become effective upon Software shipment and terminate at such time as Licensee discontinues use of Software on the Configuration, or upon sale, lease, or transfer by operation of law or otherwise, of the Configuration.
7.2 If Licensee fails to cure any breach of this Agreement, including failure to pay any required licence fees, within ten (10) days after receipt of written notice of such breach, the licence(s) as to which the breach exists shall be terminated.
7.3 Upon termination of any licence, Licensee shall immediately terminate use of Software for which the licence has been terminated and immediately either return or destroy all copies of such Software and other proprietary materials and certify in writing as to such destruction or return. Sections 3, 4, and 5 shall survive termination of this Agreement.

8. NON-WAIVER
The failure or delay of either party to exercise any right or remedy provided for herein shall not be deemed a waiver of that right or of any other rights or remedies available hereunder.

9. MISCELLANEOUS
9.1 Licensee agrees not to export Software, or re-export or resell Software from or in country of installation, without first complying with all applicable export laws and regulations. The Software may not be downloaded into any country which the United Kingdom has prohibited export.
9.2 Software support shall be provided under terms and conditions specified and in a separately executed Macmillan Software located in Support Agreement.
9.3 Where Licensee is located in the United States, its agencies or instrumentalities whether located within or outside of the United States, all Software and Documentation furnished hereunder is Commercial Computer Software and Commercial Computer Software Documentation provided only with the rights specified in this SLA customarily provided to the public by Macmillan in accordance with FAR 12.212 (a) and (b) (OCT 1995) or DFARS 227.7202-3(a) (JUN 1995) as applicable.
9.4 The Software may contain an electronic version of this SLA intended to have the same force and effect as a hardcopy SLA.
9.5 This Agreement shall be governed by English law. The United Nations Convention on Contracts for the International Sale of Goods is specifically disclaimed. Licensee's order documents shall state that the terms and conditions of this Agreement are the sole terms and conditions governing such order. This SLA states the entire understanding between the parties as to Software licensed by Licensee and shall take precedence over any omitted, conflicting or additional terms in any Licensee purchase order. If any provision of this SLA is determined to be invalid or unenforceable by a court of competent jurisdiction hereunder, the remaining provisions of this SLA shall not be affected and shall remain in full force and effect as though said invalid or unenforceable provision were not contained herein. The English language version of this Macmillan End-User Software Licence Agreement shall prevail and any translation into other languages other than English is for convenience only. No third party may enforce any of its terms under the Contracts (Rights of Third Parties) Act 1999.
9.6 Written notices required by this SLA shall be sent to the following:

Legal Department	Digital Publishing Unit
Macmillan Publishers Ltd	Macmillan Education
4 Crinan Street	Between Towns Road
London N1 9XW	Oxford OX4 3PP
United Kingdom	United Kingdom

9.7 Notwithstanding anything to the contrary provided herein, in the event of a change in control of all or substantially all of the assets of Macmillan, Macmillan may assign any or all of the rights and obligations under this Agreement to its successor in interest or to a third part assignee.

This product contains Adobe® AIR™ Runtime by Adobe® Systems Incorporated. All rights reserved. Adobe® and Adobe® AIR™ are trademarks of Adobe® Systems Incorporated.

© Macmillan Publishers Limited 2013

Macmillan Education
Between Towns Road, Oxford OX4 3PP
A division of Macmillan Publishers Limited
Companies and representatives throughout the world

ISBN 978-0-230-44375-4

© Macmillan Publishers Limited 2013
First published 2013

All rights reserved; no part of this publication may be reproduced, stored in a retrieval system, transmitted in any form, or by any means, electronic, mechanical, photocopying, recording, or otherwise, without the prior written permission of the publishers.

Written by Robert Campbell, Rob Metcalf, Julie Moore and Mike Hogan, with additional material by Amanda Jeffries, Amanda Leigh and Jonathan Coxall

The authors have asserted their rights to be identified as the authors of this work in accordance with the Copyright, Designs and Patents Act 1988.

Cover design by Macmillan Publshers Limited

Design of booklet and worksheets by emc design ltd

Video production by It's Magazines

Cover Credit: Bananastock, Digital Vision, Getty, Image Source

The authors and publishers would like to thank the following for permission to reproduce their photographs:
Apple Inc; Bananastock; Brand X; Comstock; Corbis; Creatas; Digital Stock; Digital Vision; EYEWIRE; Fancy; Getty; Goodshot; Grapheast; Image 100; Image Source; iStock; Macmillan Publishers Ltd; Medio images; Pathfinder; PhotoAlto; PhotoDisc; PhotoDisc/Getty Images; stockbyte; SUPERSTOCK

The author(s) and publishers are grateful for permission to reprint the following copyright material:
Sound Recording Rights for '*Mr Blue Sky*' performed by ELO, courtesy of Sony Music Entertainment UK Limited. Licensed by Sony Music Commercial Markets UK; '*Mr. Blue Sky*' - Words and Music by Ivy Jeff Lynne © 1977, Reproduced by permission of EMI Music Publishing Ltd, London W8 5SW; Sound Recording Rights '*Night Boat in Cairo*' performed by Madness. Licensed courtesy of Union Square Music, London; '*Night Boat To Cairo*' - Words and Music Michael Barson and Graham McPherson © 1979, Reproduced by permission of EMI Music Publishing Ltd, London W8 5SW; Sound Recording Rights for '*Dancing in the Street*', performed by Martha Reeves and The Vandellas. Courtesy of Motown Record Company. Under license from Universal Music Operations Limited; '*Dancing In The Street*' – Words and Music by Ivy Jo Hunter, Marvin P Gaye and William Stevenson, copyright © 1964. Reproduced by permission of Jobete Music Co. Inc/EMI Music. London W8 5SW.

These materials may contain links for third party websites. We have no control over, and are not responsible for, the contents of such third party websites. Please use care when accessing them.

Although we have tried to trace and contact copyright holders before publication, in some cases this has not been possible. If contacted we will be pleased to rectify any errors or omissions at the earliest opportunity.

Printed and bound in Thailand

2017 2016 2015 2014 2013
10 9 8 7 6 5 4 3 2 1